A Relational Moral Theory

A Relational Moral Theory draws on neglected resources from the Global South and especially the African philosophical tradition to provide a new answer to a perennial philosophical question: what do all morally right actions have in common as distinct from wrong ones? Thaddeus Metz points out that the principles of utility and of respect for autonomy, the two rivals that have dominated Western moral theory for the last two centuries, share an individualist premise. Once that common assumption is replaced by a relational perspective given prominence in African ethical thought, a different comprehensive principle, one focused on harmony or friendliness, emerges. Metz argues that this principle corrects the blind spots of the Western moral principles, and has implications for a wide array of controversies in applied ethics that an international audience of moral philosophers, professional ethicists, and similar thinkers will find compelling.

Thaddeus Metz is Research Professor of Philosophy at the University of Pretoria. He obtained his PhD from the Sage School of Philosophy at Cornell University in 1997. Since then he has become known for driving the application of an analytic method to topics in continental and African philosophy. He is the author of around 300 publications include *Meaning in Life* (Oxford, 2013) and *Jurisprudence in an African Context* (Oxford, 2017). In recognition of having brought African philosophy to global audiences, *Prospect Magazine* designated Metz one of The World's Top 50 Thinkers in 2020.

A Relational Moral Theory

African Ethics in and beyond the Continent

THADDEUS METZ

OXFORD
UNIVERSITY PRESS

OXFORD
UNIVERSITY PRESS

Great Clarendon Street, Oxford, OX2 6DP,
United Kingdom

Oxford University Press is a department of the University of Oxford.
It furthers the University's objective of excellence in research, scholarship,
and education by publishing worldwide. Oxford is a registered trade mark of
Oxford University Press in the UK and in certain other countries

First published 2022
First published in paperback 2025

Published in the United States of America by Oxford University Press
198 Madison Avenue, New York, NY 10016, United States of America

British Library Cataloguing in Publication Data
Data available

Library of Congress Cataloging in Publication Data
Data available

ISBN 978–0–19–874896–0 (Hbk.)
ISBN 978–0–19–896499–5 (Pbk.)

DOI: 10.1093/oso/9780198748960.001.0001

Printed and bound by CPI Group (UK) Ltd, Croydon, CR0 4YY

The manufacturer's authorised representative in the EU for product safety is
Oxford University Press España S.A. of El Parque Empresarial San Fernando
de Henares, Avenida de Castilla, 2 – 28830 Madrid
(www.oup.es/en or product.safety@oup.com). OUP España S.A. also
acts as importer into Spain of products made by the manufacturer.

Preface

Although this book is about ethical theory of a sort that is intended to be of interest to a philosopher working in any major tradition, it owes much to my having come to live in an African country and becoming acquainted with indigenous sub-Saharan worldviews and ways of life. It unnerves me to think that I would have remained ignorant of them and not been in a position to compose this book had I stayed in the United States, which was my likely path in life. I might not have found my intellectual home, or at least one of them, had I not wandered away from where I grew up.

It was upon first moving to South Africa in 1999, and especially upon starting to lecture there in 2004, that I began to study African ethics, the characteristic mores and the philosophical interpretations of them that have been prominent amongst black peoples south of the Sahara desert and that did not come largely from, say, Europe or the Middle East (which have, of course, had important influences on the African continent). Lecturing to students at the University of the Witwatersrand in Johannesburg, it seemed not merely apt, but also morally essential, to teach them something from the local intellectual tradition. So, I intensively read and spoke to philosophers, theologians, anthropologists, and sociologists about indigenous, pre-colonial, or 'traditional' Africa, and considered what sub-Saharan cultures could contribute to contemporary debates amongst those studying moral philosophy anywhere in the world.

At first I wanted to see what a theory of right action grounded on African norms would look like in comparison to 'modern' Western ones such as the principles of utility and of respect for autonomy. In the African philosophical literature I did encounter theoretical statements of morality, which I quote in this book, but they were usually intended to be descriptive, i.e., to represent the ways that many sub-Saharan peoples have thought about right and wrong behaviour. I, however, have been interested in articulating a prescriptive theory, a principle with a sub-Saharan pedigree that promises to account comprehensively for how one morally ought to act. In addition, I have sought an African normative ethical theory that is backed by strong credentials relative to competing accounts, and, moreover, that would be prima facie attractive to philosophers working both in and beyond the African tradition. In 2007 I deemed one particular interpretation of the African tradition, which treats harmonious or communal relationship as an end, to be the most promising in these respects. Since then, I have developed that relational approach in a variety of ways, and argued that it plausibly captures a variety of moral intuitions shared by many ethicists around the world. Needless to say, it did not take long for me to come to believe my own theory; I soon found it more philosophically compelling than the Western principles that had previously governed my thinking about right and wrong.

As an American white guy who still does not know an indigenous African language well, some elements have likely been 'lost in translation'. However, my aim has not been to recount the intricate details of a sub-Saharan people's moral beliefs and practices, let alone a group of them. My project has not involved representing indigenous African morality; instead, I have drawn on salient aspects of it, at least as interpreted by contemporary African philosophers, to *construct* a moral theory that should be taken seriously by those in a variety of global philosophical traditions. I have sought to create and defend a principle of right action informed by facets of culture recurrent amongst a wide array of sub-Saharan peoples, or at least by the philosophical expressions of them in the post-independence era, ranging from the Zulu and Xhosa peoples in South Africa to the Basotho in Lesotho to the Shona in Zimbabwe to the Batswana in Botswana to the Nso' in Cameroon to the Gikuyu and the Luo in Kenya to the Oromo in Ethiopia to the Acoli in Uganda to the Chewa in Malawi to the Dinka in Sudan to the Baluba in the Congo to the Bemba in Zambia to the Yoruba, Igbo, Tiv, and Hausa in Nigeria to the Akan in Ghana. Although I have studied the cultures of these and still other African peoples, I remain an outsider. My hope is that African readers will appreciate my attempt to grapple with their philosophies and cultures for a specific purpose: developing a normative ethical theory that a multicultural audience of moral philosophers, professional ethicists, and related scholars would find compelling and, in particular, would appreciate as giving utilitarianism, Kantianism, and similar Western theories a run for their money in applied contexts. Another hope is that, when African readers critically engage with this book, they will use their superior knowledge of indigenous languages and cultures to contribute to global thought about the nature of right and wrong.

In this book I argue that a number of indigenous sub-Saharan philosophers have fastened onto relational facets of moral thought that many other traditions around the world, particularly those in Anglo-America, Europe, and Australasia, have insufficiently understood and appreciated. Most people know that Africa is a continent rich in minerals, and, indeed, that it has been cruelly coerced and exploited for them for centuries. However, relatively few scholars beyond Africa are aware of what this part of the world has to contribute philosophically. The principal aim of this book is to demonstrate the importance of certain relational, and specifically communal, ideas salient in the sub-Saharan philosophical tradition for anyone wanting to understand many theoretical and applied aspects of morality.

This aim—which I do not take to be the only sensible one—is outward, by which I mean a matter of considering which characteristically African understandings of morality would be reasonable to believe by thinkers both indigenous to the continent and from a wide array of other philosophical backgrounds.[1] This orientation differs from the more inward aims of, say, recovering facets of culture that had been denigrated by colonialists or seeking to protect local ways of life from the encroachments of globalization.[2] Such aims are important, but they have not substantially been mine. What contemporary philosophers throughout the world are likely to find prima facie appealing about African ethical thought is unlikely to be everything one might find of interest about sub-Saharan cultures.

In pursuing this outward aim, I have sought to balance two desiderata, positing an ethic that is sub-Saharan, on the one hand, and one that is philosophically defensible to a global audience, on the other. Although there do seem to be some thinkers who contend that a view is to be believed if and only if it is African (whether for reasons of relativism or resistance), I am not one of them. In the course of developing a recognizably African moral theory that could give moral theories from other (especially Western) philosophical traditions pause, I have sometimes had to trade off what some would consider Africanness for what could be received by non-Africans. For instance, ancestors—i.e., wise and influential members of a clan who have survived the deaths of their bodies and who continue to live on Earth and guide the clan—play no essential role in my favoured interpretation of African morality. If such ancestors exist, the ethic in principle provides instruction about how a moral agent should act in respect of them. However, the ethic does not by definition say that one should treat ancestors a certain way, as I have sought to set aside metaphysical claims that cannot resonate amongst philosophers with an array of multicultural backgrounds.

Some African readers might find these kinds of judgements to be offensive—just another criticism of their cultures by a white settler. However, the primary goal of this book is to argue that sub-Saharan ethical philosophy has been unjustly neglected around the world. I hope readers will appreciate that one major claim here is that the African tradition grounds a moral theory that is more attractive than predominant modern Western ones—and on terms that even Western moral theorists should find compelling.[3] In addition, readers should remember that there is no single African ethic; there are instead many interpretations of sub-Saharan morality, inviting the use of philosophical judgement to choose between them or to construct one that tries to avoids all their apparent weaknesses.

[1] For some discussion of why I believe it is worth taking this sort of outward approach in respect to Africa, see Metz (2022a).

[2] For one scholar who clearly believes inward aims are more important than outward ones, see Lamola (2019).

[3] I have also begun to put African ethics into critical dialogue with East Asian views, on which see, e.g., Bell and Metz (2011); Metz (2016a, 2017a).

What I have sought to do here is to provide a definitive and comprehensive analysis, application, and defence of my favoured principle of right action that has been heavily influenced by African philosophy. My ideas have shifted somewhat from initial statements made nearly fifteen years ago, and there have been too many piecemeal essays of mine published and in a variety of places for a given reader to absorb. It is time for a firm, unified treatment. For me to undertake that project has meant downplaying concerns about, say, whether I should have rather undertaken some other project. I wish I could have done more in what follows to respond in particular to the published critical discussions in the literature, but, for a variety of reasons, if I had tried to engage with them systematically here, I would have been unable to complete this book.

I am thankful to the many students and colleagues from Africa who have supported my work. Their interest and encouragement have helped to keep me going. Although my intellectual horizons have been broadened because of my exposure to Africa, it has been difficult at times.[4] I would like those of African descent to know that I have been buoyed by their willingness to engage with my project. The kind words and other forms of support that I have routinely received from my sub-Saharan students and colleagues over the years, beyond sharing their constructive criticisms, are partially responsible for the appearance of this book. It was also heartening to have been appointed to a South African parastatal, the National Heritage Council, because of my work on the southern African ethic of *ubuntu* (humanness in the Nguni languages there), as well as to have been commissioned by senior African scholars to compose a piece titled 'What Africa Can Contribute to the World' for the United Nations' *General History of Africa* project.

My research into African ethics began as a lecturer at the University of the Witwatersrand, but really took off once I accepted a research post at the University of Johannesburg in 2009. I am grateful to the latter institution for having proactively structured a position that would suit my temperament and support my aims. I hope that it finds some measure of return in this book, the draft for which I overhauled upon joining the University of Pretoria in 2020.

Another source of support has been the South African National Research Foundation (NRF), which awarded me Incentive Funding, grant money with which I was able to purchase books, organize workshops, travel abroad, and support postgraduate students, postdoctoral fellows, and other lecturers in the field of African philosophy. This book is based on work that was supported financially by the NRF, and any opinion, findings, conclusions, or recommendations expressed in it are those of the author, with the NRF not accepting any liability in regard thereto.

[4] For a reply to some of the political criticisms, see Jones and Metz (2015).

A Relational Moral Theory includes an array of parts of journal articles, book chapters, and encyclopaedia entries published since 2007 that I have reconsidered, revised, and sewn together into what is meant to be a unity, not a patchwork. I thank the many people who provided input on these previously published essays, acknowledging here those (besides anonymous referees) who took the time to share written comments or to speak with me one-on-one with the aim of mutual understanding and learning, of whom I recall the following: Martin Ajei, Lucy Allais, Tom Angier, Aribiah Attoe, Caesar Atuire, Oladele Balogun, Kevin Behrens, Daniel A. Bell, Mfuniselwa Bhengu, David Bilchitz, Alex Broadbent, Bénézet Bujo, Munamato Chemhuru, Jonathan Chimakonam, Luis Cordeiro-Rodrigues, Drucilla Cornell, Louise du Toit, Mbongisi Dyantyi, Edwin Etieyibo, Cornelius Ewuoso, Nir Eyal, Michael Onyebuchi Eze, Douglas Farland, Ademola Fayemi, Katrin Flikschuh, Yaw Frimpong-Mansoh, Joseph Gaie, Robert Goodin, Anke Graneß, Lawrence Hamilton, Shireen Hassim, Nimi Hoffmann, Kai Horsthemke, George Hull, Elvis Imafidon, Ward Jones, Aryan Kaganof, Simon Keller, Stephen Kershnar, Reuel Khoza, Hugh LaFollette, Chenyang Li, Kirk Lougheed, Dirk Louw, David Lutz, Cheryl Macpherson, Nkosinathi Mahlangu, David Martens, Erasmus Masitera, Dismas Masolo, Bernard Matolino, John Mbiti, Eusebius McKaiser, Sarah Clark Miller, Yvonne Mokgoro, Motsamai Molefe, Olusegun Morakinyo, Pius Mosima, Pascah Mungwini, Ronald Munson, Munyaradzi Murove, Mechthild Nagel, Amasa Ndofirepi, Joel Netshitenzhe, Uchenna Okeja, Abraham Olivier, Oritsegbubemi Oyowe, Brian Penrose, Thomas Pogge, Henry Richardson, Samuel Segun, Jeffrey Sehume, Augustine Shutte, Marta Soniewicka, Dan Stein, Raymond Suttner, Sharlene Swartz, Pedro Tabensky, Olufemi Taiwo, Godfrey Tangwa, Monica Taylor, Paul Taylor, Mark Tschaepe, Ogbo Ugwuanyi, Isaac Ukpokolo, Stan Van Hooft, Neil Van Leeuwen, Jason van Niekerk, Samantha Vice, Christopher Wareham, Kwasi Wiredu, Allen Wood, and Charles Yeats.

With regard to the book *qua* book, I am pleased to acknowledge the input of my editor, Peter Momtchiloff, who is invariably a source of good advice (and enormous patience), and two anonymous reviewers for Oxford University Press, whose comments have helped to strengthen the manuscript. Special thanks go to Darrel Moellendorf for having organized a workshop devoted to a draft of the book manuscript at the Normative Orders Cluster of Goethe Universität. My work benefited greatly from not only his input, but also that of Lara Denis, Dorothea Gädeke, Jimmy Lenman, Uchenna Okeja, and Frans Svensson. Special thanks also go to Hennie Lötter, who convened a similar gathering at the University of Johannesburg. The active participation there of him, Colin Chasi, Dylan Futter, Nyasha Mboti, Tristen Taylor, and Nikolai Viedge has also made this a better book, even though not what many of them would have liked to see.

I am glad to be able to acknowledge the help of Dee Cohen, Vanessa Freerks, Dimpho Maponya, and Asheel Singh, who over the years have organized many of the references and secured the permissions to use materials from the following essays:

- Metz, Thaddeus (2019) 'Neither Parochial nor Cosmopolitan: Cultural Instruction in the Light of a Communal Ethic', *Education as Change*, 23: 1–16.
- Metz, Thaddeus (2018) 'An African Theory of Good Leadership', *African Journal of Business Ethics*, 12: 36–53.
- Metz, Thaddeus (2018) 'An African Theory of the Point of Higher Education', in *Contemporary Philosophical Proposals for the University*, Stoller, Aaron and Kramer, Eli (eds), New York: Palgrave Macmillan, pp. 161–86.
- Metz, Thaddeus (2017) 'A Bioethic of Communion', in *The Ethics of Reproductive Genetics*, Soniewicka, Marta (ed.), Cham: Springer, pp. 49–66.
- Metz, Thaddeus (2017) 'Ancillary Care Obligations in Light of an African Bioethic', *Theoretical Medicine and Bioethics*, 38: 111–26.
- Metz, Thaddeus (2016) 'Exploring the Ethical Foundations of Nkrumah's *Consciencism*', in *Disentangling Consciencism*, Ajei, Martin (ed.), Lanham, MD: Rowman & Littlefield, pp. 213–27.
- Metz, Thaddeus (2015) 'African Ethics', in *The International Encyclopedia of Ethics*, LaFollette, Hugh (ed.), Malden, MA: Blackwell Publishing Ltd, pp. 1–9.
- Metz, Thaddeus (2015) 'How the West Was One: The Western as Individualist, the African as Communitarian', *Educational Philosophy and Theory*, 47: 1175–84.
- Metz, Thaddeus (2014) 'Dignity in the *Ubuntu* Tradition', in *Cambridge Handbook on Human Dignity*, Düwell, Marcus et al. (eds), Cambridge: Cambridge University Press, pp. 310–18.
- Metz, Thaddeus (2013) 'Questioning African Attempts to Ground Ethics on Metaphysics', in *Ontologized Ethics: New Essays in African Meta-ethics*, Imafidon, Elvis and Bewaji, John (eds), Lanham, MD: Rowman & Littlefield Publishers, pp. 189–204.
- Metz, Thaddeus (2013) 'The Ethics of Swearing', *Review of Social Economy*, 71: 228–48.
- Metz, Thaddeus (2013) 'The Western Ethic of Care or an Afro-Communitarian Ethic?', *Journal of Global Ethics*, 9: 77–92.
- Metz, Thaddeus (2012) 'An African Theory of Moral Status', *Ethical Theory and Moral Practice*, 15: 387–402.
- Metz, Thaddeus (2012) 'African Conceptions of Human Dignity', *Human Rights Review*, 13: 19–37.
- Metz, Thaddeus (2011) '*Ubuntu* as a Moral Theory and Human Rights in South Africa', *African Human Rights Law Journal*, 11: 532–59.

- Metz, Thaddeus (2010) 'For the Sake of the Friendship: Relationality and Relationship as Grounds of Beneficence', *Theoria*, 57: 54–76.
- Metz, Thaddeus (2010) 'African and Western Moral Theories in a Bioethical Context', *Developing World Bioethics*, 10: 49–58.
- Metz, Thaddeus and Gaie, Joseph (2010) 'The African Ethic of *Ubuntu/Botho*: Implications for Research on Morality', *Journal of Moral Education*, 39: 273–90.
- Metz, Thaddeus (2007) 'Toward an African Moral Theory', *The Journal of Political Philosophy*, 15: 321–41.

Having already dedicated my first sole-authored and lengthy book, begun in the United States, to my first son who was born there, it is apt to dedicate my second one, begun in South Africa, to my second son who was born there. Jamil Metz, although you were a young person at the time that I began to write this book, your empathy, compassion, generosity, and gregariousness had already taught me a lot about what it means to relate communally. This work is for you.

Contents

1
Introduction

1.1 'The Great Gift from Africa'

For much of my academic career as a professional philosopher, I have been aware of patent gaps in contemporary Western moral theory about how we should treat others.[1] I have thought that animals matter for their own sake but not as much as human beings, that many human beings have a dignity but that pain is morally relevant insofar as it reduces a person's quality of life, and that, despite everyone mattering from a moral point of view, an agent is obligated to do more for those related to her in certain ways. And I have found it extremely difficult for Kantianism, utilitarianism, and related Euro-American-Australasian principles of right action to account for these judgements.

It is sometimes said that a useful strategy by which to make headway in a philosophical debate is to reject a premise shared by its major interlocutors. In this book, I have applied this approach to normative ethical theory, the project of advancing a basic principle that plausibly entails and best explains what all morally right (and, conversely, wrong) actions have in common. I maintain that the major moral theories of the past 200 years in the Western tradition, ranging from egoism to utilitarianism to Lockean natural rights to respect for autonomy to respect for human life, share a certain, individualist claim. Once individualism is rejected, one can develop a relational alternative that fills in many of the gaps left open by these competing theories. Or so I argue here.

The idea that morality is a function of relational properties is not new. Confucianism in the East Asian tradition is an instance of this view, as are the ethic of care and some of Karl Marx's ideas in the Western tradition. However, it is only lately that relationalism has been articulated as a distinct kind of ethic in English-speaking philosophy, despite having predated more individualist views by many centuries. In addition, adherents to the above relational perspectives have eschewed my project of systematically developing and defending a theory of morally right action, for reasons that I address below.

Although I construct a relational moral theory by drawing occasionally on the work of Confucians and care ethicists, the sub-title of this book is telling.

[1] I focus on interpersonal morality in this book and do not systematically address institutional matters of law, politics, or economics, on which see some brief remarks in the Conclusion (13.4).

A Relational Moral Theory: African Ethics in and beyond the Continent. Thaddeus Metz, Oxford University Press.
 DOI: 10.1093/oso/9780198748960.003.0001

It is principally the African philosophical tradition (and then its large English-language and literate vein) that I have considered for insights. That is partly because I find the ideas in this tradition particularly promising, and partly because I believe it is important for African ideas to contribute meaningfully to world philosophy. About the only thing that most non-African philosophers seem to know about indigenous sub-Saharan worldviews is that they are characteristically communitarian. While that has sometimes taken the unfortunate form of corporatism, which assigns moral primacy to a community in the sense of a group, it is more promising to think of morality as a function of communal relationship, a way that individuals can and should interact. In this book I work to systematize this relational approach to right action by creating and arguing for a moral theory with a recognizably sub-Saharan pedigree that should be weighed up against at least contemporary Western moral theories. The salient African idea that morality is a function of prizing communality is what I develop into the form of a normative theory, apply to a variety of practical debates, and advance as something that an international philosophical audience should take seriously as a rival to Kantianism, utilitarianism, and the like.

Although the principle I advance is largely *from* Africa, it is not meant to be only *for* Africans. I argue here that it does better than influential Western theories at accounting for a wide array of uncontroversial moral judgements that Westerners themselves (amongst others) hold. Note that I do not argue that the Western tradition of moral philosophy is utterly bankrupt; any long-standing body of thought should be expected to have some kernels of truth in it. And I indeed draw on some salient Western ideas, particularly Kantian ones about human rights and respectful treatment, when developing a relational moral theory. However, by the same token, the African tradition, which is grossly under-represented on the global stage, should be expected to have some kernels of truth in it, and my claim is that its focus on communal relationship can be understood in a way that grounds a promising foundational ethic.

The South African intellectual Steve Biko predicts that sub-Saharan Africa's keen appreciation of relationship will eventually be recognized by other parts of the world:

> We believe that in the long run the special contribution to the world by Africa will be in this field of human relationship. The great powers of the world may have done wonders in giving the world an industrial and military look, but the great gift still has to come from Africa—giving the world a more human face.
> (2004: 47)

Other Africanists have made similar claims for about 100 years (du Bois 1897, 1924; Busia 1962: 108; Mutwa 1964: 552, 691; Kaunda 1966: 22; Iroegbu 2007: 151). I do not know whether Biko's prophesy will come true. However, in this book I do what I can to help make it come true in respect of a global audience of moral philosophers.

In the rest of this chapter, I do more to explain and motivate the project of advancing a moral theory with an African content (1.2), after which I provide an overview of what I seek to accomplish in each of the three major parts of this book. Part I of the book concerns meta-ethical issues about how I aim to justify my favoured moral theory (1.3), which is roughly with argumentation that appeals to moral intuitions and avoids contested metaphysical claims. Part II of the book argues for the best African theory of morality, contending that a certain communal principle of right action is most philosophically defensible compared to others suggested by the sub-Saharan tradition such as vitalism (1.4). Part III argues for the best moral theory, which happens to be from Africa; it contends that the communal ethic developed in the second part of the book is more defensible than the most influential Western moral theories such as utilitarian and Kantianism when it comes to implications for a wide array of contemporary interpersonal controversies (1.5).[2]

1.2 An African Moral Theory

Many will be either unclear or sceptical about the nature of my project in this book, and I briefly address some of the more common and important concerns. In particular, some will not understand, or will reject, the aim of developing a moral theory (1.2.1); others will be unfamiliar with what words such as 'African' mean, or will contend that they should not be used (1.2.2); and still others will doubt that it makes sense to speak of an 'African moral theory', or will argue that it is pointless to seek one out (1.2.3). In this section, I try to allay these worries.[3]

1.2.1 Theory in Moral Thought

Intuitively, it is usually immoral to kill innocent people, to lie, to rape, to exploit, to kidnap, and to torture animals for the fun of it. Some of these actions can be permissible to perform on occasion and would not warrant guilt, resentment, punishment, or other negative reactions. However, my point is that these

[2] In terms of reader interest, those concerned with matters internal to African philosophy might focus on Chapters 2–7, while those particularly wanting to see how the ethic weighs up against Western moral theories could principally consider Chapters 6–12, picking whichever applied topics from Part III they prefer. Each applied chapter is relatively self-contained, but does cross-reference where that would be useful.

[3] Readers who already understand and appreciate the nature of my project may wish to skip this section and move directly to the overview of the book's major parts (1.3–1.5).

actions seem wrong in most contexts. Would it not be interesting if there were just one thing in virtue of which these actions are wrong as well as all others that are wrong?[4]

A moral or normative ethical theory is an attempt to specify what that one property might be. It is an account of which basic, general duty purportedly grounds all other, more particular duties. The project of seeking the most defensible moral theory has been systematically undertaken in the Western tradition at least since the work of Thomas Hobbes, who in 1651 argued in *Leviathan* that wrong actions are identical to those expected to harm the agent who performed them. Since then, a number of familiar moral theories have been developed and critically explored, amongst them the ideas that an action is wrong just insofar as it: fails to maximize the general welfare; would be forbidden by a rule that, if generally adhered to, would maximize the general welfare; does not give people what they deserve; treats rational nature or the capacity for autonomy disrespectfully; is part of a maxim that cannot be universalized without contradiction; violates natural rights of self-ownership; degrades the sanctity of human life; would be forbidden by a rule that would be agreed to by all reasonable parties to a social contract; is what God has forbidden; is not what the agent would want done to herself; is what a majority of society has forbidden.

One might think that since so many moral theories have been postulated, and since debate still rages about whether any one of them is the best, let alone whether any is adequate, the project should be abandoned. In the face of deep disagreement about general principles, we should favour 'anti-theory' or particularism, so the objection goes.

However, there are several reasons why I have spent much of my professional career so far searching for the most plausible moral theory. For one, I share Derek Parfit's view of the field, according to which it is still fairly young (1984: sec. 154). Despite its seventeenth-century origins with Hobbes, not very many professional philosophers have devoted their lives to thinking theoretically about wrongness, at least from a secular standpoint, and it is only since the massification of higher education in the 1960s that a respectable number have been hired to do so.

For a second point, since that time, some degree of convergence has arguably been obtained. Even if the field has not homed in on the best or most promising general principle, it has begun to weed out some views as not all that promising, or at least as less promising than others.

A third reason I remain sanguine about the prospect of finding an attractive moral theory is that, up to now, it has overwhelmingly been philosophers working

[4] I focus on right and wrong action in this book, and do not address good and bad character systematically. Mostly that is for reasons of focus, but it also because I believe that a large part of what makes people bad is having engaged in wrongful behaviour. For some suggestions about how one might appeal to communality to capture moral virtue, see the Conclusion (13.3) and Metz (2022b).

in the Western tradition who have sought one out. My hunch is that the most plentiful theoretical resources in that tradition are limited and could usefully be supplemented with insights from other parts of the world. That has yet to be done systematically when it comes to the construction of a moral theory, and is what I seek to do here mainly by drawing on values and norms salient in the African tradition, many of which will resonate with other cultures in the Global South. A theoretical perspective informed by a long-standing body of philosophical thought promises to shed light on the nature of morality.[5]

Note that even if the field were never to find a single most defensible moral theory, or even a small cluster of ones deemed adequate by nearly all moral philosophers, it could know with confidence that such does not exist only upon having searched diligently for it. And, finally, even if the search failed in the end, philosophers would have learned much about morality in the course of having undertaken it.

Some of those who favour a relational approach to ethics have advanced other reasons, beyond the lack of convergence of expert judgement, for doubting that one should seek out a moral theory. Some maintain that relationality gives one reason to highlight particularity and context, and to downplay abstract principle. If moral action consists of sustaining or otherwise honouring certain relationships between people, then it will rarely be enough to treat them strictly in accordance with the deliverances of a rule about how to divide benefits and burdens, say, according to desert, rights, or the maximization of utility. Instead, developing, enriching, and more generally prizing relationships requires close attention to the details of specific people's different histories, self-understandings, and perspectives. For expressions of this view in an African context, consider the suggestions that sub-Saharan morality is to be apprehended on a 'know it when I see it' (Mokgoro 1998: 16) or a 'who feels it knows it' (Mboti 2015: 134) basis.

I accept that a given person's intuition in a specific situation can be some evidence of how to proceed, but I doubt that it is often sufficient. The process of setting given, apparent duties in the probabilistic and explanatory contexts of other intuitive ones, in effect seeking a coherent theory, appears to be a crucial means by which to know whether one is justified in accepting them. For example, it was in part through moral theorization that post-war Americans came to learn that they have no reason to believe that interracial romantic relationships are immoral. Feeling disgusted upon encountering mixed-race couples was not a great reason to judge them to be wrong. Over time, Americans learned that a purported duty to love erotically only those of one's race was not analogous to other, uncontested duties, was not entailed by what they have in common, was not

[5] Indeed, two scholars suggest that, from a bird's-eye view of the globe, harmony is what they call the 'mother of all values', and not either utility or autonomy as per much of the contemporary Western tradition (Bell and Mo 2014).

essential to account for other duties, and so on. It did not fit with what else Americans reasonably thought they knew about morality, and so was aptly dropped by a large majority who put their minds to the issue in a theoretical manner. Particularism too greatly risks parochialism.

There is no doubt that acting rightly requires judgement in the light of a given set of circumstances, including an awareness of who people are and what they believe. And it is true that some moral theorists have suggested that a general principle can and should be applied like an algorithm. However, a moral theory need not be understood as something so mechanical. Although a moral theorist believes that all particular duties should ultimately be derivable from a single general duty, he need not think that the derivations are deductive or certain. More often than not, the best that a moral theorist can hope for is uncertain, probabilistic evidence that a specific action is what a principle prescribes, especially in a specific context. Appeal to analogies and inference to the best explanation are common both in everyday life and in the field of philosophy, even when a moral theory is being invoked.

Here is another reason why adherents to a relational approach to morality have often doubted that theorization is apt. Seeking out the best moral theory has usually been done by a philosopher sitting alone in his armchair. However, there is reason to deny that solitary reflection can produce reliable judgements about how to resolve dilemmas, if relationship is the key to morality. Instead, friends of relationality tend to favour dialogue, ideally amongst affected parties, in order to determine the right way forward (in the African context, Bujo 2001 has made this point with care). Because relationships are complex, a person cogitating on his own is unlikely to be able to figure out how to improve them. Instead, success on that score is much more likely when many heads are put to the task, especially those of the people who are involved in the matter.

One thing to note, in reply, is that this point strictly speaking does not tell against the project of seeking out a moral theory. At most, it shows that moral theorization should not be undertaken by an isolated individual. However, typical academic ethicists, including myself, have engaged with many other people in the course of formulating their principles. We have often received feedback from university colleagues, colloquium interlocutors, conference attendees, peer reviewers, journal editors, postgraduate students, postdoctoral fellows, and thousands of undergraduates.

Critics doubt that this sort of input is enough; they worry that these people by and large share the same background and hence suffer the same blind spots. The point is fair, but in my view calls for engagement with experts from other backgrounds. Precisely because morality is so complex, if one is going to seek out a *theory* about it, it would be most productive to engage with those who are most familiar with the relevant evidence. That need not mean having a university degree or holding a post in a philosophy department, but does involve some kind of expertise. Hence, in my view, Western philosophers have erred, not in seeking out moral theories, but mainly in failing to engage with philosophers and similar intellectuals from other traditions. In this book, I aim to help rectify that to some degree by taking up characteristically African approaches to right and wrong, particularly as expounded by contemporary sub-Saharan ethicists and moral philosophers in literate English works.[6]

1.2.2 How Geographical Labels Are Used

In this sub-section, I indicate what I mean by 'African' and similar terms such as 'sub-Saharan', 'Western', and the like when applied to philosophers, theories, reasoning, and ways of life. Some believe that such terms are usually descriptively inaccurate, while others contend that they are normatively suspect, say, for being racist or narrowing people's conceptions of how they could live. Since I freely use geographical labels in this book, I respond here to these concerns.

The term 'African' has been employed in a variety of ways. Here is one theoretically useful way to use the term, and those like it such as 'Western': to refer to features that have been salient in a locale over a substantial amount of time. In general, I use geographical labels to pick out properties that have for a long while been recurrent in a place in a way they have tended not to be elsewhere. They denote long-standing characteristics in a region that differentiate it from many other regions. Kwame Gyekye appears to hold a similar view when he remarks that 'in many areas of thought we can discern features of the traditional life and thought of African peoples sufficiently common to constitute a legitimate and reasonable basis for the construction (or reconstruction) of a philosophical system that may properly be called African' (1995: 191). I add that commonality is not quite enough, for then properties such as breathing or eating would count as African; hence, the common features need to be prominent in the sub-Saharan region relative to many other parts of the world.

Such a view is not essentialist, for it does not imply that the relevant properties are to be found only in a certain location, throughout that location, or invariably in it. Such a view is also not constructivist, for it implies that there is a mind-independent fact of the matter about the frequency with which certain properties are present in places, about which one or one's group could be mistaken.

Consider this example: marsupials are Australian. That is true, I submit, even though one will find a number of marsupials in South America, one will not find marsupials in downtown Sydney, and the day could come when there are no marsupials in Australia. Hence, a natural reading of the statement is not

[6] The ways that East Asian, Indian, Islamic, and Latin American perspectives (amongst others) might bear on moral theory also merit consideration, but need to be considered in some other book.

essentialist. In addition, it is not constructivist, for what makes it the case that marsupials are Australian is not merely that people believe it to be; if a group asserted that marsupials were not Australian but rather African, that would be incorrect. Instead, the claim that marsupials are Australian appears true in virtue of the objective fact that marsupials have for a long while been frequent in Australia in a way they have tended not to be elsewhere. Basically, they have stood out there.

Here is another example: baseball is American. Again, I suggest this claim is true, but not true 'essentially'. After all, the Cubans and Japanese are well known for playing baseball; it is of course true that not all Americans play it or even appreciate it; and there is nothing preventing Americans from giving up this sport entirely. The fact that baseball is American is also not 'constructed', for if a sociologist of sport failed to mention baseball when aiming to provide a general account of sport in the United States, she would be epistemically guilty of having made a glaring omission. Baseball is American insofar as it is salient there.

Consider, now, some geographical labels that are central to this book. The combination of markets, science, and constitutionalism is Western. That is true even though one will find it in places beyond Europe, the United Kingdom, and North America, such as in South Africa and Australia, and even though one will not find it deep in the Amazon jungle amongst, say, the Yanomamo people.

Similarly, according to the way I use geographical labels in this book, it is African to hold a belief in the need to respect ancestors—wise progenitors of a clan who have survived the death of their bodies, now live in an invisible form on Earth, and continue to interact with human beings. That is true despite the facts that not all people in Africa hold this belief and that some other traditions, especially in the East, also include reverence for ancestors. What makes the label 'African' apt is that a belief in ancestors has for a long time been part of the worldviews of a great many peoples indigenous to the African continent, unlike many other parts of the world. It is particularly frequent or noticeable in Africa, at least compared to North America, Europe, the Middle East, and Russia.

Beyond a belief in the need to respect ancestors, peoples indigenous to Africa are well known for having tended to share certain ways of life.[7] They *characteristically*—not universally, not uniquely—have:

- been small scale in number, so that everyone knows everyone else, with little approximating the size and anonymity of a metropolis
- been oral cultures, without a long-standing corpus of written works

[7] Here, I tightly summarize anthropological and sociological findings from many sources, amongst them: Fortes and Evans-Pritchard (1940); Forde (1954); Abraham (1962); Carlston (1968); Wiredu (1980, 1992, 2008); Mbiti (1990); Gyekye (1995: 191–210); Magesa (1997).

- maintained that ritual, initiation, and custom have some moral importance of a sort generally unrecognized in 'modern' societies
- adopted worldviews that are holistic in the sense of not differentiating between the religious, aesthetic, moral, legal, and the like
- held that there are two dimensions of a single reality, the perceptible and the imperceptible, which are in constant interrelation
- believed in the existence of witches, and have often attributed injuries and illnesses to them (or to angry ancestors)
- thought that one's character is imbued with a destiny
- invoked maxims such as 'A person is a person through other persons' and 'I am because we are', which not only describe interdependence, but also prescribe self-realization through positive relationships with others
- held land in common, parcelling it out to households based on need or clan membership
- lacked sophisticated science and complex technology, with the economy based largely on agriculture, cattle, or hunting/gathering
- contended that there are weighty duties to aid other persons that far transcend the nuclear family, centred on what Westerners would call 'extended family'
- used terms such as 'father' and 'sister' to refer to people whom those in the West would deem to be merely friends or associates
- found some moral significance in greetings, especially to those who are known, but also to visitors
- accepted a duty to wed and to procreate, viewing solitariness and celibacy as problematic
- been governed by (male) chiefs, who tended to seek counsel from elders
- resolved political conflicts affecting society by consensus, at least amongst elders, rather than submitted to either majority rule or the non-consultative will of a monarch
- demonstrated respect for elders, i.e., the wise, where age has been taken as a reliable indicator of wisdom
- responded to infraction not mainly with retribution, but with an eye towards reconciliation between the offender, his family, the immediate victim, and the broader community.

These traits—which are not meant to be exhaustive—all count as African, by my use of the term, as they have been recurrent across a broad range of space, viz., from southern to eastern to western Africa, and over a long period of time there, having been present several hundreds of years before colonialists began to settle and continuing to influence philosophical thought in the twenty-first-century.

For all I can tell of the social scientific literature, these features have been salient south of the Sahara desert amongst indigenous peoples. For those sceptical of the accuracy of this body of literature, I can hedge to say that at least post-independence professional philosophers from Africa have often ascribed these features to their respective peoples, where I am addressing myself principally to these philosophers. For the purposes of this book I do not question their ascriptions, leaving that for historians and anthropologists.

I of course recognize the banalities that 'traditional' Africa has not been uniform, i.e., that there have been some exceptions to the above, and that sub-Saharan societies have changed (frankly becoming more 'Western' in my sense of the term) over the past 100 years. The claim that geographical labels are sensibly used to pick out properties that have been salient in a region of space-time means that I am using the word 'African' neither to describe the way those on the continent have lived in comprehensive detail nor to capture how a contemporary person who calls himself an 'African' conceives of himself. In calling a property 'African' (or 'sub-Saharan') it is important to see that I am not seeking to explain to a particular individual who he is, and a reader could well fail to 'find himself' reflected in the normative ethical theory I construct. It is one thing to use the term 'African' for the sake of contemporary self-understanding or identity politics, and it is another to use it to pick out a swathe of long-standing beliefs and practices in a certain region on which to ground a general moral principle.[8]

Using geographical labels along the latter lines has several welcome implications. First, as I have already shown, it does not commit one to essentialism. If the word 'African' merely picks out features that are characteristic of that place, then it is clearly possible for it to apply neither universally in Africa nor necessarily there. What counts as 'African' can change, at least over a long span of time.

In addition, it follows that calling something 'African' should not be taken to mean that it is utterly unique to that part of the world. Too often academics suggest that there is no sense in calling something 'African' since it can invariably be found in some places other than Africa (e.g., Yurkivska 2001; Parker 2003; Horsthemke and Enslin 2005). However, that is too strict a way to use geographical labels, which can be useful if employed in the looser way that I do, viz., to refer to features that have been salient in a location over a long time span, features that might not be utterly distinct to Africa.

Another advantage of using geographical labels in this way is that it invites a plausibly gradient conception of what is African. For something to be African is not an all-or-nothing matter. Instead, something counts as *more* African the more it exhibits properties that have been salient there, or particularly in the sub-Saharan region, for a long while in contrast to many other parts of the world.

[8] Some in the Black Consciousness movement have suggested that my views do not count as 'African' since they do not capture the identity of living African people. However, as an *ad hominem*, I refer them to Biko's essay from which I quoted at the top of this chapter. Biko, too, sometimes uses the word 'African' in a sociological way (2004: 40–7), and precisely to contrast what has been salient in sub-Saharan societies with what has been salient in Western ones.

As will become clear below, my favoured moral theory does not inherently include reference to either a realm of imperceptible agents wherein one will find ancestors or a view of the world as consisting of interdependent vital forces, some of which are perceptible and some of which are not. My theory is therefore *somewhat less* African than an ethic that does include such conditions (such as in Magesa 1997; Bujo 2001; Murove 2007).[9] However, I submit that the theory I advance remains African to a substantial degree, insofar as it is informed by a wide array of other properties that have been prominent on the continent over a long time and across a broad space.[10] After all, the moral theories of Kwasi Wiredu (1996) and Kwame Gyekye (1997) are invariably accepted as African despite a similarly secular content. If their respective doctrines of sympathetic impartiality and moderate communitarianism count as African despite the utter absence of any reference to ancestors or vital forces, so can my ethic.

Finally, using a label such as 'African' to indicate long-term predominance in that part of the world should not be unattractive to those concerned about racist or colonialist uses of the term. Some suggest that since some white people have used 'African' derogatorily, one such as myself must also be doing so when using the term. Others contend that since Europeans were the initial ones to group peoples together as Africans, and not people on the continent themselves, it is epistemically imperialist to continue to speak of 'Africans'. Still others maintain that to speak of 'Africans' is necessarily to homogenize them, that is, to fail to treat them as particular individuals or peoples.

I believe the knockdown point to make in response to these concerns is that nowadays many people in Africa, including those in the field of philosophy, are happy to label themselves 'Africans' and for public purposes. They do so without disparaging connotations, without expecting white people to avoid the word, and without invariably failing to be aware of differences among individuals and peoples. The African National Congress and the African Union are just two examples. Notice I am not claiming that so long as a certain group uses a word to describe itself, outsiders may invariably use the same word. I do not believe that; the fact that African-Americans sometimes use a word beginning with the letter 'n' to refer to themselves does not give me ethical licence to do so. But notice that African-Americans have never to the best of my knowledge created an organization with this word in the name of the organization, which would invite others to

[9] By the same token, if it were true that African cultures have characteristically been sexist, then it would follow that a rigorously egalitarian moral and political philosophy would be *less* African than an inegalitarian one. It would not necessarily follow, however, that it would be downright unAfrican (*contra* Oyowe and Yurkivska 2014).

[10] In addition, recall that I seek to balance the Africanness of my ethic with plausibility to twenty-first-century philosophers and related thinkers both in and beyond Africa. So, what my approach has lost in Africanness it is supposed to have gained in other important dimensions.

call them with that word. In contrast, the word 'African' is routinely used by philosophers and related thinkers who describe themselves as 'African' to name themselves for public purposes.

It is true that I do not focus on particular African peoples in this book. I instead construct a general moral principle that purportedly best justifies features that have been recurrent amongst many sub-Saharan cultures over a long span of time. However, that does not mean I am unaware of differences or believe they are unimportant for purposes other than constructing a moral theory of interest to philosophers across and also beyond Africa.

If the reader continues to think that I am not entitled to the 'African' label for my theory, how should I label it? Am I really to call the moral theory I have articulated and defended by appealing to properties salient in sub-Saharan Africa 'Metz's view'? If I never labelled the theory 'African', I believe I would be stealing or plagiarizing, failing to give credit to the rich tradition from which I have learned so much about communal ways of relating. In part I mean to pay tribute and to acknowledge the source of some of my ideas with the term 'African'.

1.2.3 Western Method, African Content?

The sort of philosophical work in this book is unusual, as it applies a strictly normative analytic approach to sub-Saharan ideas. Although, as I will show in this book, African philosophers have themselves mentioned general principles pertaining to morality, they have often done so descriptively and not prescriptively. In addition, they have not worked systematically to differentiate between prescriptive principles with an African pedigree, and have not argued rigorously that one is philosophically best in relation to competitors. From my perspective, the lack of such an approach has led to statements about how best to interpret African morality that seem contradictory or that I at least find difficult to reconcile. To illustrate what I see as a problem, consider the following quotations from influential African philosophers; I find it hard to tell from them which values are intended to be basic, which are meant to be derivative, and which are supposed to be equivalent.

• From John Mbiti, the magisterial Kenyan historian of African philosophies and religions:

> Because of this great emphasis on one's relationship with other people, morals have been evolved in order to keep society not only alive but in harmony. (1975: 175)

> Whatever strengthens the life of the community is held to be good and right. What weakens the life of the community is held to be evil and wrong. (1975: 177)

The first quotation suggests that harmony is at least a (if not the) point of moral behaviour, which is beyond life, but the second quotation, summing up morality for society, focuses on life and does not mention harmony. Does harmony tend to produce more life in a community, or is harmony perhaps one and the same thing as a community's life? Or are life and harmony two distinct basic goods?

• From Peter Kasenene, the Ugandan theologian who has published studies of African morality:

> [I]n African societies, immorality is the word or deed which undermines fellowship.... Immorality in African ethical thought refers to a disruption of fellowship. (1998: 21, 67)
>
> A person is good in so far as he or she promotes, supports or protects his or her life-force and the life-force of his or her neighbours. Alternatively, a person is bad or evil in as much as he or she undermines or destroys this life-force. The quest for life and its enhancement is the most fundamental value in African religions which governs all the other values. (1998: 25)

If wrong actions are identical to those that undermine fellowship, should not one's conception of good (and bad) individuals be largely informed by that view, so that people are good insofar as they fulfil duties to support fellowship as opposed to fostering life-force?

• From Pantaleon Iroegbu, a theologian from Nigeria who has addressed a variety of ethical topics in his writings:

> The conclusion is that the purpose of our life is community-service and community-belongingness. (2005a: 442)
>
> Life is such an important value that it is rightly described as the ultimate *raison d'être* of all other activities of the human person. It is thus most valuable, indeed a *mega-value.* (2005b: 447)

If life is the highest value, then should not the purpose of our life be to produce, sustain, or respect it, and not so much to belong to a community?

• From Dismas Masolo, the Kenyan historian of African philosophy, in his book that focuses on moral themes:

> We have seen that the basic ideas of African socialism and *palabre* as well as the idea of *juok* as a moral concept are strategies for forging a state of social cohesion. To achieve this state, people invest in cultivating and striving to live by forms of conduct that are deemed to help bring it about.... A life of cohesion, or positive integration with others, becomes a goal.... In light of this goal, the virtues listed above also become desirable. (2010: 240)

> [I]ndividual and group security is fostered through a network of social relations ruled by a strong sense of unity and caring.... [W]ell-being is complete when (apart from material prosperity) people feel that they are in an atmosphere of positive relations with other members of society or neighborhood.
>
> (2010: 216, 250)

The first quotation says that promoting people's well-being is morally desirable insofar as it is part of fostering cohesive or communal relationships, which is the ultimate end that accounts for other moral properties. However, the second quotation suggests that cohesive relationships are a means to the end of improving well-being. Which value is fundamental, or are both independent final goods?

• From Edwin Etieyibo, a moral philosopher originally from Nigeria who has been based in South Africa for a long while and written on *ubuntu*, the Nguni term for humanness that is widely used to capture sub-Saharan morality:

> [A]n action's moral rightness or wrongness is determined by how well it promotes human flourishing. This makes African ethics teleological in the sense that it derives duty or moral obligation from what is good or desirable as an end to be achieved, the end being human flourishing. (2014: 73)
>
> [R]ight action and conduct are evaluated by how well they promote smooth relationships on the one hand, and uphold social structure and order, on the other. An action or conduct is good to the extent it promotes these ends and bad to the extent it detracts from the ends. (2014: 78)

The first quotation says that flourishing or interest satisfaction is the final end to be pursued when acting rightly; our ultimate goal should be to make people better off. The second, in apparent contrast, says that relationships, structure, and order are the ends to be pursued for their own sake when acting rightly; our ultimate goal should be to promote certain kinds of interaction between people.[11]

Some might contend that I have not read a given philosopher's text closely or carefully enough. Perhaps. My hope, though, is that readers will at least agree that it should be easier to interpret the field. I submit that it would be useful to demarcate competing candidates for basic duties more clearly and rigorously than has been done up to now, and then to consider whether one is to be philosophically preferred to the others. Which is the most promising candidate for a sole fundamental moral value in the African tradition: well-being, vital force, or harmonious (communal, cohesive) relationship?

[11] One way to reconcile these views might be to define flourishing in terms of relating in certain ways, as Etieyibo sometimes suggests (2014: 75–7). However, at other times he appears to define the relevant relationships as those that promote flourishing (2014: 73–4).

Since such an enquiry, at least systematically undertaken, has not been common in the field of African philosophy, some would contend that it does not count as African (Owolabi 2001; Ramose 2007). Indeed, my own account of what the word 'African' means appears to suggest the same: insofar as my style and method are not characteristic of the way philosophers below the Sahara have practised their craft over the past few hundred years, my philosophy is not African.

In reply, I note that dozens of African philosophers have suggested general accounts of morality or views of basic goods and ends; see the many quotes above, as well as myriad citations to similarly comprehensive or foundational statements about the nature of sub-Saharan ethics in this book. So, one might reasonably think that my approach is a normative extension of what African philosophers have already begun, even if they have often been representations of what sub-Saharan peoples have purportedly believed about morality. In addition, as I make clear in the next section, the argumentative defence of my favoured theory appeals, in large part, to moral judgements that are much more common in Africa than in the West and in many other places around the world. That gives my ethic a clear African pedigree.

Note that even if I had to accept that my *method* is not so African, making my ethic or philosophy overall *less* African than it could have been, it would not necessarily be disqualified from carrying the 'African' label altogether. Consider an analogy. Suppose that medical research as developed outside of Africa showed that a certain plant indigenous solely to South Africa has healing powers. It would be sensible to call the treatment a 'South African' one, despite the existence of non-African evidence that it is effective. Similarly, in this book I work to show that a moral principle that is informed by the ideas of certain African philosophers and by salient features they ascribe to many sub-Saharan societies can be justified using the methods of analytic philosophy. The method alone, if it is best labelled 'Western' or 'non-African', is not sufficient to rule out the 'African' label for the ethic.

So far in this sub-section I have addressed the objection that talk of an 'African moral theory' is in effect contradictory, as moral theorization is not African. I close it by considering the objection that, although the project might be coherent, it is not worth undertaking. Recently, some philosophers from Africa have contended that salient sub-Saharan norms, particularly ones pertaining to harmony or communality, are anachronistic, appropriate (if ever) only for a bygone time (Oguejiofor 2007; Matolino and Kwindingwi 2013). According to them, a focus on harmonious or communal relationship perhaps can make sense for small-scale, pre-industrial, oral societies, but surely not urban, technologically advanced, literate ones. Given a fundamental interest in improving people's quality of life, mores that prescribe cohesion, togetherness, belonging, and the like should be dropped.

Ultimately, my reply to this concern is this book as a whole; it attempts to demonstrate that a communal ethic makes the best sense of a wide array of moral judgements that clearly apply to twenty-first-century or 'modern' societies (amongst others). However, I also note that the present objection begs the question by presuming that a certain, welfarist morality is true. It is an open question whether the most promising account of right and wrong is grounded on (in rough catchwords) utility, vitality, or communality (or something else). I argue in this book that, in the light of many comparatively less controversial judgements about morality, communality wins out.

1.3 Meta-Ethics: Identifying the Best Moral Theory

Part I of the book is largely meta-ethical or methodological, focused on the way that I seek to justify my favoured moral theory. As indicated in the previous section, my analytic approach to African ethics differs from what has been the norm, and so I spend two chapters addressing mainly my African philosophical colleagues, explaining it and motivating it relative to methods they might find more familiar and attractive on the face of it.

Many in the African tradition believe that ethical claims follow immediately from metaphysical ones that must be established first. For example, Kwame Nkrumah (1970) maintains that an egalitarian ethic follows directly from a prior physicalist ontology, Henry Odera Oruka and Calestous Juma (1994: 115) suggest that a duty to respect nature is entailed by the purported fact that everything in the universe is interrelated, and Kwame Gyekye (1997: 35–76) contends that his 'moderate communitarian' moral and political philosophy is derived from a certain conception of the self. In Chapter 2, I aim to show how these and similar attempts fail to clear the 'is/ought gap', as it is known in Western meta-ethics, and how various strategies one might use to bridge the gap do not work. In addition, I argue that even if I were incorrect, so that appealing to ontological foundation was a viable strategy by which to defend an ethic, an additional one, strictly employed in the book, is to argue 'internally' to morality by appealing to 'intuitions', i.e., by starting from relatively uncontroversial normative judgements about cases. That is, I defend (and then in the rest of the book employ) the approach of determining which comparatively more controversial general principle about morality is justified by invoking less controversial particular moral claims.

In Chapter 3 I explain in some detail the precise analytic method that I use to evaluate theories of morally right action. There I spell out what is involved in seeking to articulate a moral theory with a recognizably sub-Saharan pedigree and to defend it with normative argumentation. In particular, I indicate the central criteria I use to determine whether a theory counts as both African and plausible, namely, the extent to which it entails and explains two classes of intuitions. One sort consists of moral judgements that are widely accepted particularly by sub-Saharan peoples or at least their contemporary philosophical exponents, e.g., that reconciliation is the proper end of criminal justice and that consensus-seeking is apt in politics. The other sort comprises moral judgements generally accepted across the globe, especially as they figure into contemporary English-speaking philosophical discussions of morality. I also point out that I elect to set aside essentially imperceptible (what Westerners would call 'spiritual') conceptions of right and wrong action. Even though they have traditionally been prominent in African philosophy, I do not consider them because they rest on metaphysical claims that are highly contestable and so are inappropriate for my particular purpose, which is to construct an ethic with a broad scope, one that could be appreciated by a multicultural audience.

1.4 Normative Ethics: The Best African Moral Theory

Having specified my method in Part I, in the rest of the book I employ it. In Part II, I engage in normative ethical theorization, distinguishing between three major secular moral principles suggested by the African literature and arguing that one is stronger than the other two. The overall aim in this part is to establish the most defensible moral theory with an African pedigree, which is basically a matter of finding the principle that best captures the intuitions presented in the previous chapter. The three good candidates in the sub-Saharan tradition for grounding a principle of right action are the common good (well-being), vital force (life), and communal relationship (harmony), which are often inadequately distinguished from each other (1.2.3). In this part of the book, I argue that the latter one is more promising as an independent foundation for right and wrong than the former two.

In Chapter 4 I address the common good, and critically explore most closely the views of Kwame Gyekye, one of the two or three most widely discussed African moral and political philosophers of the past twenty-five years. He has argued with sophistication that what unifies characteristic sub-Saharan moral thought is, in his terms, the 'master value' of well-being (2004: 41), or, more carefully, the prescription to promote the common good (1997, 2010; related views include Wiredu 1992, Sogolo 1993, and Bewaji 2004). This perspective is close to, but differs in some important ways from, Western utilitarianism. Interestingly, one cannot argue against Gyekye's view merely by invoking well-known criticisms of Western utilitarianism, such as the fact that the latter permits sacrificing the urgent interests of the few for the sake of the greater good. I advance fresh reasons for rejecting a welfarist approach to African morality that I maintain hit their target.

In Chapter 5 I take up vital force, a second value often invoked to ground African thought about morality, with three prominent thinkers in this vein being Noah Dzobo (1992), Bénézet Bujo (1997, 2001, 2005), and Laurenti Magesa (1997). From this perspective, 'In no way is any thought, word or act understood except in terms of good and bad, in the sense that such an attitude or behavior either enhances or diminishes life' (Magesa 1997: 58). Such a principle is a globally under-explored approach to ethics that deserves much more consideration than it has received. However, I ultimately conclude that it is unable to account for a variety of comparatively uncontroversial claims about ethics, including many that will appeal widely to Africans.

In Chapter 6 I begin to articulate the key elements of the third major suggestion to be found in the literature about what is fundamental to sub-Saharan ethics, namely, communal or harmonious relationships. Desmond Tutu remarks of morality for African people, 'Harmony, friendliness, community are great goods. Social harmony is for us the *summum bonum*—the greatest good' (1999: 35), and several others have suggested something similar. I provide a detailed reconstruction of typical sub-Saharan understandings of communality or harmony as an ideal to be achieved, and point out that, as the combination of sharing a way of life with others and caring for their quality of life, it is similar to what English-speakers label 'friendliness'.

I appeal in Chapter 7 to the conception of communality from the previous chapter to articulate a new deontological moral theory that instructs agents to honour beings insofar as they are by nature capable of communing as a subject or being communed with as an object. From this standpoint, what typically makes actions wrong is, roughly, that they are not friendly towards or harmonious with innocent parties, where particularly wrongful behaviour is downright unfriendly or discordant in respect of them. I draw out a variety of corollaries from rightness as friendliness, such as that one normally should not promote harmony using a very discordant means, and that having befriended someone provides extra reason to go out of one's way for him compared to a stranger. I demonstrate that this moral theory, in the light of its corollaries, accounts better for the key intuitions than the African welfarist and vitalist approaches.

1.5 Applied Ethics: The Best Moral Theory, from Africa

In Part II I will have argued for the most defensible normative theoretical account of morality with an African pedigree. In Part III I argue that the relational principle of right action is more plausible than two theories that have dominated English-speaking and more generally Western philosophy for the past two or three centuries, or at least that it must be taken seriously as an alternative to them. I address a variety of topics in applied ethics in order to illustrate the communal ethic, to show that its implications powerfully rival extant approaches to them in contemporary Western moral philosophy, and to shed some light on debates about what a moral agent owes others.

In particular, in the third major part of the book I argue that, when applied to a variety of interpersonal controversies, the principle of right action defended in the second part is often to be preferred to standard versions of utilitarianism and Kantianism, where the latter is identified with the principle of respect for autonomy (or the Formula of Humanity). I highlight the relational character of rightness as friendliness, bringing out how that feature often enables it to improve on, or at least compete reasonably against, the two principles of right action that have been the most influential in the modern Euro-American-Australasian tradition. I do not explore ways of interpreting the Western moral theories to make them stronger, instead aiming to show that the communal ethic is a powerful rival for providing plausible answers to a wide array of questions in applied ethics. I leave it to utilitarians and Kantians to see whether they can develop an interpretation of their view with an explanatory power that is comparably comprehensive.

In Chapter 8 I take up issues in environmental ethics, and, in particular, focus heavily on articulating and defending a novel account of moral status that is the companion to the theory of right action from the previous chapters. I advance the view that an entity is directly owed moral consideration roughly to the degree that it is by nature capable of being party to a communal relationship, and I argue that it is attractive in comparison to dominant accounts of moral status in the West. If moral status depends on the degree of a being's capacities to commune with us or to be communed with by us, then many animals do have a moral status but one that is not as high as ours. Such partial moral status for animals is what many, if not most, readers will find attractive at least upon reflection, and it is what is difficult for utilitarianism and Kantianism to accommodate. I also show that the relational element of the African theory grounds a promising response to the 'argument from marginal cases' purporting to show that animals have the same moral status as incapacitated humans; for even if two beings have identical intrinsic properties, they can differ in the extent to which they can relate to us and hence plausibly differ in their degree of moral status.

In Chapter 9 I address a variety of bioethical controversies as they concern medical practitioners such as doctors and nurses. I argue that the communal principle is at least no worse than, and is often to be preferred over, more Western principles when it comes to how to understand their obligations. Amongst other things, I argue that the sub-Saharan ethic makes good sense of whom a medical professional is obligated to treat and for which purposes, and also that it grounds moderate, intuitively compelling positions on abortion and euthanasia in ways that rival principles such as utilitarianism and Kantianism cannot easily do.

In Chapter 10 I turn to the duties of researchers, particularly those in the medical field, again contending that communality is revealing relative to Western competitors. For instance, I proffer a novel account of free and informed consent to participate in a study, as something to be upheld not so much as a way to promote health (utilitarianism) or to avoid degrading autonomy (Kantianism), but more as a way to respect people as capable of communal or friendly relationship. In addition, I argue that the African moral theory grounds a powerful account of ancillary care obligations, roughly duties to compensate for harms that have befallen study participants that the study did not cause, particularly in relation to an influential autonomy-based theory of them.

In Chapter 11 I reflect on the obligations of educators and what it is they owe their students and the broader society when it comes to which knowledge to teach. I point out how utilitarianism and Kantianism naturally ground a cosmopolitan approach to instructing matters of culture, whereas the communal ethic does not, an implication that I argue is reasonable. I also note how the relational moral theory probably entails that it is right to strive to develop students' virtue in ways that are not salient in the works of those who adhere to the Western moral principles.

In Chapter 12, the last applied ethics chapter, I consider some issues in business. For example, I argue that the communal ethic does a better job of accounting for intuitions about who counts as a stakeholder and how to prioritize amongst competing stakeholder interests than does either utilitarianism or Kantianism. I contend further that, when it comes to the workplace, the relational moral theory seems uniquely able to explain why there is strong moral reason for a firm to temper a managerialist production process.

Chapter 13 concludes the book. In it I first highlight some of the key advantages of the communal ethic for moral philosophers, recalling, for example, how it grounds the judgements that: animals have a moral status, albeit one less than that of human beings; many human persons have a dignity of a sort that explains why reducing their quality of life matters morally; and despite a kind of impartial consideration being demanded by people's dignity, an agent has duties to do more for those who have related communally with her. Then, I note some ways in which the relational moral theory might be of interest to social scientists, suggesting that it can ground an empirical understanding of morality that gives Lawrence Kohlberg's influential account a good run for its money. In this chapter I also point out certain limits of the position I will have advanced in this book and mention some topics that merit undertaking in future work. For instance, the focus of the book will have been on right action, and not good character, where I conclude by sketching what a communal account of moral virtue might look like. In addition, the book will have addressed rightness and wrongness in the contexts of interpersonal or otherwise small-scale relationships. Another book to write would address issues of justice in legal, political, and economic institutions.

In the Epilogue I consider what the implications of the African moral theory are for my project of having sought one out and defended it relative to major competitors in Western philosophy. Upon having first come to South Africa from the United States in 1999 for personal reasons and then taken up a lectureship at a public university in Johannesburg, I judged myself to have had a moral obligation to undertake a critical study of the sub-Saharan philosophical tradition. I would have felt guilt, and aptly I believe, had I not done so as a lecturer and researcher. I close by bringing out how my favoured communal ethic makes good sense of why I have had a duty to write this book.

PART I

META-ETHICS

African Ethics without a Metaphysical Ground

2
Reconsidering Ontology's Relevance

2.1 Minding the Is/Ought Gap

The default position amongst African philosophers is that ethics is to be grounded on metaphysics. An entire book has been devoted to exploring this approach (Imafidon and Bewaji 2013), and amongst the four basic themes in traditional African religion, one scholar includes 'an ethic that flows from ontology' (Mulago 1991: 120, 125–6). Note that this is not merely the view that an ethic should avoid false or unjustified metaphysical views (a view that I accept). It is instead, at least on many occasions, the much stronger view that a theoretical claim about how to act morally follows immediately from a broad metaphysical claim about what exists.

Here are two examples. Marcel Onyibor says that 'the principle of participation in African ontology is sustained by a common life force giving rise to a hierarchy of forces in the universe.... This co-participation in turn generates social and metaphysical responsibility on the part of man' (2007: 168), while Elvis Imafidon remarks, 'Since the African community is an aggregate of interacting cosmic forces, it would imply that such a community, conscious of the nature of its being, would establish structures to foster and sustain the much needed interaction among entities' (2013: 42–3). In addition to these claims that we have a responsibility to aid others because we are essentially life-forces that interact, it is common to encounter the similar argument that we must respect nature because everything in the cosmos is interdependent.

Most contemporary Western philosophers would view such argumentative strategies with suspicion, as illegitimately attempting to cross what is called the 'is/ought gap'. Speaking of Kwame Nkrumah's attempt to justify a certain moral-political view, which I address in detail below, Paulin Hountondji is similarly critical:

> It is just as arbitrary to found socialism on materialism as on idealism, as arbitrary to found oligarchy on idealism as on materialism (or on any other metaphysical system for that matter). Our political choices stand on their own feet. If they need justification, it must be political justification, belonging to the same level of discourse and not to what is the completely different (*ex hypothesi*) level of metaphysical speculation. (1996: 153–4)

On this issue, I side with Hountondji, as opposed to many other African philosophers. In this chapter I intend to bolster Hountondji's position by systematically

A Relational Moral Theory: African Ethics in and beyond the Continent. Thaddeus Metz, Oxford University Press.
 DOI: 10.1093/oso/9780198748960.003.0002

arguing that nothing moral *straightaway* follows from any *purely* ontological view, that is, a view about the nature of reality that includes no evaluative elements (about what is good/bad) or normative elements (about what an agent should/not do). I cannot ascertain how an inferentially strong argument can move directly to morality from mere ontology, given widely accepted principles of logic.[1] If one is interested in providing an epistemic justification for a general moral principle, I believe one must do so in some other way, centrally by supporting it with other, more particular moral claims, i.e., intuitions in the 'same level of discourse'.

In order to show that attempting to ground ethics directly on a pure metaphysics is not promising, I focus closely on two of the most influential attempts. I start with Nkrumah's view that an egalitarian ethic follows 'suddenly' (in his words) from a materialist metaphysic (2.2). After arguing that Nkrumah's argument is unsound as it stands, I consider whether various 'bridge premises' could be inserted to close the gap between is and ought, effecting an indirect route from ontology to morality through a claim explicitly linking an egalitarian moral theory to a physicalist ontology.[2] However, I argue that no such premise is plausible enough to provide reason to draw Nkrumah's moral conclusion. Then I turn to Kwame Gyekye's purported derivation of what he calls 'moderate communitarianism' from his conception of the nature of the self (2.3). Basically, Gyekye claims that agents have strong duties to aid others in ways that do not violate human rights since such a view 'immediately' (in his words) follows from the dual nature of the self as both social and individual. Again I note that the inferential structure of this direct reasoning is weak, and then try to find a bridge premise that would make sense of how Gyekye's ethic indirectly follows from his metaphysic, but fail to find one that is defensible. Next, I quickly run through similar arguments in the field, to show that they fall prey to the same problem (2.4). Perhaps someone else will find a suitable bridge premise to link a specific moral theory uniquely to claims about what exists in a plausible way. For now, however, I conclude that the most promising strategy by which to justify a moral theory epistemically is by appealing to intuitions about morality that are less controversial than it and involve no reliance on thick ontological claims about the nature of the self or the world (2.5). That is my approach in Parts II and III of the book.

2.2 From Materialism to Egalitarianism?

In this section I critically discuss Nkrumah's characteristically African attempt to ground ethics on metaphysics in his book *Consciencism*, and, specifically, his claim

[1] Perhaps some other, radically different logic could make sense of the inference. For those interested in pursuing such a strategy, consider Chimakonam (2019).

[2] The useful distinction between direct and indirect strategies comes from Oyowe (2018), who critically discussed a previously published version of the material in this chapter.

that an egalitarian morality is alone paired with a materialist ontology. As he puts it, 'Idealism favours an oligarchy, materialism favours an egalitarianism.... It is the basic unity of matter, despite its varying manifestations, which gives rise to egalitarianism' (1970: 75, 96). Granting Nkrumah that reality is ultimately physical and that the physical is unitary, I argue that nothing logically follows about whether human beings have an equal worth or a dignity in particular. Although I, too, am both a materialist and an egalitarian, and while I believe they are compatible, I do not think that the former metaphysic provides any evidence, neither direct nor indirect, for the latter ethic.

2.2.1 Nkrumah's Materialism

In *Consciencism*, Nkrumah discusses two major metaphysical views of the world, and he believes they entail different moral perspectives. First off, there is idealism, the view that the mental either is alone what exists or is fundamental in some way relative to other things that exist. Canvassing a number of idealist philosophers and their moral-political views, Nkrumah posits not merely an historical correlation between idealism and elitism, but also a logical relationship between them. That is, he holds that if one believes that the nature of reality is fundamentally mental, then one is committed to a view of human beings as having differential moral worth. In Nkrumah's words, 'idealism favoured a class structure of a horizontal sort, in which one class sat upon the neck of another.... Idealism favours an oligarchy' (1970: 75; see also 76).

The contrasting metaphysics is of course materialist: the independent existence of physical forces that move according to objective laws, without being propelled by an independent spiritual being (1970: 79, 96–7). Nkrumah distinguishes two instances of this general view. On the one hand, there is an extreme version of materialism, according to which the only things that exist are ones expressible in physical terms, such as atoms, space-time, and chemical reactions. On the other, there is a moderate version, according to which there exist some things that cannot be captured in the language of physics, chemistry, and similar disciplines, but that are constituted by (or at the very least determined by) the latter.

Nkrumah favours the moderate version of materialism, maintaining that minds exist, and are made up of (or are at least a function of) the physical, even if not able to be fully understood in those terms (1970: 84–90). His well-known phrases for the nature of the mental are that it is an instance of 'categorial conversion' or is an 'emergent property'. In the language of contemporary Anglo-American philosophy of science, Nkrumah appears to be a proponent of what is called 'non-reductive materialism'. His view is not that only matter exists, in the sense that everything can be reduced to the language or theories of physics, chemistry, and related academic fields, but instead that matter is 'primary', meaning that other categories, such as the mental, are ultimately determined by it.

2.2.2 Nkrumah's Materialist Defence of Egalitarianism

According to Nkrumah, the moderate form of materialism entails not only egalitarianism, but one of a certain kind, according to which human beings have an equal dignity, a non-instrumental, superlative value. Consider, first, how it is that 'materialism favours egalitarianism' (1970: 75). According to Nkrumah:

> Egalitarianism is based on the monistic thesis of materialism. Matter is one even in its different manifestations.... It is the basic unity of matter, despite its varying manifestations, which gives rise to egalitarianism. Basically, man is one, for all men have the same basis and arise from the same evolution according to materialism. This is the objective ground of egalitarianism.
>
> (1970: 96; see also 35, 75–7)

It is the standard materialist view that all matter is part of a single, interrelated system that, for Nkrumah, grounds the idea that human beings have an equal moral standing: 'The unity and fundamental identity of nature suggests the unity and fundamental identity of man in society' (1970: 75).

The moderate form of materialism appears essential to ground Nkrumah's thesis that humans are equal specifically in virtue of their dignity. Nkrumah seems to believe that our dignity inheres to some large degree in our mental life, for he approvingly remarks that 'man is regarded in Africa as primarily a spiritual being, a being endowed originally with a certain inward dignity, integrity and value' (1970: 68; see also 97). If the extreme version of materialism were true, then there would be no category of the spiritual, i.e., roughly the self-conscious, and hence no dignity.

Nkrumah is clearly aware of the 'is/ought gap' as it is known in Western ethics, even mentioning Hume's famous inclination to question the fact that many 'ethical philosophies begin with statements of fact and suddenly seek to base statements of appraisal thereon' (1970: 96). In addition, Nkrumah is aware that Kant shared Hume's concern, and is explicit that he is rejecting their common viewpoint:

> [P]hilosophical consciencism, though it has the same cardinal principle of ethics as Kant, differs from Kant in founding ethics on a philosophical idea of the nature of man. This is what Kant describes as ethics based on anthropology. By anthropology Kant means any study of the nature of man, and he forbids ethics to be based on such a study. It is precisely this that philosophical consciencism does. (1970: 97)

Nkrumah wants to ground morality on ontology, and specifically a moderate materialist anthropology.

2.2.3 Evaluating Nkrumah's Argument

However, it is not clear *how* Nkrumah can plausibly cross the is/ought gap. Set aside the technicalities of Hume's and Kant's philosophical views about the nature of the mind and how it acquires its content. Simply as a matter of *logic*, it is difficult to understand how one is to move from factual claims that exclude any 'statements of appraisal', i.e., those about what is good or what an agent should do, to statements that do include the latter.

Abstractly put, how can one move from statements about A to statements about C, without an intermediary statement B that links the two (and without C being part of the definition of A)? For instance, from the claim that all people are mortal (A*), one logically *cannot* immediately conclude that Socrates is mortal (C*). In order to infer the latter, one requires a 'bridge premise' linking elements of the two statements, in this case something like the claim that Socrates is a person (B*). Similarly, I submit that, from the claim that all humans are composed of matter (A'), one logically *cannot* immediately conclude that all humans have an equal worth (C'). In order to infer the latter, one requires a bridge premise linking the metaphysical and the ethical, but I cannot find such a premise in *Consciencism*.

Some will be tempted to suggest that the unity of matter is such a bridge premise. However, upon reflection, one sees that it is not, for it is merely about the metaphysical, and fails to include any ethical terms that would entail the moral-egalitarian conclusion. The claim that matter forms a unity, recall, is just the idea that there is a 'continuity of nature' (1970: 96). Just as '[t]here is a route from any twig of a tree to any other twig, such that the route never leaves the tree' (1970: 96), so any instance of matter in the world is related to some other instance, sometimes by being a proximate cause, but other times quite circuitously. This is a purely descriptive statement about the nature of reality that lacks mention of anything evaluative or prescriptive, and hence cannot do the logical work of providing epistemic reason in favour of the latter sort of statement. From the claim that all people are composed of matter (A') and that all matter is unified (B'), one still logically *cannot* immediately conclude that all people have an equal worth or should be treated as ends in themselves (C'). One still needs a bridge premise grounding the equal worth of human beings on the unity of matter in them.

Can the needed premise be supplied on Nkrumah's behalf? Yes and no. Although it is easy to construct a premise that, *if true or justified*, would permit one to infer egalitarianism from materialism, it is hard to see why one should believe that the premise is indeed true or justified. Specifically, the natural form of the bridge premise would be this: *if human beings are all made of matter that is interrelated, then all human beings have an equal worth* (B^). If this premise were known, then, granting the truth of the other premise, that human beings are all made of matter that is interrelated, one would have strong reason to conclude that human beings do have an equal worth. Indeed, one could be certain of this conclusion, via *modus ponens*. However, the key question now is what motivation there is for believing B^.

The problem with B^ is that being composed of the same bits of substance that are related to each other is compatible with there being differential value amongst the bits. After all, a plant is composed of the same material stuff as we are and is presumably no less related to us as part of the grand, evolutionary system of nature, but human beings are intuitively worth more than plants. If one had to choose between running over a flower and a human being, with no third alternative available, one ought to mow down the former, not the latter; and the best explanation of this fact is that human beings have a greater value or status than flowers from a moral point of view.

In fact, note that Nkrumah's belief in human dignity *itself* provides reason to doubt B^. Nkrumah himself recognizes that, despite the continuity of nature, some parts of nature are worth more than others. In particular, for him, those material beings that are 'spiritual', i.e., more or less have self-aware minds, have a dignity and hence 'should not be treated by another merely as a means but always as an end' (1970: 97), whereas other material beings lack a dignity. Hence, it is implausible to think that the equal value of human beings is merely a function of the fact that they are all made of matter that is interrelated, as per B^.

I conclude that Nkrumah is incorrect to think that materialism 'through its being monistic, and its referring all natural process to matter and its laws... inspired an egalitarian organization of society' (1970: 75). Instead of our equal worth being a function of the fact that we are material beings bound up with other beings made of the same stuff, it must be a matter (so to speak) of the *kind* of material beings we are. In order to demonstrate that human beings have a dignity, an inner worth higher than what is in the mineral, vegetable, and animal kingdoms, it must be shown that our particular configuration of matter is different from other configurations, is realized to a comparable degree amongst human beings, and is what counts morally speaking.

2.3 From the Social Self to Communitarianism?

Kwame Nkrumah was a 'first-generation' African professional philosopher, by which I mean one of the first from the sub-Saharan region to study African philosophy at a university and to produce written works on the subject. Kwame Gyekye was from the second generation, and continued the trend of maintaining that axiology follows from ontology. Gyekye says, 'Moral questions... may, in some sense, be said to be linked to, or engendered by, metaphysical conceptions of the person' (1997: 36), and 'The natural relationality of the person thus immediately plunges her into a moral universe' (1997: 67). As I did with Nkrumah, I first point out that Gyekye's reasoning is on the face of it a *non sequitur*, then consider ways to reconstruct it, and conclude that none of them provides an attractive way to ground a moral-political theory on metaphysical claims about the nature of the self.

2.3.1 Moderate Communitarianism

The most influential African moral and political philosophy of the past twenty-five years has been Gyekye's moderate communitarianism. Even where critics have found it wanting, it has stimulated the most debate and is the most well known of any sub-Saharan theory of how individuals morally should behave and of how the state justly ought to function. What makes a normative theory rightly called 'communitarian', by Gyekye's lights, is principally that it requires both participation in a shared way of life and substantial action for the sake of the common good (1997: 42–6, 66–7, 70, 142). The common good is a kind of interest that is both universal and basic amongst human beings. It is basic in that it is a matter of meeting urgent needs, providing items essential for any human being to function, such as food, water, healthcare, and clothing (Gyekye 1997: 45). The common good is also universal in that actions that promote it are those that at the very least make no one worse off, and, in the typical case, make everyone better off (Gyekye 1997: 46, 2004: 117). Communitarianism contrasts with what Gyekye calls 'individualism': the view that a moral agent by and large need neither participate with others nor do much to help them (1997: 45).

Communitarianism and individualism admit of degrees, and Gyekye famously defends a moderate form of communitarianism. Gyekye argues that moral agents have a basic duty to promote the common good as much as possible (1997: 70–5, 2004: 105–11), and so what makes his view moderate is not that its burdens are light. Instead, the moderation is a function of two other facets of Gyekye's view. First, although an agent must do all he can to improve others' well-being, he may not do so in ways that violate individual rights. Gyekye believes that there are human rights to life as well as to civil liberties regarding free expression of opinion (1992: 251), bodily integrity (2004: 36), and even lifestyles that the majority might frown upon (1997: 65). A radical or extreme form of communitarianism would permit agents to perform whichever actions would most promote the common good, which, as contemporary discussion of Western utilitarianism has shown, could involve objectionably treating an individual merely as a means to an end.

The second facet that makes Gyekye's communitarianism moderate rather than extreme is that, although individuals are required to do all they can to improve others' welfare, they need not utterly conform to the ways of life that are dominant in their society. When criticizing extreme forms of communitarianism, Gyekye rejects the idea of a 'cramped or shackled self, responding robotically to the ways and demands of the communal structure' (1997: 55–6). Instead, he appreciates the 'viable and telling pursuits of individuals who can appropriately be described as idealists, visionaries, or revolutionaries' (1997: 57).

What these two elements have in common is the idea that 'moderate communitarianism acknowledges the intrinsic worth of the individual and the moral (natural) rights of the individual that the acknowledgment can be said to entail' (1997: 69). Unlike the extreme form, moderate communitarianism accepts that individuals have the right not to be used as a mere means to the promotion of the common good, on the one hand, and the right to choose idiosyncratic ways of life for themselves, on the other. Gyekye's view remains fundamentally communitarian, and not individualist, insofar as agents must do everything in their power to promote the common good (without degrading individuals) and they have some (defeasible) obligation to cooperate with others and share their fate (1997: 75–6).

Elsewhere I question moderate communitarianism as a moral theory (4.3). Here, in contrast, I cast doubt on the way Gyekye seeks to defend it.

2.3.2 Gyekye's Defence of Moderate Communitarianism

Gyekye's main rationale for moderate communitarianism is that the self has a dual nature as partially independent of the community and partially dependent on it. To spell this out, it is useful to distinguish between two basic elements of Gyekye's moderate communitarianism. On the one hand, individuals have the obligations to lend some support to their society's culture and to do all they can to promote the common good. On the other hand, individuals are entitled to choose their own lifestyles and not to be treated as mere means to the end of improving others' lives. Gyekye favours this combination of duties and rights because they are supposed to follow from the fact that there are two metaphysical aspects to ourselves—an individual nature and a social one. Our duties are a product of our nature as communal beings, whereas our rights follow from our nature as beings who are not utterly determined by the community. Gyekye says:

> [M]oderate communitarianism offers a more appropriate and adequate account of the self and its relation to the community than the unrestricted or extreme or radical account, in that the former sees the self both as a communal being *and* as an autonomous, self-assertive being with a capacity for evaluation and choice, while the latter sees the activity of what I have referred to as the 'mental feature' of the person as *wholly* contingent upon, and determined by, the communal structure itself. (1997: 59; see also 41, 53)

Against a radical communitarian ethic, Gyekye makes these purely descriptive claims: 'The individual is by nature a social (communal) being, yes; but she is, also by nature, *other* things as well' (1997: 47), and 'The powers of inventiveness, imagination, and so on are not entirely a function of the communal culture; they are instead a function of natural talents or endowments, even though they can only be nurtured and exercised in a cultural community' (1997: 59). Since part of us is determined by our inner biology and part of us is determined by our external society, Gyekye maintains that the correct ethic is one that requires us to do a lot for others, albeit in ways that do not degrade individuals' mental features, which include criticism, creativity, and the like.

More specifically, Gyekye maintains that the self is an *equal* product of nature and nurture, the inner and the outer, the individual and the social, which, in turn, requires giving *equal* weight to rights and duties. An individualist morality, which lays great emphasis on a person's rights and rejects the idea of weighty duties to help others, would purportedly follow from a metaphysical view of the self as atomistic and self-sufficient (1997: 38–9, 45). And a radical communitarian normative theory, one that recognizes no individual rights, would be suitable for a self that is completely determined by society, a view that Gyekye (1997: 47–8, 52–9) ascribes to Ifeanyi Menkiti. In contrast, according to Gyekye:

> [I]n view of the fact that neither can the individual develop outside the framework of the community nor can the welfare of the community as a whole dispense with the talent and initiative of its individual members, I think that the most satisfactory way to recognize the claims of both communality and individuality is to ascribe to them the status of an equal moral standing.
>
> (1997: 41; see also 67)

The attempt to ground ethics on metaphysics is clear in Gyekye's key argument for moderate communitarianism. I now maintain that this argument is fallacious; nothing moral can follow from anything *merely* metaphysical. Furthermore, there is no plausible premise that I can find that would show how moderate communitarianism is uniquely suitable, given the dual nature of the self.

2.3.3 Evaluating Gyekye's Argument

One readily sees that Gyekye's direct reasoning, as expressed in the quotations above, is not merely invalid, but also weak, upon presenting it in standard form:

P1: The human self is equally the product of the natural (biology) and the social (culture).

C: Therefore, the correct ethic for us is one that ascribes equal weight to individual rights and communal duties.

C does not follow necessarily or even probabilistically from P1. The conclusion is not logically implied by the premise, which it would have to be in order to follow without another, intermediate premise. In the absence of a bridge premise mediating P1, which is solely about the source of the self, and C, which is instead about the content of morality, the latter gains *no* epistemic support from the former.

To be fair to Gyekye's project, I now consider what a bridge premise might look like and whether it is attractive. The intermediary would have to speak of both the sources of the self and the content of morality, and I can think of three ways one could try to specify it.

Here is one indirect strategy by which to move from a metaphysic of the self to a moderate communitarian ethic:

P1: The human self is equally the product of the natural (biology) and the social (culture).

P2: The correct ethic for human selves is one that reflects the source of the human self.

P3: The ethic for human selves that reflects the source of the human self *qua* equal product of the natural (biology) and the social (culture) is one that ascribes equal weight to individual rights and communal duties.

C: Therefore, the correct ethic for human selves is one that ascribes equal weight to individual rights and communal duties.

I have not found an explicit statement of P2 in Gyekye's most sustained defence of moderate communitarianism (1997), but it has some intuitive pull, and it turns out to be similar to the kind of argument that another major political philosopher, John Rawls (1999: sec. 5, 6, 30), once used to support his theory of justice that includes substantial individual rights. With the insertion of P2 along with P3, the argument has become valid; one cannot logically reject the moderate communitarian conclusion while accepting the premises.

Before evaluating the premises, I pause to clarify them. What is it for an ethic to 'reflect' certain facts about human beings? I presume that for a principle to reflect (or mirror) an object is for the principle to be contoured to it or to replicate it. To reflect something is to match or duplicate features of the thing. Perhaps for Gyekye our individual rights replicate our natural origins as biological beings with mental features, and our duties towards others fit our social origins as beings brought up in a culture, or so P3 should be understood to say.

One might question whether moderate communitarianism indeed 'reflects' the factors that determine who we are, i.e., whether P3 is true, but I set that issue aside in favour of casting doubt on P2. It is far from clear that the correct ethic for us, or more generally the correct norm for an object, is necessarily one that reflects. Instead, sound norms are intuitively understood to be those that direct or constrain their objects in accordance with good reasons.

Consider, for example, norms of prudence. When it comes to self-interested behaviour, people often tend to act on strong desires against their better judgement, and they also tend not to give enough weight to their long-term interests, focusing too heavily on the short-term. It would be odd to think that norms governing how one *ought* to act with regard to one's own good should *reflect* these wayward dispositions of human nature.

Of course, norms that are meant to regulate people's decisions ought to *take account of* human nature—they cannot be overly idealistic or utopian, for example, or else the dictum of 'ought implies can' will tell against them. Plausibly, we can have no reason to do what we simply cannot do. However, that point differs from the idea that norms ought to *reflect* human nature, which is the idea of P2.

Let me try a second way to reconstruct, on Gyekye's behalf, the inference from the metaphysical claim about the nature of the self to the moral conclusion of moderate communitarianism. In the book Gyekye published just prior to the major defence of moderate communitarianism, one finds: 'If sociality is in fact fundamental to human nature, then the type of social order that ought to exist is that which would conduce to the full realization of that nature' (1995: 156–7; see also 161–2). Instead of moral rules mirroring what humans are already like, perhaps they ought to serve the function of helping us to develop what we essentially are. This sort of idea is expressed in the following argument:

P1: The human self is equally the product of the natural (biology) and the social (culture).

P2*: The correct ethic for human selves is one that, when followed, would realize the human self.

P3*: The ethic for human selves that, when followed, would realize the human self *qua* equal product of the natural (biology) and the social (culture) is one that ascribes equal weight to individual rights and communal duties.

C: Therefore, the correct ethic for human selves is one that ascribes equal weight to individual rights and communal duties.

Once again, the argument is now valid, requiring us to consider whether the premises are true. It is worth questioning P3*—the claim that Gyekye's combination of rights and duties would, if followed, do the best job (or even an adequate job) of realizing human nature. However, I elect to focus on P2*.

P2* might appear attractive in light of some familiar Aristotelian ideas about ethics. It is not uncommon for ethicists to hold perfectionism, which is broadly the idea that our aim as moral agents should be to develop human nature—either one's own, as per Aristotle's *eudaimonist* or self-realization ethic, or everyone's nature generally, a view that Thomas Hurka (1993) has advocated with sophistication.

Now, perfectionism admits of two distinct varieties, one of which is much more plausible than the other. Perfectionism$_1$ is the view that a moral agent ought to develop human nature, whatever it metaphysically is as distinct from what, say, animals are. In contrast, perfectionism$_2$ is the view that a moral agent ought to develop the *valuable* aspects of human nature, features of us that are good for their own sake and that animals lack.

The difference between the two varieties is revealed upon consideration of features of human nature that are not good, i.e., that are either downright bad, on the one hand, or neutral, on the other. For an instance of the latter, it appears to be a part of human nature *simpliciter* to have been born from a woman impregnated by a man, which would not be true of a 'test-tube baby'. Perfectionism$_1$ would naturally entail that there is some moral reason not to have such a baby because it would not be a characteristic human being, whereas perfectionism$_2$ could easily avoid that implication.

I realize that there are those who might bite the bullet and deem a test-tube baby to be wrong to create, and precisely because it would be 'unnatural'. Therefore, consider another, more telling example: that of our deep disposition to divide human beings along racial, ethnic, and related characteristics, to be paranoid of those we deem 'other', and to work to 'cleanse' ourselves of them.[3] On the face of it, perfectionism$_1$ would prescribe rearing human beings who do exhibit that divisive tendency, since it is part of human nature *simpliciter*, and probably because of our evolutionary history, whereas any plausible version of perfectionism$_2$ would rule that out.

I presume the reader shares my judgement in finding the implications of perfectionism$_2$ to be more attractive than those of perfectionism$_1$. However—and here is the rub—Gyekye's P2* is expressive of the latter, and not the former. P2* says that the function of morality ought to be to realize human selves, where, in order to do epistemic work in conjunction with the purely metaphysical P1, the notion of human self at play must be free of any evaluative or prescriptive elements and instead be purely descriptive. Insofar as P2* expresses perfectionism$_1$ and we find that conception of ethics unattractive, we must reject P2*.

Here is a third idea I have about how to help Gyekye shore up the inference from a metaphysical judgement about the self to a moderate communitarian conclusion about morality and politics. Although I will argue that it, too, is unsuccessful, it should be revealing to address it:

P1: The human self is equally the product of the natural (biology) and the social (culture).

P2†: The correct ethic for human selves is one that has us pay back those responsible for the course of our lives in proportion to their contribution.

P3†: The ethic for human selves that has us proportionately pay back those responsible for the course of our lives, where we are equally the product of the

[3] For two philosophically informed discussions of this tendency, see Koestler (1967) and Nussbaum (2012: 27–46).

natural (biology) and the social (culture), is one that ascribes equal weight to individual rights and communal duties.

C: Therefore, the correct ethic for human selves is one that ascribes equal weight to individual rights and communal duties.

The idea behind P2† will perhaps be attractive to those familiar with an influential version of the Divine Command Theory. According to this view, our most basic obligation is to pay back God as our creator, which entails that we have moral reason to do whatever He commands us to do (cf. Lombardi 1991). P2† is similar, indicating that we owe a debt of gratitude, or otherwise a debt of repayment, to whatever is responsible for our existence.

P1 proposes that, with respect to a given individual, both she and her community are comparably responsible for the course of her life. And the rest of the argument expresses the idea that the way to pay back the individual and her community is to ascribe her both rights and duties of the sort Gyekye does. She owes it to herself to take advantage of rights to exercise her mental features of criticism, imagination, and the like, and she owes it to others in her society to participate in their way of life and promote the common good.

Consider, now, whether P2† is true or not or at least plausible. One clear problem with it is that it cannot serve as a complete ground for morality. Intuitively, I have some obligation to help distant foreigners and even animals in distress when I can do so at little cost to myself, but distant foreigners and animals are in no respect responsible for the course of my life. So, whatever duties I have to aid compatriots, those who have benefited me, must be tempered against the duties I have to aid those who have not, potentially blocking the inference to acting in a moderately communitarian way towards compatriots.

Another problem concerns P3†, which, upon reflection, appears unsupported by the logic of the argument. While the rationale appears able to make sense of why *one ought to take advantage* of a right, it does not, upon reflection, make sense of why *another ought to accord* one a right. Note, first, that P2† and P1 entail that, since I am partly responsible for my existence and the path my life has taken, I owe it to myself (or, strictly speaking, to the inner part of myself) to guide my life partially on the basis of my mental features. P2† and P1, secondly, entail that, since others are partly responsible for my existence and the path my life has taken, I owe something to them. However, what is it that I owe them?

Setting my parents or legal guardians aside, it appears that I primarily owe other members of society something related to the culture they have maintained and imparted to me. It might also be that, insofar as others have supported an economic system enabling me to meet my needs, I owe members of my society behaviour that would help them meet their needs. So, if the logic of the current argument is sound, Gyekye can fairly derive the conclusion that I owe others in my society support for their culture and promotion of the common good.

However, it is unclear how he can derive the idea that I owe others respect for their individual rights to live as they see fit, for *it is not in virtue of those rights that others have benefited me.*

Again, others have helped me in terms of conferring meanings, values, and more generally a way of life on me that grounds my sense of self, and by supporting an economy that meets my needs, and so I should return the favour with regard to fostering a society's culture and well-being. However, others have not helped me (or, at least, not very much) insofar as they have taken advantage of rights to live idiosyncratic lifestyles. It therefore appears, from the logic of the present argument, that I do not generally owe it to them not to violate their individual rights to choose their own ways of life.

Before concluding this section, I advance a further reason for doubting that any attractive reconstruction is available, i.e., for thinking that it is fruitless to try to ground a moral-political theory on claims about the nature of the self in the way Gyekye attempts. Consider that debate amongst scientists still rages about the extent to which nature and nurture are respectively responsible for who we are and what we do. It is not so clear that nature and nurture are equal sources of our selves, or even that they are comparable sources. Appealing to shaky descriptive claims about our human nature is, for the foreseeable future, out of place as a defence of the firmly held claim that one should accord an 'equal moral standing' (1997: 41) to the claims of individuality and communality.

2.4 More Instances of the Gap

So far I have argued Nkrumah's and Gyekye's arguments are fallacious. There is a gulf between ontological claims about what is or exists, on the one hand, and ethical claims about what is good or how agents ought to act, on the other, in the sense that nothing about the latter is justified *merely* on the basis of the former. Furthermore, I have argued against a variety of attempts to bridge the is/ought gap with premises that explicitly ground ethical claims on metaphysical ones. Although the positing of such premises can resolve the problem of invalid inference, the premises themselves have been implausible.

The attempt to move from pure ontology to morality is not unique to these two Ghanaian philosophers, but is characteristic of the field of African philosophy more generally. I now point out some other kinds of arguments in the literature similar in form to Nkrumah's and Gyekye's, and contend that the criticism I have made of the latter applies with equal force to the former.

First off, recall the quotes from the Nigerian philosophers I started with at the outset of this chapter. Those quotations suggest that, according to widely shared sub-Saharan perspectives on metaphysics, the world as a whole is composed of forces that interact with one another. These forces can be in either a perceptible realm or an imperceptible one, and they are constantly in motion and affecting one another both within a given realm and between realms. Onyibor and Imafidon say that duties to help other persons are 'generated' from or 'implied' by this purely metaphysical view of the fundamental nature of reality, a view that several other philosophers appear to share. Here are additional examples of this approach: 'African morals lay a great emphasis on social conduct, since a basic African view is that the individual exists only because others exist' (Mbiti 1975: 175), and 'Existence in Africa cannot be any other thing outside "in-relation", that is communal. The individual's life is inseparable from that of the other or his community. This breeds the idea of collective responsibility' (Ogugua 2007: 33; see also Nze 2007; cf. Oladipo 2004: 356; Ogbujah 2007).

However, *does* necessary interdependence between an individual and his society really 'breed' the idea of collective responsibility? How *could* it, logically speaking? Consider the following thought experiments to see that there is a gulf between the metaphysical claim and the moral one, in the sense that no specific axiology follows from an ontology.

First, imagine that individuals were self-sufficient and did not need each other and were not influenced by one another. Imagine that the individual person is 'prior to the community and equipped with conceptions of the good perhaps totally different from the purposes of the community, individual conceptions of the good *wholly* and *always* arrived at independently of the system of values available in a community' (Gyekye 1997: 45). My claim is: nothing yet follows with respect to the way we ought to treat people. In particular, one need not hold the individualist view that there are no duties to assist others. It could still be, for instance, that atomistic individuals would have a dignity that warrants respectful treatment from a given agent, one form of which would be helping them to achieve whichever ends they have set for themselves. Or it might be that atomistic individuals are capable of feeling pain, giving us moral reason to help them.

Second, now imagine the opposite. Suppose, for the sake of argument, that the way Gyekye reads Menkiti were true, i.e., that little, if anything, about us is the result of our natural endowment, and that nearly everything about us is instead a product of socialization and other external influences. My claim is: nothing yet follows with respect to the way we ought to treat people. In particular, one need not hold the radical communitarian view that there are no individual rights and that one is obligated to conform blindly to the community's extant norms, whatever they happen to be. It could still be, for instance, that, although everything about us is a product of society, what society has produced are beings with a dignity that warrants respectful treatment, one form of which would be to avoid using coercion or deception to force us to adopt a given way of life.

What these thought experiments demonstrate is that argumentatively settling questions about how we are obligated to treat other persons cannot be done *immediately* on the basis of *purely* metaphysical descriptions of human nature.

Instead, one invariably has to take up irreducibly evaluative or normative considerations, some of which might be whether we have a dignity and what is involved in treating it with respect.

Turn now to a similar kind of argument, regarding how to treat non-persons, that has been advanced by other African philosophers. Some of them have ascribed a moral status to nature as a whole, or to many non-human beings in it, on the basis of the purported metaphysical fact that everything in the world is interrelated—indeed, interdependent. Often the suggestion is that, according to a Western ontology, human beings are separate from nature, which allegedly entails the view that it is permissible to dominate it, whereas, according to an African metaphysics, human beings are dependent on or otherwise tied to nature, from which it is said to follow that they must treat it or large parts of it with respect of some kind.

For an example of such a rationale, consider these remarks from the influential Kenyan philosophers Henry Odera Oruka and Calestous Juma:

> The Judaeo-Christian ethic has placed humans apart from nature, a fact that has contributed to global environmental degradation. There is a need for a shift towards a new epistemological outlook in which humankind is viewed as part of a complex and systematic totality of nature . . . an ecophilosophical approach which recognizes the totality of (spatial, temporal and other) interlinkages in nature. (1994: 115)

For a similar view, consider this remark from an intellectual working in the southern African tradition of *ubuntu*:

> Cosmic unity means that everything is perpetually in motion, influencing and being influenced by something else. From this perspective has evolved the view that knowing is a relational act. . . . Knowing involves participation in the dynamic process, which involves interaction between parts and the whole. . . . From this belief emerges an ethic that prioritises social obligations to others, to one's community and to the cosmos in general. (Mkhize 2008: 38; see also 35–6)[4]

My problem with these rationales should be clear: from the bare fact that everything in the natural world is interrelated, nothing immediately follows about how to respond to nature. It could be that, although human beings are dependent on nature, nature should be exploited, as much as is consistent with a long-term anthropocentric interest in promoting human lives and well-being. Conversely, it could be that, even if human beings were not dependent on certain

[4] See also remarks by Sindima (1989: 538–9) and Murove (2004: 205), as well as the critical discussion in Behrens (2013: 58–62).

natural objects, the latter have a moral status and should be accorded moral treatment for their own sake, perhaps because they can feel pain.

As with Nkrumah's and Gyekye's rationales, it is worth considering whether there is a bridge premise that can plausibly ground respect for nature on it purportedly consisting of interlinked forces. My hunch, though, is that my inability to find an attractive bridge premise for the former views bodes ill for finding one for the latter view.

2.5 How Not to Fall into the Gap

My argumentation in this chapter is not meant to suggest that metaphysical claims are never relevant to accepting or rejecting a moral conclusion. In denying that purely ontological claims about what exists can on their own entail a specific moral theory, I should not be read as saying that ontology should be completely ignored when doing ethical philosophy. After all, it would be a bad idea to make reference to the Flying Spaghetti Monster inherent to one's moral theory, or to maintain that one ought to be suspicious of the alien lizards posing as human beings when making hiring decisions. It is one thing to try to show that a certain general moral principle is true because it is uniquely paired with a certain account of the nature of the self or the universe, and it is another to argue that certain moral claims are implausible because they rest on unjustified or false claims about what exists.

In addition, there is another type of from-metaphysics-to-morals reasoning salient in the African tradition that is still viable, for all I have said here. Specifically, one might hold an 'impure' metaphysics, i.e., one that inherently includes evaluative or normative elements. Such a perspective is typical of Aristotelian views of what exists, according to which a thing's nature is constituted at least in part by its purpose, i.e., by what would be *good* for it or by how it *ought* to function, and some African philosophers have also held such a view (e.g., Chemhuru 2016). If what it essentially is to be a human being *just is* to be the sort of being that *ought* to treat others or nature in a certain way, then this sort of metaphysics would be prima facie relevant to ethics. No bridge premise would be needed linking the metaphysical statement with a moral one since the metaphysical statement itself includes moral considerations. This so-called 'metaphysics' differs from the kinds explored in this chapter that are pure, i.e., shorn of anything evaluative or normative. While I am not inclined to believe a teleological approach to ontology, insofar as it conceives of the is itself in terms of ought, it does not objectionably try to *infer* the latter from the former.

As noted above (1.1), often a promising strategy by which to transcend a debate between two positions is to reject a premise that both of them share. Both radical and moderate communitarians have often assumed that the way to treat others is a function of the extent to which society is ontologically prior to the individual (or vice versa). I have argued that this common assumption is incorrect, clearing the way for a resolutely normative approach to moral disputes in African philosophy of the sort Hountondji suggests at the start of this chapter. In the rest of the book I strictly use such an approach, usually evaluating general moral principles in the light of particular moral claims.

Finally, note that, even if I am incorrect in this chapter, and a purely ontological claim about what exists somehow can directly or (more plausibly) indirectly entail a specific theoretical account of how to act morally, there is no reason to think that *only* such a strategy is available if one wants epistemic support for a moral theory. For all that has been said, it appears sensible to think that at least one viable way to argue for a general principle about what makes actions right as opposed to wrong is to consider the extent to which the principle can make sense of particular cases of right and wrong that are less controversial than it. I spell out this favoured approach in the following chapter.

3
Analysing African Ethics

3.1 Justifying an African Moral Theory

In the first chapter I (amongst other things) pointed out that I use the term 'African' and cognate words to pick out properties that have been recurrent in at least the sub-Saharan region for a long while, and in the second I contended that a moral theory cannot be epistemically justified by immediate appeal to metaphysical considerations utterly shorn of evaluative or normative judgements, as has often been attempted in the African philosophical tradition. What I do in the present chapter is to specify those properties that I deem to be both African and relevant to constructing a moral theory as well as to indicate how I propose to justify belief in an African moral theory.

I begin by clarifying the elements of the analytic methodology that I employ to articulate and defend my favoured moral theory, drawing analogies between scientific enquiry and my moral theorization (3.2). Next, I note the fact that, unlike many African philosophers who would place imperceptible agents such as ancestors, God, and the not-yet-born at the heart of their ethical thought, I do not (3.3). Kwasi Wiredu and Kwame Gyekye are well known for having argued that the African ethical tradition is descriptively best understood as humanist, but I do not make that hermeneutic claim. Instead, I contend that, even if they were incorrect, it would be worth creating a principle with a sub-Saharan pedigree that a global audience of philosophers could take seriously in the light of their own backgrounds, which means taking a secular approach.[1] I then list the comparatively uncontroversial moral judgements that I invoke to determine which secular moral theory informed by characteristically African beliefs and practices is most defensible (3.4). In Part II of this book, I mainly evaluate African moral theories by ascertaining the extent to which they entail and explain moral judgements about particular cases that are less controversial than the theories and that can be reasonably considered common ground by African philosophers. There I argue for a certain relational moral theory relative to African competitors, and do so largely by appeal to the intuitions about what is right or wrong from this chapter that I expect them to share. I noted earlier that I am seeking to mirror neither the ways that contemporary Africans understand themselves nor the ways that

[1] Those familiar and comfortable with an analytic and secular approach to moral thought may wish to skip 3.2 and 3.3.

A Relational Moral Theory: African Ethics in and beyond the Continent. Thaddeus Metz, Oxford University Press.

DOI: 10.1093/oso/9780198748960.003.0003

indigenous African peoples have lived (1.2.2). Instead, I selectively draw on features that have been prominent in much of the sub-Saharan region for a long while in order to construct a moral theory that can be found attractive by a multicultural philosophical audience in the twenty-first-century. In the conclusion of this chapter I note the way in which this chapter will have driven this point home (3.5), briefly returning to the question of whether the 'African' label is appropriate for my project.

3.2 An Analytic Approach

One way to think about an analytic approach to ethics is to consider how it is similar to some features of the natural sciences. In the latter disciplines, enquirers are careful to define their terms (3.2.1), often seek to discover fundamental laws (3.2.2), evaluate hypotheses in the light of publicly accessible argumentation (3.2.3), and consider such evidence to consist of probabilistic inferences, and especially inference to the best explanation, where hypotheses are judged in the light of their ability to entail and explain a wide array of comparatively uncontroversial data (3.2.4). I do not purport to demonstrate or even suggest that analytic ethics in fact is a kind of scientific enquiry,[2] but rather indicate ways in which the two are similar, so as to clarify my method in this book.

3.2.1 Definitions

When a scientist is seeking to discover a fact or to explain an event, she typically is careful about how she formulates what it is that she wants to know. For example, if she were to test whether animals are sentient, it would be important for her to indicate what she means by the word 'animals' (all living organisms or something narrower such as all vertebrates?) and even what she means by 'sentient' (the ability to feel pain, or to be aware of the environment, or both?). If she were to leave these terms open, then the meaning of her hypothesis would be unclear, it would be difficult to tell whether the hypothesis was supported by the data, and those inclined to question her research would risk evaluating something she did not have in mind.

For similar reasons, I believe it is worth being specific about the meaning of terms when engaging in moral philosophy. Often in southern Africa, people will speak of the 'spirit' of *ubuntu*, the Nguni term for humanness that is often invoked to sum up morality. I am not denying that there is a spirit of *ubuntu*, i.e., a collection of various ethical connotations typically associated with the term by

[2] Although I confess that I am sympathetic to such a claim; cf. Metz (2013a: 88–97).

(especially southern) African indigenous peoples. However, in this book, I do not rest content with invoking the spirit, and instead aim to be specific about why I believe something counts as African and morally sound.

Some in the African tradition have explicitly eschewed the project of seeking to define its core terms on the ground that it cannot be done. For instance, Yvonne Mokgoro, a former South African Constitutional Court justice who appealed to *ubuntu* when ruling on the death penalty, has remarked that it cannot be articulated with precision. As she puts it:

> To define an African notion in a foreign language and from an abstract as opposed to a concrete approach [is] to defy the very essence of the African world-view and can also be particularly elusive. I will therefore not in the least attempt to define the concept with precision. That would in any case be unattainable. (1998: 16; cf. Praeg 2014)

In sum, for Mokgoro and some others, the definitional facet of my project is both unAfrican and unattainable.

Regarding the former charge, I accept that carving out well-defined meanings of terms might be *less* African than another sort of philosophical method. However, I believe the philosophy remains African to a large degree, in the light of the source and content of the terms. As for the other charge, of being impossible to carry out, note that my project does not attempt to seek clear and distinct analyses of the myriad properties that a particular people associates with the word '*ubuntu*' or cognate terms. Instead, it draws on that collection of properties selectively in order to construct and defend a general moral principle. The latter, as I like to think this book shows, is possible, even if the former is not.

Some will think that, even if such an approach is possible, it amounts to 'killing the spirit' of *ubuntu*, akin to an entomologist pinning down a butterfly for observation.[3] I appreciate the force of the metaphor.

However, by carefully defining moral words, I am not seeking to *replace* the vernacular or ordinary language with philosophical terminology. The butterfly can and should remain at large while I go about developing a specialized vocabulary for professional purposes, including enabling those around the world who are unfamiliar with African cultures to appreciate some of their intellectual insights.

Talk of the 'spirit' of *ubuntu* is just one example of what I aim to avoid. Another includes the ubiquitous claim that the community is 'prior to' the individual. My question is: 'prior' in what sense? Temporally? Logically? Metaphysically? Causally? Evaluatively? Normatively? This kind of careful specification is rarely provided in the field. Similar remarks go for the commonly cited maxim, 'I am because we are and we are because I am.' This statement means a number of

[3] An incisive metaphor that Aryan Kaganof suggested to me in conversation.

different things to Africans who use it, and my approach involves avoiding using language ambiguously and asking interlocutors to specify what they have in mind when using such a sentence.

3.2.2 Laws

It is typical of natural scientists to seek out laws of various kinds. Some aim to establish property identities, e.g., that water is necessarily H_2O, while others are interested in causal necessities, e.g., that a plant must grow if it has water, sunlight, carbon dioxide, and soil. Isaac Newton and Albert Einstein, for just two examples, are rated highly because of the extent to which they were able to justify fundamental laws of motion, ones governing the behaviour of an enormous array of physical objects and events across the universe.

Analogously, I seek to ascertain lawfulness when it comes to morality here on Earth. Similar to the way scientists have taken themselves to have established that something is water if and only if it is H_2O, analytic ethicists tend to seek out a similar formula for wrongness. In the West, utilitarians maintain that an act is wrong if and only if it fails to maximize the general welfare and Kantians contend that an act is wrong if and only if it treats rational nature disrespectfully. In this book I argue that the African tradition can ground a moral theory that is more attractive than these and related ones, and even on grounds that adherents to rival principles would appreciate. It would be intellectually fascinating to discover that all wrong actions have one basic thing in common, and it would also be practically useful when it comes to resolving applied controversies.

There might be grounds to doubt that an attractive moral law is forthcoming from any philosophical tradition, perhaps because the world purportedly consists of forces that are constantly in flux (e.g., Ramose 2005). However, even if the world does consist of fluctuating and interdependent forces, that complexity has not precluded the establishment of many scientific laws, including that water is H_2O and $E = MC^2$. If water can have an essence in the face of constant change, perhaps morality can, too. In any event, we can really know that there is no plausible moral theory only upon having searched for it, particularly in the light of heretofore neglected intellectual resources (cf. 1.2.1).

3.2.3 Public Argumentation

Beyond differentiating between various moral theories and articulating a novel one, in this book I am also interested in epistemically justifying one relative to the others. The sort of justification on which I focus is publicly accessible argumentation, as opposed to merely private or otherwise fairly parochial considerations, where the relevant public includes philosophers from a variety of intellectual traditions.

An appeal to perception is a clear case of widely accessible evidence in descriptive matters. If one wants to know whether there is a cup on the table, a good approach would be to ask those nearby to use their vision. If those with a reliable sense of sight all agree that there is a cup on the table, that is strong evidence that there indeed is one. Convergence of minds from a variety of backgrounds on a subject constitutes strong justification for belief, tending to reveal mind-independent facts of the matter about it. I therefore appeal to widely shared intuitions about right and wrong as an analogous source of justification in prescriptive matters.

It is, however, a recurrent part of the African tradition to believe that the most reliable sources of moral knowledge are ancestors, i.e., wise forefathers who have survived the deaths of their bodies, continue to live on Earth in an imperceptible form, and, unlike us, are able to know God's mind. Ancestors are frequently thought to be the ones who provide moral instruction to their people and punish members for violating moral norms. Furthermore, it is common to maintain that only a traditional healer or diviner priest who has undergone many years of training can receive or at least understand messages from ancestors—say, by throwing bones or entering a trance.

I do not invoke any of this moral epistemology in this book. Indeed, I could not do so according to this epistemology itself, which includes the claim that one needs to be an 'insider' to be able to access the evidence sent by imperceptible agents. Since I am an 'outsider', and since my audience is meant to be a global one, I must work with some other mode of justification.

In this book the kind of evidence I can proffer for or against moral theories is a certain kind of argumentation. An argument is a collection of claims in which some claims putatively provide epistemic reason to believe another claim, part of which reason is constituted by the fact that the supporting propositions are less controversial than the proposition being supported. An argument is good if the premises are true or at least justified, lend evidentiary support to the conclusion, and are weaker for interlocutors than the conclusion. When I present arguments, the kinds of premises I appeal to are ones that are not meant to be justified by appeal to revelation, divination, or some other way of receiving information from ancestors or other imperceptible agents. Instead, they are ones that both insiders and outsiders such as professional philosophers around the world can be expected to find plausible. Sometimes they are claims already accepted by nearly everyone party to the debate, while other times the premises are claims that could be taken seriously by a wide array of disputants, upon some reflection on them.

3.2.4 Probabilistic Inference

In the epistemic project that is science, it is typical to aim for conclusions that probably follow from their premises, where the premises are themselves probably true or justified. Certainty features prominently in mathematics, but not so much in science.

In particular, it is common in science to seek to undermine a hypothesis about a law by providing a purported counterexample. Since to posit a law, such as all swans are white, is to make a kind of general claim, one can provide some reason to doubt that the proposed law holds by pointing to an apparent exception, e.g., a black swan. Conversely, to provide evidence in favour of a general claim, one could sensibly note many instances in which it appears to be true, i.e., one could use induction. Or one could use abduction; that is, one could show that the proposed law, in comparison with others sensibly under consideration, more easily entails fairly uncontroversial data and provides a better explanation of them.

I work with a similar model of inference when it comes to ethics. Seeking out a plausible moral theory in this book is similar to testing an empirical hypothesis. In both cases, one is seeking to establish a general claim, with the moral case being a matter of establishing whether all wrong actions have something in common in virtue of which they are wrong.

One strong sort of evidence to posit against a moral theory is to show that it has a counterintuitive implication, for instance that it entails that an act is wrong that is for all we can tell right, or that it entails that an act is right that is incontestably wrong. If it followed from a moral theory that it is permissible to be cruel to babies for fun, that would be a major strike against the theory.

Conversely, strong evidence in favour of a moral theory is that it clearly entails and powerfully explains a wide array of less controversial claims about what is right and wrong. Often these take the form of what I sometimes call 'intuitions', comparatively uncontroversial judgements of particular actions as to whether they are, say, morally required or forbidden (or to what degree). If a moral theory entailed that it is wrong to be cruel to babies for fun whereas a rival could not, or if it provided an explanation of that judgement that was better than those of a rival, that would be some grounds for believing the theory compared to it.

3.3 A Secular Content

There are additional salient features of the sciences that I also take on board, but that are not inherent to an analytic method per se. They involve a disinclination to appeal to in principle imperceptible agents and forces in relation to them. This approach sets me apart from some of my colleagues working in the African philosophical tradition, and I need to explain my motivation.

To be more specific, the sciences do posit unobservables but ones that are not agents and that appear essential to explain or predict observables. That is, most science starts with what has been or at least can be perceived (or introspected). That does not mean it takes what one has viewed or heard as infallible; it just means that such sensations are deemed to be a comparatively uncontroversial, even if provisional, place to begin enquiry. Presuming one has perceived certain things under the right conditions, scientists are then willing to consider whether imperceptible things exist only as necessary to account for what has been perceived.

So, for example, scientists have not *started* seeking to understand nature by positing gravity or causation, which are in principle beyond our perception, but rather have invoked these properties insofar as they are required to explain events that we have perceived. In addition, when seeking to understand nature by positing unobservables, scientists tend not to appeal to imperceptible agents and instead to appeal to physical facts. Newton could have said that angels pushed planets according to the laws he discovered, but instead, *qua* scientist, he maintained that gravity operates according to them.

Although some African philosophers, most famously Gyekye and Wiredu, have held that indigenous sub-Saharan morality does not make essential reference to anything beyond the perceptible, that is not obviously true. And it is definitely true that indigenous African worldviews recurrently posit imperceptible agents, particularly ancestors, as well as forces, such as divine energy (vital force) and magic. Now, my book is addressed not merely to those who hold such worldviews, but also to those who do not. My intended audience includes professional philosophers beyond Africa, with my aim being to construct a moral theory that they, too, could find powerful. I therefore avoid invoking highly contested metaphysical matters, to try to establish some convergence on ethical ones.

Imagine an adherent to African ethics addressing the United Nations. What would she reasonably emphasize as something that sub-Saharan cultures can contribute to global thought about morality? She should not pitch the idea that relationships with ancestors are at the heart of right action, requiring us to remember them, to sacrifice animals to them, and to share libations with them regularly to keep them strong and disposed to treat us well. After all, relatively few of the world's people think that much of day-to-day life consists of interacting with imperceptible agents who have continued to live with us in a certain place on Earth after the deaths of their bodies and are still thirsty for beer. She would also be unwise to suggest that zombies should be deployed as suicide bombers during wartime (Mutwa 1964: 657) or that the energy discharged by witches should be harnessed to power local economies (Mawere 2011: 98). Such suggestions have their place for certain audiences, but not, I submit, for a multicultural readership wanting to appreciate something from the African moral tradition.

Since my goal is to articulate, in a principled form, those moral elements of sub-Saharan cultures that could be found attractive by philosophers who are not just from Africa but also from other backgrounds, I abstract from controversial issues about the nature of reality. African philosophers readily believe in the perceptible, while Western and many other kinds of philosophers are quick to accept the physical. Although these realms are not identical, e.g., there can be imperceptible physical properties, they admit of much overlap and are deemed real by most philosophical traditions.[4]

Although my theoretical interpretations of African morality do not essentially include reference to anything beyond the natural, note that they can be read as not essentially *excluding* such reference either. When I consider moral theories grounded (in rough catchwords) on utility, vitality, and communality, respectively, I construe these properties in physical terms, but a broader interpretation is available. Although I bracket the issue of whether imperceptible agents exist, the moral theories could be read as providing guidance about what our duties would be to them if they were to exist.

3.4 The Key Intuitions

In this book I aim to distinguish between and critically explore the most promising secular moral theories suggested by the African tradition, to argue that one is more promising in terms of both Africanness and philosophical plausibility (Part II), and then to show that it is more attractive than key rivals in the Western tradition, often enough even in terms of judgements that Western ethicists would themselves appreciate (Part III). Often when I evaluate theories, I either present a counterexample against one or make an inference to the best explanation for one. Both types of argument involve an appeal to moral intuition. Here, I say more about what I mean by the word and what role intuition plays in my defence of a moral theory (3.4.1), after which I specify the core moral intuitions I invoke in the book. One group of them is shared widely across the globe, or at least by both Western and African philosophers (3.4.2), while another group is more common to the African tradition (3.4.3).

3.4.1 Intuition and Justification

In the context of evaluating principles of right and wrong action, an intuition counts as a judgement that a particular act has some moral feature such as permissibility or a certain degree of wrongness, where that judgement is meant to be less controversial than the principles it is being invoked to evaluate. I do not consider intuitions to be beyond doubt, self-justifying, or anything so strong as a foundationalist epistemology would suggest. Instead, they are beliefs that are

[4] One interesting exception is a certain strain of Hinduism, according to which the visible or physical is merely *māyā*, i.e., illusion or not the most fundamental reality.

firmly and commonly held by most informed interlocutors, and for this reason are sensibly taken as provisional starting points for debate; they are judgements that could be overridden in principle, but only with substantial evidence.

Although there is fair debate about *which* intuitions are reliable (with those about remote possible worlds being prima facie more dubious), it looks difficult, if not impossible, to make philosophical headway without them. How else can one provide substantial evidence either in favour of or against a general principle without appealing to its implications for a wide array of particular cases deemed to be less contested than it? I argued that trying to draw an inference from non-moral considerations, such as metaphysics, is not promising (Chapter 2), where the straightforward major alternative is inferring the correctness of a moral theory in the light of its implications for a variety of comparatively uncontroversial moral judgements.

In any event, in this book I seek to advance a principle of right action that will clearly entail and best explain many intuitions about morality, and especially ones by and large shared by both the Western and African traditions. More carefully, I distinguish between two classes of intuitions: those held by the African tradition and many other traditions to more or less the same extent, and those more often held by the African than by many other traditions, particularly the Western. The better that a moral theory accounts for both groups, the more justified it is both as an African principle and to a multicultural audience of philosophers.

3.4.2 'Global' Intuitions

Since I am engaging in cross-cultural philosophical debate, it would be ideal to ascertain some common ground between at least the Western and African philosophical traditions, though ideally more than just them. Uncontroversially for at least both groups, it is typically *pro tanto* immoral:

(a) to kill innocent people without their consent for money
(b) to have sex with someone against her will so as to feel pleasure or a sense of power
(c) to deceive a person, at least when not done in self- or other-defence
(d) to discriminate on a racial or gendered basis when allocating opportunities, at least when not redressing a previous comparable discrimination
(e) to express ethnic, sexual, or similar epithets towards others
(f) never to fight hunger, poverty, displacement, or the like suffered by those outside one's in-group, when one could do so at little cost to oneself
(g) never to prevent serious crimes done to others, when one could do so at little cost to oneself
(h) to torture an animal for the fun of it.

Note that I do not and need not claim that these actions are *always* immoral; perhaps there are some cases in which, say, deception is perfectly justified for purposes other than defence of innocents. In addition, I am not contending that these actions, when they are immoral, should *never* be performed. It might be that even when they are *pro tanto* wrong, one morally ought to do some of them in order to avoid a greater wrongdoing. My point is that, for most in the Western and African philosophical traditions and a wide array of others, these actions are *usually* wrong to *some* degree.

The above intuitions hardly exhaust the arguments I shall employ in support of the conclusion that my favoured African theory is more defensible than Kantianism and utilitarianism. This list merely constitutes an initial filter through which any adequate moral theory ought to pass. In Part III of the book, I appeal to many additional intuitions to adjudicate between these competitors, ones that, while often not as uncontroversial as the above list, are still less contested than the theories and, hence, fair and useful to invoke when evaluating them.

3.4.3 'African' Intuitions

In addition to the territory shared by the African and other traditions, I also evaluate moral theories springing from the African tradition in terms of how well they account for intuitions that are much more commonly held in it compared to others—the Western one in particular. If I am to develop a moral theory that merits the 'African' label, it would not be enough merely to draw on a principle that has been suggested by philosophers from Africa; in addition, it should capture moral judgements that are salient in Africa but not in the West. Here, I not merely list them, but also spell them out a bit for the reader who is not so familiar with sub-Saharan cultures.

Before sketching the so-called 'African' intuitions, I urge the reader to recall what I mean by geographical labels (1.2.2). By 'African' I am referring to features recurrent in much of the sub-Saharan region of the continent over several hundred years, and not, say, the views of a given twenty-first-century resident of Johannesburg. Such an individual might not accept what I am labelling 'intuitions' below. In addition, when I describe an intuition as 'African', or as *more* African than Western, recall that I do not mean to suggest that all indigenous sub-Saharan peoples have held it. What I claim are moral judgements more common amongst indigenous Africans than Westerners are ones that have been long-standing and more widespread in particularly the sub-Saharan part of the continent than in at least Europe, the United Kingdom, North America, and Australasia. They are mores that stand out not only in a wide array of sub-Saharan space, from Ghana to South Africa to Kenya, but also a long span of time there, from pre-colonial societies to contemporary African intellectuals inspired by them. Or, if one has some doubt that one can know that pre-colonial African peoples actually held the following intuitions, they are at least ones that recur more often in the post-independence, English-speaking social scientific and philosophical literature on African ethics than in that on Western ethics.

Less controversially for African ethical thought than for at least Western ethical thought, then, it is typically *pro tanto* immoral:

(i) to resolve political conflicts in the face of continued dissent, rather than seeking consensus
(j) to fail to do what is likely to make people's lives go better, if one is politically in charge
(k) to make retribution the fundamental aim of criminal justice, in contrast to seeking reconciliation
(l) to create wealth largely on a competitive basis, instead of a cooperative one
(m) to distribute wealth in a greatly unequal way and to fail to meet everyone's needs
(n) to avoid greeting people, especially elders, upon encountering them
(o) to remain isolated or to flout long-standing norms central to a people's self-conception, as opposed to partaking in customs
(p) to fail to marry and rear children, as opposed to creating a family.

As these intuitions might be less familiar than (a)–(h) to readers not *au fait* with African cultures, I take some time to spell them out in what follows.

In the political realm, indigenous sub-Saharan societies have routinely prized unanimity, with majoritarianism typically being seen as a morally inadequate way to resolve political conflicts or otherwise to determine law and policy in the face of disagreement (i). In many small-scale African communities, discussion continues until a compromise is found and all in the discussion agree with the outcome, either amongst all adults affected by the issue or by popularly appointed (typically male) elders, to whom a monarch usually defers.[5]

One of the most fascinating and powerful contributions from African thinkers to contemporary political philosophy has been the contention that even large-scale societies should make decisions consequent to consensus. The system that is currently dominant in the West and in contemporary Africa is one in which great power lies with the majority. A candidate belongs to a political party that competes against other parties for power, and, once elected, the winning candidate can and often does represent his party alone, aiming to promote his constituency's

[5] Some of the many sources on this point include: Fortes and Evans-Pritchard (1940); Busia (1967: 28); Gyekye (1992, 1997: 124–40); Wiredu (1992: 204, 1996: 172–90, 2000); Bhengu (1996: 23–6, 40–2); Bujo (1997: 158–68); Legesse (2001); Ramose (2005: 95–101); Ayittey (2006); Ani (2014). Cf. Eze (2008) and Matolino (2018), who acknowledge the common African practice of political consensus-seeking, but reject it as unjust or impractical, at least for a twenty-first-century 'modern' society.

interests. In contrast, drawing on salient African beliefs and practices, Wiredu has proposed a 'non-party polity' in which a majority with certain views would be required to find ways to bring minorities on board before proceeding (1996: 172–90, 2000). Candidates, who might be affiliated with a political discussion group, would compete against each other for votes on the basis of values and positions. Once elected (by majority rule, such being practically necessary in an urban environment), a winning candidate would not represent a party, but instead the public as a whole. Specifically, legislators would not aim to promote a constituency's interests, but instead would share power by seeking unanimous agreement with one another in the adoption of every statute.

Turning to what a legislature should decide (in contrast to how it should come to a decision), for most contemporary intellectuals inspired by indigenous sub-Saharan cultures, the intuitive point of governance is to promote the human good (j). That is understood to include not merely well-being, but also virtue and perhaps even meaningfulness. That might not sound particularly unique, until one compares it with other approaches to politics that have been taken by other traditions. For example, on the African continent there is no long-standing and widespread practice of using politics to prompt people to conform to God's will as revealed in a book or by a prophet. Although it is characteristic of sub-Saharan peoples to believe in God, they typically do not believe that God's will has been revealed to any human beings in particular (Gyekye 1995: 129–46; Wiredu 1996: 61–77), let alone that a government should be enforcing it. Also alien to the African context is political liberalism: the idea that conceptions of the good life are akin to religious views on which the state must remain neutral, such that the state's only job is to protect people's rights to live as they see fit. Despite human rights of a sort routinely having been observed amongst sub-Saharan peoples and often prized by African philosophers, it is rare to encounter the idea that the government would be wrong to strive to improve the quality of life of those in its charge.

Much more common are views such as the following from a South African intellectual who has sought to ground public policy on *ubuntu*:

> Neo-liberal theory insists on state neutrality that unduly constrains the legitimate sphere of government action, barring consideration of policies designed to develop or restore a strong sense of national unity. The state should stay out of the business of telling citizens what constitutes a valuable life, the theory goes.... But this view has bizarre and undemocratic consequences. Should we erase all non-neutral policies meant to increase social responsibility and sustain the social attachments that give meaning to our lives, even if such policies have the overwhelming support of the citizenry? (Nkondo 2007: 95)

To use the jargon of contemporary Anglo-American political philosophy, African peoples, or at least political philosophers from them, are generally 'welfarist' and 'perfectionist' when it comes to the proper aims of the government. The recurrent intuition is that political decisions should aim not only to make people objectively better off, such as by fulfilling their needs and perhaps improving meaning in their lives, but also to make them better people, which might mean realizing their nature as communal beings or fostering their vitality.[6]

With respect to criminal justice, African legal philosophers, following the societies from which they have come, largely eschew retribution as the primary response to wrongdoing (k). By 'retribution' I mean punishing an offender because he deserves or otherwise merits a harm proportionate to his offence. Although retributive sentiments are not entirely absent from the behaviour of people in African societies (e.g., Mutwa 1964: 630),[7] it is not the dominant philosophical theme when it comes to how a government or society ought to respond to wrongdoers.

In contrast to such a backward-looking rationale for punishment, many African communities and thinkers influenced by them have the intuition that it is appropriate to respond to crime with the expectation of a good result of some sort. In particular, sub-Saharan philosophers generally believe that the proper function of criminal justice is the forward-looking one of mending a broken relationship between the offender, his victim, and the broader community (traditionally understood to include imperceptible agents such as ancestors); on this score, talk of 'reconciliation' or 'restoring harmony' is common.[8] Apology and compensation are central to such an approach, although punishment can be justified when done with an eye to reforming the offender and enabling him to become reintegrated into society. For two examples of how such a characteristically African approach to wrongdoing has informed contemporary South African practice, an *ubuntu* ethic is usually credited for helping to ground a largely restorative response to apartheid-era political crimes in the form of the Truth and Reconciliation Commission (Tutu 1999; Bell 2002: 85–107; Krog 2008), and the justices of the Constitutional Court of South Africa (1995) uniformly judged *ubuntu* to be incompatible with the death penalty or any retributive reasoning that could underwrite it.

In terms of economic production, the widespread view amongst indigenous African peoples has been that the point of labour, innovation, and other forms of wealth creation should be to satisfy not merely one's own interests—say, by amassing profit—but also those of one's extended family or of society in general (l).

[6] For just a few additional examples, see Senghor (1964: 79); Ake (1987); Gbadegesin (1991); Paris (1995: 114–17, 152–3); Gyekye (1997: 35–76, 2004); Siame (2000); Bujo (2001: 101–2); Ikuenobe (2006: 265–87).

[7] Mutwa's comment on what he sees as a strong retributive urge amongst the Zulu people is the exception when it comes to most discussions of criminal justice as an ideal amongst indigenous African peoples. Note, too, that retaliation undertaken in order to protect the society from harm in the future (as discussed in Bujo 2001: 136) is distinct from retribution, which imposes harm merely because of an action in the past, without requiring a future good to come from doing so.

[8] Representative examples include: Aja (1997); Magesa (1997: 234–40, 267–76); Tutu (1999); Ramose (2001); Wiredu (1992: 204); Murungi (2004); Idowu (2006); Villa-Vicencio (2009).

Bénézet Bujo, a Congolese theologian who has published two important books on sub-Saharan ethics, notes: 'It is a well-known fact that in traditional Africa, work had nothing to do with "salary." The development of the clan's community life is what was emphasized' (1997: 164). Similarly, Augustine Shutte, in one of the first books devoted to southern African moral and political ideals, remarks: 'In an ethic of *ubuntu* ownership and property... only get their meaning and purpose from their relation to work as a means to personal growth and community.... They are justified insofar as they enable productive work for the common good, unjustified insofar as they prevent it' (2001: 159).[9]

Work in African contexts has often been more cooperative than competitive, not merely in terms of the end of benefiting others beyond oneself that Bujo and Shutte highlight, but also with respect to its means. For a key example, able-bodied people have been characteristically expected to help one another harvest their fields. Instead of those living on the land being solely responsible for gathering up the produce from it, all those who had harvesting to do would collectively move from field to field to undertake the labour together.[10] For another example, in contrast to a banking model, it has been natural for those inspired by indigenous African values to pool their resources and then loan them out either without seeking interest or on a profit-sharing basis (Okem and Stanton 2016); such cooperatives are widely known as '*stokvels*' in southern Africa and '*tontines*' in West Africa. Similarly: the burden of building a house is not shouldered solely on those who will live in it (Kasenene 1994: 142); 'when one is sick, the whole community comes to one's help or aid' (Ikuenobe 2006: 294); the task of overcoming grief is not deemed to be the responsibility merely of the one in mourning (Wiredu 1992: 204; Bhengu 1996: 7); and, finally, consider the internationally recognized African maxim that it takes a village to rear a child (e.g., Ikuenobe 2006: 300).

These considerations likely help to explain why so many African societies adopted centrally planned economic systems after independence from colonialism. Free markets seemed, if not inherently wrong, then at least something that would hinder the morally desirable behaviours of working for the sake of improving others' quality of life and doing so in a cohesive manner. One continues to find contemporary African thinkers railing against Western capitalism's 'unbridled individualism' (Dzobo 1992: 226), 'single-minded commercialism' (Wiredu 1992: 202), and 'morally blind, purely economic logic' (Tangwa 2005: 181).

Turning from economic production to distribution, it has been rare for 'traditional' Africans to allow private property in the Marxist sense where a small group

[9] See also Samkange and Samkange (1980: 80–7); Gbadegesin (1991: 225–9); Murove (2009a: 231–2).

[10] E.g., Samkange and Samkange (1980: 101–2); Gbadegesin (1991: 65–6, 259–61); Wiredu (1992: 201–2, 2009: 16); Bujo (1997: 164); Letseka (2000: 183–4); Koenane (2019); Setlhodi (2019).

owns large swathes of the means of production and hires the majority to work at them in exchange for a wage (m). Although people in sub-Saharan societies have had different amounts of land and wealth and have used markets (on which see Gyekye 1997: 146–61; Ayittey 2006: 317–31), they have usually not been so unequal as to facilitate full-blown capitalism. Instead, wealth has often been purposely distributed precisely so as to prevent such great inequality. Just as liberalism is largely alien to the African political tradition, so libertarianism is foreign to African accounts of how to distribute economic goods. Redistributivism and even egalitarianism are instead the clearly dominant themes. For instance, speaking from an African perspective, the influential Kenyan philosopher Henry Odera Oruka says: 'Part of the aim of egalitarian fairness is to suppress and eradicate, as a matter of cardinal ethical principle, any development toward inequality in wealth and liberty. Equality in egalitarian terms is an end in itself and inequality an evil to be eliminated, even at a high price' (1997: 120).[11] When it comes to possessing natural resources such as land and cattle, pre-colonial sub-Saharan societies have generally considered clan membership to be sufficient to ground a claim to a decent portion, supposing one makes good use of it and does not let it go to waste. For example, those recently married and needing help to get started would often receive a parcel of land from the chief and some cows from those with a surplus of them.

People in the West tend to think that individual claims should largely determine the resources one may possess; for example, one may keep what one deserves for having been productive or one has a right to keep what one has received by voluntary transfer from a previous owner. Giving to others what they have no right to is not thought of as upholding a duty but as being generous. In contrast, a much greater percentage of Africans think that one is morally obligated to help others, roughly to the extent that one can and that others need, with rights or desert not figuring into the analysis of how much one ought to transfer wealth, time, or labour.[12] Relatedly, it appears to be more African than at least Western to think that it is permissible to take goods such as food without others' consent, so long as one does not overdo it (e.g., Verhoef and Michel 1997: 399; Tangwa 2005: 180). Note that such taking would not count as 'stealing' since the person in possession of the item is presumably not its rightful owner in the light of the other's need for it.

Moving away from economic matters now, the (n) intuition is about acknowledging someone who has entered one's presence and asking about how they are,

[11] For more discussion of the tendency of African societies to meet the needs of all and to discourage great economic inequalities, see Nyerere (1968: 2–7); Gbadegesin (1991: 65–6, 203–4, 242–3, 249–61); Kasenene (1994: 142); Paris (1995: 109–11, 152–3); Bujo (1997: 162–3, 2001: 38); Gyekye (1997: 142); Magesa (1997: 278); Ikuenobe (2006: 298–9); Tangwa (2010: 66–7).

[12] Busia (1962: 131, 149–50); Setiloane (1976: 66–7); Wiredu (1992: 198–202); Gyekye (1997: 61–76); Masolo (2010: 222–54).

ideally including reference to their family (say, with use of the plural 'you'). Such a practice is not merely a matter of etiquette amongst many indigenous African peoples; to greet is considered to have moral significance, such that it would be wrong, not merely rude, if one failed to do it. This is particularly so when engaging with people one knows and elders. However, it is also widely considered to apply to anyone in one's presence, including assistants at a till and even people crossing one's path.[13]

The contrast with everyday life and moral views in North America and Europe is patent. Of course, people there sometimes greet one another, particularly in the southern part of the United States, for example. However, the thought that there is a moral duty to enquire into another person's condition, or to pay proper respect to elders, before settling down to business in a shop is not so frequent, in neither the culture nor, especially, its salient ethical philosophies.

Not only must one acknowledge the presence of others in the African tradition, one is also expected to participate with them, in conversation, rituals, and culture more broadly (o). A nice illustration of this point is a study recounted by Shutte in his book devoted to *ubuntu* (2001: 27–8). He notes a survey that was taken of two groups of nuns at a convent. After the obligatory chores and praying were done, the study found that the German nuns often continued to work by knitting or sewing, while the African nuns did not and instead spent time in conversation. The study noted that each group of sisters deemed the other morally lacking; the Germans judged the Africans insufficiently diligent, while the Africans considered the Germans to objectionably care more about practical matters than about people.

More generally, it has been common amongst African societies for a long while, and more so than amongst at least Western ones, to think that one has some obligation to engage with one's fellows and not to disrupt the community's way of life.[14] As John Mbiti remarks, 'To be human is to belong to the whole community and to do so involves participating in the beliefs, ceremonies, rituals and festivals of the community' (1990: 2). This does not mean that African values forbid individuality, creativity, or nonconformity; indeed, tolerance is typically regarded as an important virtue, and aiming to improve the lot of another person requires one to 'exercise *individual* care for each member of the community' (e.g., Bujo 2001: 93). However, it does mean that some weight in moral thinking should be given to whether one's behaviour would be downright disruptive or otherwise

[13] Onwuanibe (1984: 185); Mbiti (1990: 208–9); Wiredu (1996: 62); Murove (2004: 205); Dandala (2009: 260); Mnyaka and Motlhabi (2005: 219); Ngwainmbi (2009); Nkulu-N'Sengha (2009: 143). Although Wiredu points out that failing to greet is a 'serious lapse from good behavior' for his Akan people in Ghana, he denies that greetings are properly described as 'moral'; for he too narrowly restricts this term to whatever is essential to 'avoid the collapse of human community' (1996: 63).

[14] E.g., Busia (1962: 130); Mutwa (1964: 554–5, 615, 657); Wiredu (1980: 10–1); Mbiti (1990: 2, 208–9); Dzobo (1992: 229); Bujo (2001: 135); Gyekye (2004: 39); Ogbujah (2007: 132–3); Masolo (2010: 225–6, 234, 244).

disrespectful of core norms in terms of which one's society identifies itself. Furthermore, isolation from others has often been viewed with suspicion, with just one proverb, from the Kom people in Cameroon, saying that 'aloofness is good only for a witch' (Tosam 2014: 12; see also Mnyaka and Motlhabi 2005: 222). The contrast with 'modern' Western cultures and their philosophies is stark, here, with little to no weight characteristically ascribed to participating in a shared way of life and seclusion not being viewed as wrong to any degree, at least if one finds ways to help others from afar.

Finally, the (p) intuition is that many African peoples, or at least their philosophers, have thought that there is some strong moral reason to create familial relationships by finding a spouse and rearing children with him or her.[15] Polygamy is often permitted, and indeed welcomed, because of its effectiveness at generating more children than monogamy would. The point is not merely that, having wed, one is morally obligated to keep one's vows, or that, having had children, one is obligated to ensure they are loved and socialized. These norms are of course widespread in Western societies and amongst philosophers whose thoughts are grounded on the norms salient in them. The point is rather the stronger claim that one has some obligation to wed, at least in part in order to raise children, in the first place—intuitions that are much less common in at least the Western philosophical tradition.

Some might suggest that African societies have valued procreation merely because of scarcity in an agricultural society, such that it would not be supported outside of that context (cf. Wiredu 1992: 205). Others might be concerned that advocating a duty to procreate would lead to people having children when they cannot afford to do so. However, African philosophers clearly do not value children merely as a means towards labour on a farm and without regard for their quality of life. Instead, these thinkers often appeal to the dignity of human life or the importance of family as what prescribes procreation, where they would readily accept a rider that one must expect those procreated to have worthwhile lives.

In addition, notice that the intuition does not quite say that one must 'create' children, but rather that one must at least 'rear' them. Although many Africans would maintain that the best way to rear children is first to create them, the reader may elect to focus on the weaker reading, in which adoption would satisfy the obligation.

More troublesome, I think, is that it is well known that African societies have tended to frown upon homosexuality, not merely because of the influence of Christianity, but also because of the perceived lack of contribution towards values

[15] For discussion in the context of many different African peoples, see Jahn (1961: 109); Mutwa (1964: 625, 634); Mbiti (1975: 98–100, 104–7); Dzobo (1992: 225–7, 233); Wiredu (1992: 205); Kasenene (1994: 141, 1998: 71–2, 77–80); Paris (1995: 79–80, 113); Tangwa (1996: 194–5, 2010: 62–3); Bujo (1997: 108–14, 2001: 6–7, 34–54); Magesa (1997: 63, 89, 120–35, 167); Okyere-Manu (2016); cf. Ramose (2003: 385).

of life and community (Bujo 2001: 6, 2015; Asante 2003: 72–3; Tangwa 2010: 62). However, I do not take on this 'African' intuition as one that a moral theory must capture, supposing it has indeed been salient. In adumbrating the (i)–(p) intuitions that are more prominent in the sub-Saharan moral-philosophical tradition than in the Western and other traditions, I have not listed literally all those that I have encountered. That is not merely to keep the discussion tight, but also to keep it philosophically promising in the light of contemporary global reflection on morality. When selecting beliefs and practices that have been salient amongst sub-Saharan peoples, I have chosen those that, although not often accepted by moral philosophers from other cultures, could nonetheless be taken seriously by them as potentially revealing something about right and wrong.

For some additional examples of 'African' intuitions that I have set aside, consider that it appears that education was often gendered in 'traditional' sub-Saharan societies, the thought having been that it is right for men to be trained for one sort of job and women for another (Adeyinka and Ndwapi 2002; Adeyemi and Adeyinka 2003). Note, too, that some African people believe that white people (whether understood racially or culturally) are incapable of exhibiting *ubuntu*, i.e., cannot display human excellence (Taringa 2007; Gade 2012). Still more, some have suggested that African ethical thought is extremely partial, according a moral status only to an in-group, and not impartially to all human persons (e.g., Sogolo 1993: 120, 124–9; Paris 1995: 87–8; Kasoma 1996: 108; Gathogo 2008: 47–9). Even if these intuitions were as long-standing and widespread as those of (i)–(p)—an empirical issue that I do not settle here—I would not invoke them, because of their prima facie implausibility to a twenty-first-century philosophical audience around the world. Leaving out these intuitions might make a theory uninformed by them *less* African than it could have been. However, recall that my project is to balance Africanness with philosophical justification in the construction of a moral theory.

Summing up, I have advanced sixteen firm intuitions about right and wrong by which to evaluate moral theories suggested by the African tradition. Eight are comparably common to philosophy in Africa and many other parts of the world, particularly the West (a–h), while eight are much more common to philosophical thought in Africa than in the West and elsewhere (i–p). In the next part of the book, I seek to discover a principle that both clearly entails and powerfully explains all sixteen, or at least ascertain which principle does better than its rivals in these respects. Such a principle would count as African for doing so and would at the same time promise to be philosophically attractive to interlocutors around the world.

3.5 'African': What's in a Name?

As Part I of the book draws to a close here, I note that recurrent themes in its chapters have been what the word 'African' means and whether the theory I create and defend warrants the label. In some ways I find it frustrating to have to engage in these debates, as they tend to prevent scholars from doing philosophy as opposed to meta-philosophy. However, these questions have arisen frequently during the course of my project, and it is reasonable for African philosophers as well as those from other backgrounds to want answers to them.

I have contended that the moral theory I advance in the next two parts of the book counts as African at least insofar as it accounts well for the (i)–(p) intuitions above. I have also argued that Africanness comes in degrees, determined by the extent to which something is informed by features that have been salient in sub-Saharan thought and practice. That construal means that my theory is *less* African than some others; all things being equal, an ethic that is grounded on a prior metaphysic of interdependence or includes essential reference to ancestors is somewhat more African than mine. Even so, I submit that mine still deserves the label, if it indeed easily entails and plausibly explains a wide array of sub-Saharan mores (ones that are prima facie morally attractive to contemporary philosophers). That is surely true at least in relation to the Western principles of utility and of respect for autonomy, as well as other major moral perspectives such as Confucianism, Islam, Hinduism, and so on.

I do take myself to be providing an interpretation of African moral thought, bringing out what a twenty-first-century multicultural audience of philosophers can find compelling about it. And as names in African cultures are characteristically imbued with significance, I would be honoured to have the 'African' title for the theory I advance in the rest of this book. However, in the final analysis, I would not be unhappy if my favoured theory were deemed to be philosophically attractive, but were denied the geographical label. What matters to me above all is finding the most defensible principle of right action, regardless of what it is called. So, if the reader prefers to name the relational moral theory that I now advance in Parts II and III 'Metz's view', so be it.

PART II

NORMATIVE ETHICS

Communality as the Ground of African Morality

4
The Common Good

> [A]ll other values are reducible *ultimately* to the value of well-being .... [W]ell-being can be considered a 'master value'.
>
> Kwame Gyekye (2004: 41)

4.1 Well-Being as the 'Master Value'

The African tradition is commonly labelled 'communitarian' in contrast to the 'individualism' prominent in Western thought and practice. Often the only thing that those beyond the continent know about sub-Saharan worldviews and ways of life is that they are focused on community in some way. This banality is true, but it is vague and admits of a variety of philosophical interpretations, the logics of which are usefully distinguished and then critically examined.

Communality, harmony, or a similar way of relating could be considered, on the one hand, a foundational value from which other values are derived, or, on the other, a derivative value that follows from some other, more basic one. The three moral theories most clearly suggested by the African philosophical literature are neatly divided in terms of this distinction (cf. 1.2.3). There is the view that communal relationship is a route by which to produce good human lives, where such lives are ones with either well-being (Chapter 4) or vital force (Chapter 5), and then there is the view that communal relationship is not a mere means to the realization of some other value, but rather is something to be pursued as an end (Chapters 6 and 7).

In this chapter I focus on the claim that, when seeking out the most promising moral theory with an African pedigree, one should favour the view that morality at bottom involves taking the well-being of everyone into account and advancing it in a certain way, which one can reliably do by entering into community (or harmonizing) with them. Two sub-Saharan philosophers particularly known for this view are the Ghanaians Kwasi Wiredu, with his principle of sympathetic impartiality, and Kwame Gyekye, whose moderate communitarianism (or rather its justification) I discussed above (2.3). As I indicate below, however, a number of other philosophers have voiced similarly welfarist accounts of African morality. These philosophers usually maintain that conceiving of right action in terms of even-handedly promoting well-being captures their respective peoples' thoughts about it, with some also contending that it is a fair representation, or the best reconstruction, of the African tradition more generally.

A Relational Moral Theory: African Ethics in and beyond the Continent. Thaddeus Metz, Oxford University Press.
 DOI: 10.1093/oso/9780198748960.003.0004

Wiredu's principle of sympathetic impartiality more or less prescribes acting according to the Golden Rule (Wiredu 1992: 198, 1996: 41, 2009: 15–6). I do not address it further since it is already familiar to an international audience of philosophers, is not particularly African as opposed to non-African,[1] and has serious weaknesses, such as the inability to justify punishment, that have usually prevented it from being taken seriously as a moral theory. I instead focus here on the ideas of Gyekye, whose moderate communitarianism prescribes promoting the common good in ways that do not violate individual rights. This moral theory has been central to African moral-political philosophy over the past twenty-plus years, but is not well known to global readers. After spelling out the essentials of Gyekye's moral theory, contrasting it with Western utilitarianism, and motivating it a bit (4.2), I advance objections to it (4.3), drawing heavily on the sixteen intuitions laid down in the previous chapter. I consider how the common good approach might be interpreted differently so as to avoid these objections, but I conclude that serious counterexamples remain. In the final section I briefly suggest how a relational theory, i.e., one that takes communality of some kind to be fundamental, need not imply that morality has nothing to do with promoting good lives; it could sensibly contend that the right relationship incorporates the aim of advancing others' welfare, amongst other things (4.4). Hence, I begin to indicate how my favoured theory promises to capture the kernel of truth in taking well-being to be central to sub-Saharan moral thought, even if, as I argue, Gyekye is incorrect to describe well-being as the 'master value'.

4.2 The Common Good as Foundation

In his first book on African philosophy, Gyekye advances the view that well-being is foundational to the moral thought of his Ghanaian Akan people and many other African societies. Here is Gyekye's first theoretical description of African ethics, that is, one that attempts to reduce all moral beliefs to a single basic property:

> Moral value in the Akan system is determined in terms of its consequences for mankind and society. 'Good' is thus used of actions that promote human interest. The good is identical with the welfare of the society.... Just as the good is that action or pattern of behaviour which conduces to well-being and social harmony,

[1] Indeed, the Golden Rule is the standard candidate for a moral norm that has been believed by *all* long-standing religio-philosophical traditions, on which see Küng and Kuschel (1993). In addition, by Wiredu's own admission, the Golden Rule cannot capture the moral importance of salient features of African society such as greetings (Wiredu 1996: 62–3), collective harvesting (Wiredu 2009: 16), or consensual democracy (Wiredu interviewed in Eze and Metz 2015: 83–5).

> so the evil (*bone*; that is, moral evil) is that which is considered detrimental to the well-being of humanity and society. (1995: 132–3; first edition published in 1987)

Although there is mention of 'harmony' here as an apparent end, the thrust of the passage is that right action has to do with improving people's quality of life and avoiding making them worse off. Gyekye continued throughout his career to support a sub-Saharan ethical theory focused on well-being, saying in his last book: 'African morality originates from considerations of human welfare and interests, not from divine pronouncements. Actions that promote human welfare or interest are good, while those that detract from human welfare are bad' (2013: 221).[2]

For just a few similarly welfarist comments about the nature of sub-Saharan ethics, consider:

> The greatest happiness and good of the tribe was the end and aim of each member of the tribe. Now, utility forms part of the basis of perhaps all moral codes. With the Bantu, it formed the basis of morality... it was utilitarian. This was the standard of goodness, and in harmony with, and conformity to, this end must the moral conduct be moulded. (Molema 1920: 116)

> [E]very Akan maxim about the specifically moral values that I know, explicitly or implicitly, postulates the harmonization of interests as the means, and the securing of human well-being as the end, of all moral endeavor. (Wiredu 1996: 65)

> [T]he Yoruba Ifa demonstrates serious efforts to show that the basis of morality lies in the concern for human welfare.... Being morally upright is not as much a matter of pleasing the supernatural forces as it is of promoting human welfare. It is in the light of this that the attitude of the Yoruba people pertaining to the place of religion and the supernatural forces in morality becomes easy to understand. Devotion to the deities is not as much in the interest of the deities as it is in the interest of the people. (Bewaji 2004: 398, 399)

These and many other statements[3] are by and large descriptive; they are meant to capture the way an African people or indigenous Africans generally have thought about right and wrong. I focus on Gyekye's theory because, at least in two of his

[2] For similar statements made between the time of Gyekye's first and last books, see Gyekye (1992: 109, 1997: 50, 2004: 38–41, 47, 90–3, 2010: sec. 5).

[3] For some similarly encapsulating statements about the welfarist foundation of sub-Saharan morality (at least in respect of the aim of right action), see Setiloane (1976: 57, 226); Gbadegesin (1991: 261); Sogolo (1993: 145–9); Bhengu (1996: 53); Kasoma (1996: 103–4); Oruka (1997: 138–40); Omoregbe (2005: 37); Ogbujah (2007: 136–7); Unah (2014: 110, 118). See also the earlier welfarist statements from Masolo and Etieyibo (1.2.3), which I suggested are juxtaposed with some non-welfarist ones in their work.

books (1997, 2004), it is also prescriptive; he advances it as something that should guide behaviour, apart from whether Africans have in fact believed it (for one of his central arguments, see 2.3 above).

Although Gyekye takes considerations of welfare to be fundamental to an attractive African ethic, and believes that rightness is action that promotes human well-being (e.g., 1997: 70–5, 2004: 105–11), he is careful to differentiate his approach from 'utilitarianism' in the sense widely used amongst contemporary English-speaking philosophers. Consider three major differences between them.

First, by 'well-being' Gyekye does not have in mind something subjective such as pleasurable experiences, satisfied desires, or positive emotions, which has been the salient way that 'modern' Western philosophers, economists, and psychologists have understood it. Instead, for Gyekye, and most other African philosophers, well-being in the first instance is constituted by objective factors such as the satisfaction of material, psychological, and social needs (Gyekye 1997: 44–6, 2004: 40, 54, 94, 116). In particular, Gyekye maintains that moral behaviour is a matter of working to satisfy 'needs that are *basic* to the enjoyment and fulfilment of the life of each individual' (2010: sec. 7). Such needs constitute a common good, for they 'can be said to be commonly—universally—shared by all human individuals, and to be essential for the ordinary or basic functioning of the human person in a human society' (2004: 53; see also 54, 94, and 1997: 41–7). Right action, for Gyekye, largely consists of promoting this common good—what is required for any human being to flourish (1997: 50, 2004: 91).

Second, Gyekye does not believe that right action is essentially what maximizes an amount of final value aggregated over all individuals. The latter, Western utilitarian approach to moral behaviour notoriously entails that it could be permissible to impose great harm on an innocent individual for the sake of a greater good to others. In contrast, for Gyekye right acts are those that meet *everyone's* needs (or are at least expected to do so), with the correct morality being one that 'seeks to promote the well-being of all people as its sole aim.... No individual person's interests and needs are neglected or sacrificed on the altar of the "principle of the greatest number"' (2004: 117; see also 2004: 54, 92, 94, 2010: sec. 7). Gyekye, along with some other African philosophers,[4] supposes that there need not be radical conflicts of interest between the individual and others in his society. Gyekye maintains that 'at least the basic interests of all the members of the community are identical' (2010: sec. 7; see also 1997: 76, 130), which suggests that there is invariably a way to meet everyone's needs.[5]

[4] See especially Wiredu (1996: 185) and Ikuenobe (2006: 65–83), but also those cited in the next note.

[5] For other philosophers working in the African tradition who prize the common good, see Asouzu (2004: 380–402); Lutz (2009); Etieyibo (2014: 73–8); Tosam (2014); Molefe (2019: 6, 84, 122, 147, 164–6).

At one stage in his career, Gyekye famously labelled his moral theory 'moderate communitarianism' (see 2.3). The 'communitarian' part consists of the obligation to do all one can to promote the common good, i.e., to meet the shared needs of all, without leaving anyone out. The 'moderate' part of Gyekye's view is that, when seeking to advance the common good for all, one may not do so in a way that violates individual rights, which constitutes a third major difference from Western utilitarianism. In particular, Gyekye emphasizes the need to protect the liberties of individuals to challenge the cultures of which they are a part, which involves rights to freedom of thought and association (1997: 52, 59–69, 2004: 38–40, 47, 93). The contrasting, 'extreme' form of communitarianism would require individuals to conform to extant social norms and permit others to force them to do so.

In taking well-being to be the end of right action (with individual rights constraining pursuit of this aim), Gyekye is committed to the view that other considerations that have been salient in the African ethical tradition are derivative. Not only does he make the general point that all other values are reducible to well-being (quoted at the start of this chapter), but he also is explicit that the specific values of communality and vitality are ultimately a function of utility (to use rough catchwords). Regarding vitality, Gyekye says: 'The African love of life is a feature of their concern for human well-being, which constitutes the warp and woof of their moral life and thought' (1995: 208). And with respect to ways of relating communally to others, Gyekye says that 'moral norms and virtues can be said to include kindness, generosity, compassion, benevolence, and respect and concern for others; in short, any action or behavior conducive to the promotion of the well-being of others' (1997: 50).

In addition to being distinct from Western utilitarianism, Gyekye's moral theory promises to capture several characteristically African moral intuitions well (3.4.3), and so merits engagement. For instance, it is plausible to think that a kind of political decision-making that requires consensus would be the most reliable way to determine what would advance the common good. After all, a policy that everyone has agreed to is most likely to be that which is in the interests of everyone. For another example, a focus on reconciliation amongst wrongdoers and victims is on the face of it well explained by a requirement to advance the common good. Aiming to fix broken relationships and move people towards mutual aid is something that would be good for all involved, certainly relative to a retributive response to wrongdoing. For a third instance, a concern for the common good accounts well for the practice of allocating wealth according to need—say, by sharing the proceeds of one's labour with the clan as a whole. Still more, promoting the common good would clearly explain the idea that the point of government is to improve people's quality of life, and not merely to protect their rights to live as they see fit.

Gyekye's ethic also merits engagement because of its prima facie ability to account for the intuitions with a more global scope (3.4.2). His prescription to advance the common good, albeit without violating individual rights to autonomous decision-making, readily makes some sense of the wrongness of murder, rape, theft, deception, discrimination, and the like.

4.3 The Limits of the Common Good

There is surely something correct about the idea that African morality, or rather an attractive normative interpretation of it, concerns the promotion of well-being. The question is whether right action is exhausted by a prescription to promote the common good without violating rights. In this section, I make the case that it is not, at least in the light of characteristically sub-Saharan views about right and wrong. There are several intuitions salient in the African tradition that either are not entailed by, or are poorly explained by, a prescription to meet everyone's needs while not interfering with anyone's liberties.

First, although it is easy to see why a requirement to advance the common good would prescribe a systematic redistribution of wealth as required to meet everyone's needs, it is harder to see why it would forbid great inequalities when everyone's needs have in fact been met (3.4.3 (m)). While large differentials in money and property are surely not as unjust as they would be if the needs of some were not met, many African philosophers hold that they would be unjust to some degree even if the needs of all were met. For example, permitting some to own the means of production would enable exploitation, where a minority does no work but instead has a majority work for it (Nyerere 1968: 3–4), and it would also foster feelings of envy on the part of those who do not own such great wealth (Magesa 1997: 278). It seems a stretch to suggest that taking advantage of others or doing what prompts envy are in themselves failures to meet the needs of others.

Second, it is difficult for a prescription to promote the common good to prescribe creating wealth in a cooperative fashion as a default orientation (3.4.3 (l)). In many indigenous African societies it might have been that everyone's interests were advanced when families would move from plot to plot helping each other to harvest a field. However, there are occasions where acting without regard for others' well-being would reliably end up performing the function of improving it, as if there were an 'invisible hand', in the famous words of Adam Smith. It is a matter of some debate when these situations arise, but, insofar as the overwhelming majority of economists believe that making exchanges in a marketplace is more efficient at producing wealth than planning, it appears that most everyday economic transactions between workers and managers (combined with state redistribution) in capitalist societies could fit the bill. In that case, a theory instructing one to perform any acts promoting the common good (without violating rights) would forbid one from *intentionally* aiming to help others and cooperating with them and would instead instruct one to aim to satisfy one's own interests on a (regulated) competitive market. However, there remains something right (not merely permissible, but praiseworthy), at least from a characteristically African perspective, about *aiming* to make others better off and cooperating with them. It is for many sub-Saharan thinkers wrong to *some* degree not to be moved by others' interests in the economic sphere and instead to be competitive, seeking the most for oneself.

Of course, labour and consumer markets might well be morally justified, all things considered. They have been central to why hundreds of millions of Chinese people have been lifted out of poverty over the past thirty years or so. The point is that, for a theory to capture sub-Saharan intuitions about how to interact, it ought to entail that there is *something* less than morally ideal about economic production being dominated by self-interested behaviour, even when that indirectly benefits others. A focus on the common good cannot account for that intuition, supposing markets (along with state intervention) were indeed marginally best for all in the long run.

Here is a third intuition that is more African than Western that Gyekye's theory has difficulty accommodating: the idea that it is immoral to fail to greet people upon meeting them, including, often enough, people one does not know (3.4.3 (n)). Of course, in a society where greeting is the norm, one could expect people to feel aggrieved if they were not greeted, where that feeling would constitute a reduction of well-being. However, African thought about the propriety of greetings cuts more deeply than that. For example, presumably it would be right for a society that does not currently greet to adopt the convention of greeting, or right for one to greet others even in the absence of such a convention.

Furthermore, when I greet a shop assistant or a gardener when I am passing by on the street, I am not thereby meeting their needs, however these might plausibly be construed. Doing so is implausibly part of 'that set of goods that is essentially or fundamentally good for human beings as such' (Gyekye 2004: 54). If one were to expand the notion of the common good to include well-being beyond the meeting of needs, then greeting a shop assistant or a gardener in passing might count. However, doing so would still not come close to advancing the good of everyone, not even in the shop or in the neighbourhood. The effects of my actions would be quite limited, and yet right all the same.

Again, one might try to alter Gyekye's moral theory, weakening the prescription to advance the common good to something like Pareto optimality, in which one should benefit some so long as one harms none. However, not even that move would fully capture why greetings seem to have a moral dimension, for part of the best explanation, I submit, is non-welfarist. For many African thinkers, greetings are required as a way to express the attitude that this is a person with a dignity and so merits acknowledgement. The point is even more stark upon considering the extra demands to greet elders, understood as those of a certain age who exhibit true personhood (virtue). One is to do so not because it is expected to make them or anyone else better off, but rather because their wisdom merits respectful treatment.

For a fourth counterexample to Gyekye's moderate communitarianism, consider the intuition that partaking in customs is *pro tanto* right and either denigrating or abandoning them is wrong to some degree (3.4.3 (o)). Gyekye himself acknowledges the intuition when he mentions the Akan maxim that 'customs are not to be destroyed' (2004: 39), and he can argue that participating in cultural life is often uplifting or meaningful not only for the one who does it, but also for others who feel a sense of connection from it. However, this rationale cannot make sense of the characteristically African intuition that it would be wrong to *some* degree to fail to participate when not participating would make everyone marginally better off than participating.

It is of course the case, as Gyekye contends, that sometimes 'a practice detrimental to human well-being ought to be repudiated' (2004: 38). My point is not that, from a typically African viewpoint, societies should never change, regardless of their cost to human welfare. My point is instead that, even when doing so is all-things-considered justified, letting go of shared ways of life can come at *some* moral cost, and that an exclusive focus on doing whatever advances the common good cannot account for this intuition. If well-being were the sole end of moral action, then there would be *nothing* morally problematic with changing harmful ways of life, but there can be, at least when they have been freely adopted and central to a people's self-conception. So, right action must involve some purpose that is not reducible to promoting well-being, if it is going to capture the moral importance of culture adequately.

Here is a fifth intuition, more African than Western, that a prescription to advance the common good has difficulty capturing, namely, the demand to both marry and rear children (3.4.3 (p)). Of course, loneliness is hardly conducive to happiness, and the prescription to have children in sub-Saharan societies has normally been qualified by the point that one must be able to ensure they have lives worth living. However, there is also good evidence that raising children fails to contribute to well-being for the parents, at least in the West; the happiest appear to be those who are married without children (e.g., Senior 2010).

Gyekye could fairly respond that the common good does not consist of subjective well-being, which is what rearing kids most clearly costs parents. However, if the African intuition is that procreation is what is required, then children cost parents and also others more than merely pleasure and satisfaction. Consider that for any needy baby whom parents create, all but the rich would be less able to meet not only one another's needs, but also the needs of all other babies, children, and adults who already exist. For the overwhelming majority of people, procreating inhibits their ability to promote the common good; creating new persons with needs means a reduced capacity to meet the needs of extant persons. Hence, a moral theory that instructs one to promote the common good as much as one can (without violating individual rights) seems to entail that creating additional needy beings should be kept to a minimum, and not that a typical person has any duty to procreate.[6]

So far I have argued that Gyekye's moderate communitarian moral theory has difficulty accounting for several intuitions from the African tradition, indeed most of the ones I had advanced (3.4.3).[7] I believe that it has some additional problems, including incorrectly presuming that one never has to make trade-offs between people's needs. Sometimes not everyone's needs can be met, as when one has to ration scarce life-saving resources—say, organs or lifeboats. However, a prescription to do what will meet the needs of all provides no guidance about what to do in such a scenario.

In addition, a prescription to promote the common good without violating individual rights has difficulty accounting for some of the more global intuitions, especially pertaining to the wrongness of insults and of mistreating animals. Gyekye's moral theory focuses strictly on human need, suggesting that no animals matter for their own sake from a moral point of view.[8] However, surely the reason it is wrong to set a cat on fire just for the thrill of watching it scurry about in agony is that we have some obligation to the cat (3.4.2 (h)). Advancing that claim need not entail that the urgent interests of cats should come at the expense of those of human persons (*contra* Menkiti 1984: 177) or that all animals, including amoebae and cats, have the same standing (*contra* Menkiti 2017: 467). Widely shared intuitions instead suggest that cats have a greater moral status than amoebae, but not one comparable to ours. Below I provide a theory that is meant to explain why (8.3–8.4), although it is admittedly open to Gyekye to broaden his principle to include the needs or well-being of certain animals.

When it comes to slurs and related derogatory expressions, note that the usual rights that Gyekye invokes are those involving the ability to step back and question the culture of which one is a part. More broadly, he can be viewed as advocating the right to live as one deems fit, subject to the condition that one indeed does whatever one can to promote the well-being of all. Such rights have little to do with the desirability of not being the target of slurs or other insults (3.4.2 (e)). Gyekye might point out that insulting people is hardly to meet their needs, but, then, so is oversleeping, where insulting people is of course morally

[6] Even if one were to broaden Gyekye's notion of well-being to include more than just meeting needs, a principle of maximizing the average well-being in society could not easily prescribe making new people when their lives would be marginally worse than those who already exist (but nonetheless would be well worth living). And I presume that a welfarist ethic ought not adopt a principle of maximizing total well-being, given that it prescribes intuitively too much procreation, viz., of beings who have lives just barely worth living, often called the 'repugnant conclusion' (Parfit 1984: sec. 131).

[7] I also suggest in 5.3 that it, like vitalism, has difficulty accounting for a reconciliatory criminal justice.

[8] Similar remarks apply to Wiredu's principle of sympathetic impartiality and the Golden Rule associated with it.

worse. More promising would be to appeal to the idea of human dignity, which is well known for being underdeveloped in his philosophy.

My central criticism of Gyekye's theory has been its inability to capture intuitions about right and wrong salient amongst African cultures or at least their philosophers. In a nutshell I have argued that an aim of promoting the common good, or even more broadly well-being, has difficulty adequately capturing the *pro tanto* moral undesirability of: great inequalities of wealth (even when that is consistent with everyone's needs being met); creating wealth for selfish reasons (even when doing so meets marginally more needs than doing so for other-regarding reasons); failing to greet people; undermining people's cultures (even when doing so marginally improves their quality of life); and remaining single and childless. I usually argued that Gyekye's theory and related welfarist principles cannot entail these intuitions.[9]

At this point, some would suggest moving to a 'two-level' or 'indirect' form of welfarism, such as advocating rule-utilitarianism or drawing a distinction between what would be the ideal act and what is prescribed in the light of human cognitive and motivational imperfections. I believe that Anglo-American reflection on these moves for many decades has shown that serious counter-examples typically remain.

However, the deeper point, and the reason I do not explore two-level/indirect welfarism here, is that even if it can entail the intuitions, I submit that it would not explain them well. The reason to greet someone is not exhausted by the idea that, say, everyone would have their needs met (or perhaps simply be happier) if everyone routinely greeted one another, particularly elders. Instead, there is something about respect that plausibly does some of the work. Similarly, the reason to avoid disparaging or interfering with long-standing ways of life central to people's identities is implausibly merely a function of the idea that, despite an omniscient arch-angel seeing that doing so need not harm anyone, we cognitively and motivationally challenged humans should normally presume that when we undermine culture we end up failing to maximize benefit. Instead, sharing a way of life seems to have some moral relevance in itself, apart from caring for people's quality of life.

Beyond two-level or indirect welfarism not being a particularly compelling philosophical explanation of the wrongness, it is, even more clearly, not a characteristically African explanation, which is what I am seeking out in this part of the book. One will search in vain for any suggestion of two-level or indirect welfarism in the African philosophical literature.

There are additional strategies that Gyekye or his defenders could explore at this point. One would be to say more about what confers a dignity on us. The deep

[9] I suggest below that several of these criticisms also apply to a vitalist moral theory (5.3).

reason why Gyekye believes that we have individual rights is that we have a dignity, but he does not explain in virtue of what we have one (1997: 63–4). Gyekye is non-committal about what constitutes our dignity, declining to specify whether it is the fact that we are children of God, capable of autonomous decision-making, or something else. Without such a specification, one cannot firmly derive all that many conclusions about how to treat people with respect; for that, one needs to know what it is about them that has a superlative non-instrumental value. Another strategy would be to interpret Gyekye's notion of human need, or at least well-being, much more relationally than I have found myself able to do in the light of his writings (see Gädeke 2020). On both counts, I submit that the reader should consider the relational moral theory below (Chapter 7), which develops an account of dignity precisely in virtue of our communal nature.

4.4 Well-Being: Neither Master nor Slave

As noted above (4.2), Gyekye is far from the only philosopher to have conceived of well-being as the basic moral value for an African ethic. It would be useful to close by sketching a big picture about the view that welfarism is the best interpretation of sub-Saharan morality. Here, in broad strokes, is what I think it captures and what it misses.

There is surely some kind of close connection between acting rightly and acting in ways likely to improve others' well-being, for any plausible moral theory with the African label. For just two examples, it is compelling to assert that consensual democracy would be more likely than majoritarian democracy to meet everyone's needs, and that reconciliation is justified relative to retributivism because the former would do some good.

Such a humanist orientation is what Gyekye and others such as Gbadegesin (1991), Wiredu (1996), and Bewaji (2004) have plausibly fastened onto in contrast to a supernaturalist reading of the African tradition. Deeming it particularly urgent to distinguish sub-Saharan ethics from one grounded on what God has revealed to a prophet or in a text, they might have been too quick to *identify* right action with behaviour that promotes human interest satisfaction (perhaps subject to certain constraints). I have suggested several respects in which such an approach cannot easily capture characteristically sub-Saharan views about right and wrong. Sometimes permitting great inequalities of wealth, being competitive in the economic sphere, undermining cultures, and remaining childless can best meet people's needs or otherwise improve their welfare, and yet many African philosophers would judge these actions to be wrong to *some* degree (even when justified on balance).

An alternative account of the close tie between right action and human welfare is worth considering. Below I maintain that right action is a matter of honouring individuals in virtue of their capacity for communal relationships, where one (but not the only) facet of these relationships involves helping others and being helped by others. From this perspective, well-being is not the master value of morality, which is instead our special communal nature. However, neither is well-being a 'slave', for it is not a mere means to some other value that is utterly distinct from it. Instead, action taken with the aim of improving others' well-being is *partially constitutive* of the fundamental duty to treat individuals as having a moral status in virtue of their capacity to be party to communal relationships. Caring for others' quality of life is one end of right action, but an additional one, essential to capture the missing intuitions, is sharing a way of life, or so I will argue.

5
Vital Force

> [A]mong Africans there was always the awareness that human life was the greatest value.... The life that is regarded as the greatest value, however, is not the vegetative and instinctual life that human beings share with plants and animals, but rather the life that is founded on the principle of syntropy.
>
> Noah Dzobo (1992: 227)

5.1 Life as the 'Greatest Value'

The above comment from Noah Dzobo appears in a chapter that he contributed to one of the most influential volumes published in African philosophy. It is the first volume of *Ghanaian Philosophical Studies*, which was edited by Kwasi Wiredu and Kwame Gyekye back in 1992. Some of the most widely discussed African works in value theory appeared in this volume. Unfortunately, Dzobo's vitalist contribution did not turn out to be one of them, having been eclipsed by the contributions of Wiredu and Gyekye.

In contrast to the welfarism explored in the previous chapter, Dzobo believes that the African tradition is best understood to be vitalist at bottom. Instead of a person's quality of life being what matters morally, for Dzobo and many others in the field it is rather life itself insofar as it is strong, complex, creative, or the like. In addition to Dzobo's work, I draw heavily on that of Bénézet Bujo and Laurenti Magesa, two theologians from the Congo and Tanzania respectively, as they too have explored the implications of vitalism for African morality with rigour and depth. Their works, along with those of some others mentioned below, suggest the principle that an act is right just insofar as it produces, protects, and develops vitality, and wrong to the degree that it ends life, fails to protect it, and causes degeneration. All three thinkers believe that such a principle best captures African moral beliefs, whereas I focus on evaluating whether we should believe such an African moral principle normatively construed.

In the following I begin by presenting the core of these and other philosophers' vitalist approach to morality (5.2), interpreting it so that it accords with the secular method I have adopted (recall 3.3). Life amongst indigenous sub-Saharans has traditionally been understood to be an imperceptible energy that has come from God and is imbued in everything in the world, including so-called 'inanimate'

A Relational Moral Theory: African Ethics in and beyond the Continent. Thaddeus Metz, Oxford University Press.
 DOI: 10.1093/oso/9780198748960.003.0005

objects. I present an understanding of vitality in terms of liveliness that, in contrast, does not rest on highly controversial metaphysical claims and thereby has greater potential to ground a moral theory of interest to a global audience. Next, I present counterexamples to the idea that right action promotes liveliness, drawing particularly on intuitions about morality adumbrated earlier (in 3.4.3), and I also argue that certain revisions to the theory do not adequately help it to account for them (5.3). I conclude this chapter by positing another strategy by which to capture the notion that life is central to African thought about ethics (5.4). I suggest that instead of communality being a means to the production of vitality, as per the philosophers explored in this chapter, vitality might well be understood to be one large facet of communality. Even if Dzobo is incorrect to maintain that life is the 'greatest value', it is not the smallest value either.

5.2 Vital Force as Foundation

Placide Tempels (1959) is well known for having been the first writer to articulate a sub-Saharan philosophical worldview with some care and to have placed vital force at its heart. Tempels notoriously suggests that his vitalist interpretation of African philosophy is true of all *bantu* language speakers, if not all Africans, and he has been taken to task for having made a hasty generalization. In addition, his aim when publishing his research was to facilitate colonialism at a cultural level. Despite these concerns, many African philosophers have found his views expressive of one major swathe of sub-Saharan normativity, and it would not be unreasonable to appeal to his work to expound a vitalist ethic.

However, I do not. Over the past forty years, intellectuals indigenous to the continent have articulated and defended intricate vitalist worldviews, and I instead draw on their publications to construct and evaluate a promising moral theory. In particular, I focus on the ideas of Dzobo (1992), Magesa (1997), and Bujo (1997, 2001, 2005), which I find of particular interest for contending that vital force makes sense of an array of recurrent African beliefs and practices. However, I do not ignore the many others who have deemed vitality to be foundational for African ethics.[1]

In Western moral thought, some have held that right action is a matter of respecting a living organism with the DNA of *Homo sapiens*. Such a view is noticeably held by many of those theorizing in the Judeo-Christian-Islamic

[1] Beyond Tempels (1959), see Jahn (1961: 116–17); Anyanwu (1984, 1987); Nwala (1985: esp. 144–5); Sindima (1989); Mulago (1991: 125–6, 131); Kasenene (1994); Hamminga (2005: 57); Ukagba (2005: 184); LenkaBula (2008); Mkhize (2008); Bikopo and van Bogaert (2010); Tangwa (2010: 186–8); Onah (2012); Molefe (2015); Etieyibo (2017); Rakotswoane and van Niekerk (2017); Uduma and Nweke (2018). See also the earlier vitalist statements from Mbiti, Kasenene, and Iroegbu (1.2.3), which I suggested are juxtaposed with some non-vitalist ones in their work.

religious tradition, who typically maintain that only human beings have been made in God's image.[2] What makes humans special, from this standpoint, is that they have a soul, a spiritual substance that originated in God and that will forever outlive the death of their bodies. Where goes a living human being, there goes a soul and hence a being that must not be degraded.

Although one can encounter this perspective in writings by African philosophers and theologians, particularly given the influence of Christianity below the Sahara desert, the conception of human life salient amongst indigenous peoples there differs from it and is less familiar to international readers. Instead of a spiritual substance—a thing—that could enjoy eternal life being essential for dignity and grounding right action, it is common for sub-Saharan thinkers to hold that morality is a function of our vital force, one that is often expected to perish at some point.

Traditionally understood, vital force is an imperceptible energy that inheres in everything in the world, including what is perceptible and also what seems 'inanimate', including rocks. God is deemed to be the source of all vital force, with everything contingent and concrete in the universe having sprung from God and taken some divine energy with it. All beings in the world are often thought to be good in themselves to some degree, by virtue of having some degree of vital force. In addition, widely held African worldviews presume an ontological-*cum*-axiological hierarchy, such that animate beings such as plants and animals have a greater degree (or kind) of vital force than inanimate ones and hence have a greater moral standing, human beings have more (or better) vital force than plants and animals and therefore are higher than them, ancestors have even more (better) than human beings, and then God, the source of all vital force, has the most (best) and so is of course the most important.

Similar to the way that, for the Abrahamic faiths, the soul is thought to carry one's personality and to outlive the death of one's body, so, for what is commonly called 'Traditional African Religion', one's vital force carries (or constitutes) one's self and survives bodily death. Although ancestors may be thought to have lived for several hundred years, there is little intimation of immortality in the indigenous African tradition, even for ancestors (e.g., Menkiti 1984: 174–5). People are generally expected to survive the death of their body by virtue of their vital force continuing to reside in an imperceptible realm on Earth, becoming one of the 'living-dead', but all or nearly all are often expected to cease to exist at some point, particularly upon being forgotten by their descendants.

Although a number of contemporary sub-Saharan philosophers expound such ideas, I invoke few of them, given my intention to avoid ontological controversies as much as possible when advancing a moral theory (3.3). Is God, as the ultimate

[2] For just a couple of examples, see Paul II (1995) and United States Catholic Church (2003).

source of vital force, in fact real? Is everything in the universe actually infused with a divine energy? Does a certain configuration of this energy constitute our self? Will this configuration of energy and hence our self survive the death of our body? If so, will we indeed continue to reside on Earth? Have ancestors really done so for centuries? Instead of engaging in the metaphysics that would be required to answer these questions by appeal to evidence, I instead work with less contested ideas about the nature of reality—ones that can be readily shared with those outside the African tradition.

Supposing that the perceptible, or roughly the 'physical' or the 'natural' in Western terms, is reasonably taken as common ground amongst a large majority of intellectual traditions, I work with a conception of life grounded on it. Such a secular orientation permits me to invoke several key elements of the traditional African approach. I work with a notion of vitality that: is construed in terms of force, not substance; is thought to be perishable, as opposed to eternal; comes in different degrees or kinds; and plausibly varies in value depending on the quantity or quality of it.

Often when African thinkers make evaluative and normative vitalist judgements, they do not appeal to religious or thickly metaphysical notions, at least not explicitly. For example, they tend to say that human beings are good in some way for exhibiting a superlative degree of health, strength, growth, reproduction, creativity, complexity, vibrancy, activity, self-motion, courage, and confidence. Or they characterize undesirable states as reductions of vitality understood as disease, weakness, decay, barrenness, destruction, disintegration, lethargy, passivity, submission, insecurity, and depression. Consider Dzobo's analysis of vitality:

> [T]here is an urge or dynamic creative energy in life . . . which works towards wholeness and healing, towards building up and not pulling down. . . . Our people therefore conceive human life as a force or power that continuously recreates itself and so is characterized by continuous change and growth which depends upon its own inner source of power. . . . Since the essence of the ideal life is regarded as power and creativity, growth, creative work and increase have become essential values. Powerlessness or loss of vitality, unproductive living, and growthlessness become ultimate evils in our indigenous culture. (1992: 227)

Such construals of vitality have sense and force when it is understood in physicalist or naturalist terms, which I often call 'liveliness'.

I presume that most readers will share the judgement that there is something strongly to be preferred about persons with more liveliness than less. They are better (more excellent) people, if not also better off (happier). So, when the following thinkers speak of 'life' or 'vital force' in their descriptions of African moral beliefs, I replace their concepts with liveliness when constructing a normative ethical theory:

> In African societies, emphasis is put on vitality. . . . Everyone strives to make life stronger and to be protected from misfortune or from a diminution of life or of being. . . . In ethical terms, any action which increases life or vital force is right, and whatever decreases it is wrong. (Kasenene 1994: 140)

> The anthropocentric dimension is the aspect of African ethics which has been most emphasized. . . . There is a large consensus that the strengthening and growth of life are fundamental criteria in the realm of ethics. The members of a clan share the obligation to contribute to the growth of life of the whole community by their moral action. (Bujo 1997: 27)

> I want to address more specifically the question of the general moral/ethical consciousness that the African view of the world engenders. . . . [I]n no way is any thought, word or act understood except in terms of good and bad, in the sense that such an attitude or behavior either enhances or diminishes life.
> (Magesa 1997: 57, 58)

Although these passages are in the first instance empirical claims about what Africans have tended to believe about morality, their adherents naturally think that these principles are attractive. My task in this chapter is to evaluate, more systematically than has been done up to now, the extent to which they are justified in the light of intuitions about right and wrong.

Before doing so, I need to address an ambiguity in the above principles. Even once talk of 'life' and 'vital force' are specified as liveliness, a prescription to perform acts that will (or are reasonably expected to) promote liveliness is still vague in a crucial respect. Specifically, it does not clearly indicate where to promote liveliness, or, in other words, whose liveliness to promote. Some theorists appear to think that one's basic aim should be to exhibit the most vitality that one can in oneself (Shutte 2001: 22–5, 30–1), while others mention oneself and others as morally relevant sites (Bujo 1997: 27, 37).

In the following, I suppose that the proper aim is not purely self-regarding, so that one should seek to advance liveliness either anywhere one can or perhaps only in others. Conceiving of right action merely in terms of maximizing one's own liveliness has two seriously unwelcome implications. First, it entails intuitively incorrect answers about certain cases of killing others or letting oneself be killed. For example, a prescription to do whatever it takes to promote one's own liveliness entails that one ought to commit murder if necessary to stay alive in the long run. Suppose that you need a new kidney to survive and that no one will give one to you. Then, to maximize your liveliness, you would need to kill another (let us presume, innocent) person so as to acquire his healthy kidney for a transplant. Or, if there is a single tiny lifeboat that seats only one person, and there are two of us who have so far survived the shipwreck, then, if I lose the coin toss, I ought to rescue myself anyway, using force as necessary; for only thereby could I promote my own liveliness.

Second, a prescription to maximize one's own liveliness faces the problem of not sufficiently permitting, let alone requiring, one to give up one's life for others, since one's life would thereby end. This appears to be true even if those at risk were one's children and one could be assured of saving their lives (only) by ending one's own.

There are a number of ways that the *eudaimonist* friend of vitalism might try to reply to these concerns. Traditionalist Africans would point out that one's life continues after the death of one's body, which, if true, might help to avoid the counterexamples. As the reader knows by now, I do not presume anything metaphysically so extravagant in this book (3.3). Abstracting, therefore, from highly contested ontological claims, some others might contend that one's own good has a narrative structure that would be irreparably marred if one were to murder or to let one's children die (van Niekerk 2007).

However, it is not so clear that a vitalist can coherently take narrative value on board, as the value of liveliness does not seem to be enhanced or diminished as such by virtue of its pattern over time. In addition, even if the vitalist could somehow make sense of narrativity, any narrative disvalue could well be outweighed by an aggregate amount of liveliness over a long time such as forty or fifty years.

In reply, one might suggest that letting others live at one's own expense would be such a high 'peak' in one's own vitality—say, for being courageous—that continuing to live could never surpass it.[3] Again, I doubt that, at least if one had decades to come during which one could consistently exhibit liveliness in less intense ways. Furthermore, note that such a strategy cannot hope to show that killing an innocent person in order to save one's own life would be such a low 'trough' in respect of one's own liveliness as to be unsurpassable by future gains.

Even if a *eudaimonist* vitalism could somehow entail the intuitively correct answers to when killing others and letting oneself be killed are permissible or not, its explanation of why they are is implausible. A further problem with a principle of promoting one's own liveliness is that it cannot avoid accounting for the wrongness of killing someone else solely in terms of its effects on oneself. If I ask why I should avoid murdering another person, the present form of vitalism is the view that the basic moral reason to avoid doing so is only ever that *my* liveliness would flourish. However, a more intuitive answer would be that the liveliness of the other person is a feature that gives me some non-instrumental reason to avoid killing him.

In any event, in the rest of this chapter I work with an other-regarding version of vitalism, according to which one's basic duty is to act in ways that are expected to increase the liveliness of either anyone or only others besides oneself. In

[3] This is the way that Aristotle deals with the problem for his version of *eudaimonia*, according to Wielenberg (2004).

contrast to this consequentialist approach, another prima facie attractive interpretation of vitalism would be a respect-based one, according to which we have a dignity inhering in our liveliness and wrong actions are those that degrade it (see Iroegbu 2005b; Molefe 2015). A striking advantage of the deontological version is that it can avoid the implication that it would be right to kill one innocent person, harvest her healthy organs, and transplant them into three other innocent people who would otherwise die without them. Although I focus mostly on the teleological version, since it has been much more prominent in the field, my objections to it usually apply with comparable force to the deontological one.

Before evaluating the vitalist moral theory, note what it entails for the other two moral categories that are salient in the African tradition, viz., utility and community. With regard to the former, many vitalists will be inclined to conceive of well-being as vitality and of woe as its absence. For instance, many would here follow Tempels when he claims of a large swathe of sub-Saharans:

> Supreme happiness, the only kind of blessing, is, to the Bantu, to possess the greatest vital force.... Every illness, wound or disappointment, all suffering, depression, or fatigue, every injustice and every failure: all these are held to be, and are spoken of by the Bantu as, a diminution of vital force.
>
> (1959: 32; for similar phrasings see Kasenene 1994: 140–1)

It would be interesting to evaluate the suggestions that well-being is reducible to liveliness and woe to its absence or reduction.[4]

When it comes to the category of community, vitalists normally ascribe it an instrumental value. They most often suggest that relating communally is what *causes* an increase in liveliness or some other construal of vitality. For just one example, consider Godfrey Onah, a Nigerian theologian, when he says:

> At the centre of traditional African morality is human life. Africans have a sacred reverence for life.... To protect and nurture their lives, all human beings are inserted within a given community.... The promotion of life is therefore the determinant principle of African traditional morality and this promotion is guaranteed only in the community. Living harmoniously within a community is therefore a moral obligation ordained by God for the promotion of life.
>
> (2012; see also Kasenene 1994: 142; Magesa 1997: 81)

If discord were to arise and relationships were to break down, then people's liveliness would be threatened.

[4] For some suggestion that they are not, since dissatisfaction, ill-health, and woe involve the presence of a substantive bad beyond the mere absence of a good, see Metz (2012: 52–3).

In addition, Bujo is well known for having argued that a certain kind of communing is expected to provide *knowledge* of which norms would enhance vital force (1997: 24–42, 2001: 45–71). When people, or at least elders, come together to deliberate and seek consensus about how to proceed, they are, so Bujo contends, particularly likely to discover those practices that would realize the 'common growth of the people' and the 'promotion of life' at the societal level (1997: 161, 166).

To begin to evaluate the principle that one ought to promote liveliness in others (if not also oneself), consider the global intuitions about right and wrong (3.4.2). It is reasonable to suspect that what killing, raping, deceiving, stealing, and the like have in common is that they reduce liveliness, compared to other actions one could normally perform. They indeed tend to cause death, injury, passivity, insecurity, reduced self-esteem, and related forms of weakness and disintegration, or in Dzobo's words, they impair people's 'creative power' (1992: 228). If one prefers a deontological approach, then one could argue that killing innocents for money, raping to feel pleasure, stealing when not necessary to meet needs, and torturing animals for fun are characteristically ways of reducing another's liveliness for something worth less than it, and hence are degrading of that superlative non-instrumental value. These explanations merit global consideration as plausible alternatives to welfarist and autonomy-based rationales, even if I ultimately deny that vitalism is the strongest contender from the African tradition.

Vitalism also appears to capture some of the more African intuitions about what is right and wrong. It can make sense of the rejection of the liberal idea that the state must be neutral in respect of conceptions of the good life, prescribing a state that instead seeks to improve people's liveliness, conceived as a matter of well-being or excellence (or both). In addition, it is not surprising to find adherents to vitalism championing procreation as one important moral obligation (e.g., Dzobo 1992: 225–7, 233; Bujo 1997: 108–14, 2001: 6–7, 34–54; Magesa 1997: 63, 89, 120–35, 167). Creating a new life, while ensuring that children are reared so as to be healthy, confident, and creative, follows straightforwardly from a basic and comprehensive duty to promote liveliness. Furthermore, it is reasonable to think that working jointly on large tasks would produce more liveliness than working in isolation or otherwise shouldering burdens as individuals. And, then, distributing money and property from those who have much more than they need to those who do not would, for familiar economic considerations of diminishing marginal utility in respect of wealth, maximize liveliness.

5.3 The Limits of Vital Force

Although an appeal to liveliness as the ground of a moral theory deserves much more attention than it has received from moral philosophers, professional ethicists, and related thinkers around the world, I argue in this section that it is vulnerable to serious counterexamples. The counterexamples are, I submit, such as to make my favoured, relational theory attractive by comparison, though I do not mean to suggest that one should dismiss vitalism. It is a live option (so to speak).

First off, I submit that a number of the objections I made to welfarism in the previous chapter (4.3) apply with comparable force to vitalism. Although procreation is prescribed by a principle of promoting liveliness, it is difficult for vitalism to explain the *pro tanto* wrongness of great inequalities of wealth, economic production undertaken through competitive means, and undermining long-standing cultural practices. Recall that I supposed, for the sake of argument, these three things would on balance best promote the common good or otherwise advance people's well-being, and submitted that many African thinkers would plausibly still find them morally problematic to some degree. Parallel thought experiments apply to liveliness. For example, a moral demand to participate with others in rituals and customs retains some force even on the presumption that mocking them or abolishing them would marginally foster liveliness.

Turning to some fresh criticisms, it is worth considering whether consensus-seeking amongst equals in the political realm (3.4.3 (i)) is in fact what is expected to maximize liveliness throughout society compared to other systems. Bujo has done the most to argue for a unanimitarian democracy on the grounds of a vitalist ethic. His central reasoning is that consensus amongst at least informed representatives, an ideal springing from traditional African chiefs having routinely consulted with popularly appointed elders before making a decision, is most likely to reveal the truth about how to promote liveliness. The 'palaver', as Bujo calls it, 'shows that norms can be and have to be found in a communal manner, hence free of domination and in dialogue' (1997: 37). I believe there are two problems with this vitalist rationale for consensus.

First, compare a requirement of consensus for a statute or policy to be valid, on the one hand, with one requiring a significant majority, on the other. Whatever extra insight might be obtained as a result of consensus, i.e., 100 per cent agreement amongst legislators or policy-makers, is likely to be small relative to that resulting from a supermajority—say, 80 or 90 per cent agreement. In addition, the extra time required to obtain unanimity would likely be too slow to respond to many situations in ways likely to foster liveliness.

The second problem concerns what is sometimes called 'plural voting', where the educated receive more votes to cast than those who are uneducated. Bujo is at pains to show that the African palaver is plausibly interpreted as requiring the equal input of all who wish to participate in it, and in that respect is more egalitarian than, and superior to, the logic of German discourse ethics (1997: 37–56). However, if one's view is that 'every action must be considered evil which prevents the fulfilment of the common, and also of the individual life'

(Bujo 1997: 37), then seeking consensus in such an egalitarian way would be wrong, if, as is plausible, giving the same number of votes to the uneducated as the educated would prevent liveliness relative to what would be obtained by giving the uneducated fewer votes than the educated. Bujo's consequentialist principle directs us to evaluate procedures in terms of their expected outcomes, and sometimes inegalitarian procedures are likely to produce better outcomes. One might at this point opt for a non-consequentialist or respect-based vitalism. However, while I accept that there is something degrading about plural voting, it is hard to see why it would degrade people's *liveliness*.

Criminal justice is another respect in which vitalism has difficulty capturing the African intuitions about what is right as opposed to wrong. Although it is clear that a prescription to promote liveliness in society would forbid punishing on grounds of retribution, it is unclear that it recommends seeking reconciliation between offenders and their victims as the alternative. If the basic aim were to promote liveliness and hence to prevent other-regarding crime, such as murder, rape, and theft, then it appears that a state should often inflict severe penalties on individuals so as to deter them and others from committing it or lock people away so that they cannot re-offend. That is, vitality seems to justify deterrence and incapacitation, not so much reconciliation.

In addition, a teleological moral theory has difficulty entailing that it should be the guilty, those who have in fact committed a crime, who should be punished. Imposing a penalty on one person so as to instil fear in others or using punishment to incapacitate differ substantially from imposing a penalty on a guilty person to prompt him to compensate his victims, to reform his character, and more generally to facilitate a mending of ties between him and his victims. The African tradition generally favours reconciliation between the guilty and the innocent, or at least it is advocated more frequently than deterrence and incapacitation, which could be applied to parties who have done no wrong, but an ethic of liveliness appears to provide no reason to include the former approach as the aim of criminal justice relative to the latter.[5]

In addition to having difficulty capturing the African intuitions, there are some global ones that vitalism does not easily entail or powerfully explain. First off, consider that a principle urging us to promote liveliness appears to permit racial and ethnic discrimination when it comes to romantic relationships, which is wrong by most contemporary philosophies (3.4.2 (d)). Nearly all professional moral philosophers and related thinkers around the world believe that, if the state is going to give people the opportunity to marry, it must do so in a way that permits them to do so with persons of another race. However, a state could rule out interracial marriage without impairing vitality. Concretely, imagine that a

[5] A similar point applies to Gyekye's welfarism and related ethics (4.3); they, too, provide no particular reason to favour reconciliation over deterrence and incapacitation.

racist state did not punish those who were to intermarry. Suppose it rather defined a valid marriage as one incapable of obtaining between members of different races and ethnicities. Mixed couples who have vowed to live together in romantic, long-term relationships simply could not count as 'legally married'. Despite the absence of punitive or 'restrictive' law in H.L.A. Hart's (1961) influential terms, the state's segregationist 'facilitative' law would remain wrongful, indeed, a human rights violation. However, supposing the separated population groups had enough people within them for everyone to find a fertile spouse, it appears that no one's liveliness would be undermined.

There are two ways the friend of vital force could try to show that such marital segregation would impair people's liveliness, but neither is compelling. Most initially tempting, one might reasonably suggest that people would become depressed and be unable to express their natural selves, if not given the opportunity to wed those of another race whom they love.

In reply, though, suppose a state encouraged people of different races not to socialize with one another, so that they rarely became lovers in the first place. If people grew up thinking that it is inappropriate to become intimate with others deemed to be of 'another kind', then a segregationist marriage law would not frustrate strong desires, let alone threaten to impair health, childrearing, or other forms of creative power. The point is that such state policies would be immoral, despite people's liveliness not being hampered.

Second, then, the friend of a vitalist ethic might plausibly suggest that 'separate but equal is still unequal', meaning that such segregationist policies would likely result in lower self-esteem on the part of the race deemed inferior. A state expressing the judgement that a certain group is not worth mixing with would harm people's senses of their own worth.

The point is fair, but now imagine a racist but in a sense 'even-handed' state, one of the sort that former President de Klerk of South Africa has maintained was the intention (albeit not the practice) of apartheid architects. Suppose the state's aim were to foster cultures, where it thinks that they flourish best when races are kept pure and distinct. Suppose the state did not maintain that, say, black African culture is inferior to white European culture, but rather that people must not intermarry for the sake of their respective cultures. In this (admittedly) hypothetical scenario, the state's discriminatory practice would not be expressing the judgement that any group is inferior to any other group, and so a loss of self-esteem would not be expected to result. However, it would still be wrong for the state not to facilitate marriage across racial, ethnic, or cultural lines.

Consider, now, another global intuition, pertaining to deception (3.4.2 (c)). It can be wrong to tell innocent people lies or to trick them, even when there is little to no risk of impairing their liveliness. For a first example, consider the case of a spouse who systematically cheats on her husband behind his back, and is so careful and conniving that he has no chance of finding out. It appears she would be enhancing the liveliness of her lover and herself, while not reducing that of her spouse. Or, second, think about a sociologist who tells study participants that he wants to know about how they choose their clothes and organize their bedrooms, but instead is out to observe sexual behaviour. Imagine he has told participants that the cameras installed will film them only during specific morning hours, but that this is a lie and they instead record them when masturbating or having intercourse. Suppose there is no reduction of liveliness on the part of the ones observed, and not even the realistic threat of such. Even so, I presume that readers, whether working in African, Western, or other traditions, believe that these actions would be wrong, at least to some substantial degree.

The natural reply to make on behalf of vitalism is that there is real risk of people discovering what the spouse and the sociologist have done, which would then make the victims feel insecure, depressed, and the like. However, upon stipulating that discovery of the deception would not happen, the actions still appear wrong. Furthermore, note that an appeal to the discovery of the deception suggests that it is not the deception that is wrong, but rather the belief that one was deceived. After all, no loss of vitality would come if one did not believe that one had been deceived but one indeed had been; conversely, a substantial loss of vitality would come if one believed that one had been deceived but one in fact had not been. Although the deception itself is what is intuitively wrong, it might be hard for vitalism to make sense of that insofar as the effects on people's liveliness depend on the beliefs of those acted upon and not the deceptive actions themselves.

So far as I know, this discussion constitutes some of the first systematic criticism of the vitalist approach to morality in the African tradition. I look forward to seeing how vitalists might respond to the objections raised here. For all I can tell at this stage of enquiry, however, a communal ethic, advanced in the next two chapters, does a better job of accounting for the key intuitions (3.4) than does the one explored in this chapter.

5.4 Life: Neither Greatest nor Smallest

Like the value of well-being, that of vital force is recurrent in sub-Saharan thought about ethics and has something attractive about it. It would therefore be ideal to find a place for it when constructing an African moral theory.

As indicated above, a vitalist ethic takes relationships to be instrumental considerations; specifically, it treats them as mere means to the production of either liveliness itself or knowledge of which actions would produce liveliness. In contrast, a relational ethic is roughly the view that relationships are to be pursued as ends, with other values being a function of them. One might suspect that I would deem liveliness to be a cause of communal relationship, reversing the vitalist's order of variables. However, such an approach would not acknowledge the intuitive respects in which liveliness of the sort described above (5.2) can indeed be something for a moral agent to seek out for its own sake, not merely as a means to a distinct end.

Hence, in the following chapters, I instead advance the view that relating with others in the morally proper way can include making them more lively. My view is that right action is a matter of honouring individuals in virtue of their capacity for communal relationships, where one (but not the only) facet of these relationships involves enhancing their creative power. From this perspective, vital force is not, as per Dzobo, the 'greatest' value, which is instead our special relational nature. However, neither is vitality the smallest value, for it is not a merely instrumental good. Instead, action taken with the aim of improving others' liveliness is *partially constitutive* of the fundamental duty to treat individuals as having a moral standing because of their capacity to be party to communal relationships.

6
Communal Relationship

> [T]he highest good in African societies is the preservation of order and harmony within the community, on the one hand, and between the community and its spiritual protectors (the divinities and ancestors), on the other hand.... Harmony is the paramount goal within and among all the possible relationships within the cosmological order, and herein lies its ethical significance (as) the source and justification of all moral obligations.
>
> Peter Paris (1995: 43, 56)

6.1 Harmony as the 'Highest Good'

In previous chapters, I have critically explored the hypotheses that the best theoretical interpretation of sub-Saharan morality is one according to which either (roughly speaking) utility or vitality is the supreme value. Here, I advance harmony or communality as a third and more promising candidate. Instead of well-being or vital force alone meriting pursuit for its own sake, I argue that harmonious or communal relationship of a certain kind is ultimately what should be pursued as an end.[1]

Peter Paris, a theologian who has studied African and African-American ethics, is empirically contending that African peoples have considered relationality to be the highest good, as is Desmond Tutu, the South African theologian who chaired the country's Truth and Reconciliation Commission, when he says of indigenous Africans, 'Harmony, friendliness, community are great goods. Social harmony is for us the *summum bonum*' (1999: 35). However, I argue in this and the following chapter for a resolutely normative conclusion: that one should consider harmony or communality, as opposed to welfare or life, to be most important if one is seeking the most defensible moral theory with an African content.

In the two previous chapters I addressed moral theories entailing that relationality has an instrumental status, viz., is good merely as a means to the advancement of either the common good or vital force. In contrast, the suggestion from Paris, Tutu, and others mentioned below is that, from an African perspective, certain ways of relating are to be treated as valuable in themselves, with other

[1] Albeit as a way to express respect for individuals capable of it, spelled out in Chapter 7.

A Relational Moral Theory: African Ethics in and beyond the Continent. Thaddeus Metz, Oxford University Press.
 DOI: 10.1093/oso/9780198748960.003.0006

values being derivative or subsidiary. In the rest of Part II, I argue that the best interpretation of the African ethical tradition is roughly that such relational properties are what matter at bottom.

I spell out my precise moral theory only in Chapter 7, in this one mainly working to specify the relevant way of relating that informs it. Here I indicate what I mean when speaking of 'harmony', 'communal relationship', and similar terms (6.2), namely, that they are the combination of identifying with others and exhibiting solidarity with them. I point out that identity and solidarity realized at the same time are more or less equivalent to what English-speakers often mean by 'friendliness' or even a broad sense of 'love'. I next explain why I do not directly adopt the principle suggested by Paris, Tutu, and others that relationship is itself a final good (or even goal) that is to be promoted (6.3). This teleological approach has seriously counterintuitive implications, which in sum amount to an inability to ground human rights. I conclude by noting the transition from Chapter 6, in which I will have advanced an account of African relationality as relevant to morality and criticized some relational principles, to Chapter 7, where I present my favoured relational moral theory, which is deontological (6.4).

6.2 Communality: Identity and Solidarity

It is not only Paris and Tutu who contend that African morality is best interpreted as a fundamentally relational ethic, and I start this long section by indicating respects in which others have also proposed such a view (6.2.1). Then, I begin to specify the way of relating that I will eventually contend grounds the most attractive moral theory from Africa. This relationship, which I usually label 'harmonious' or 'communal', is a combination of two logically distinct ways of interacting, namely, identifying with others and exhibiting solidarity with them. After spelling out separately what it means to identify with others (6.2.2) and to exhibit solidarity with them (6.2.3), I indicate how they are different (6.2.4) and what is involved in conceiving of them as a unity, viz., that together they consist of a broad sense of 'love' or, somewhat less misleading, friendliness (6.2.5).

6.2.1 The Relational as Foundational

The African tradition is routinely called 'communitarian' in contrast to the 'individualism' of Western thought and practice. Whereas in previous chapters I have criticized theories according to which communing is merely a means to the realization of some other, more basic good such as welfare or life, here I begin to consider what morality might look like if communing were itself basic in some way. In addition to the quotes above from Paris and Tutu, consider the following remarks from southern Africans inspired by indigenous values:

> We regard our living together not as an unfortunate mishap warranting endless competition among us but as a deliberate act of God to make us a community of brothers and sisters jointly involved in the quest for a composite answer to the varied problems of life. Hence in all we do we always place Man first and hence all our action is usually joint community oriented action rather than the individualism which is the hallmark of the capitalist approach. (Biko 2004: 46)

> In the moral universe of Ubuntu, humanity is conceived of as one large family that is bonded together by reciprocal ties of love and loyalty. This is, of course, an ideal conception towards which we should forever strive.... The servant leader is the chief agent of striving towards harmony in community. (Khoza 2006: 58–9)

> At the heart of these [Shona and Zulu] proverbs lies a motif of an ethical reminder that one should always live and behave in a way that maximises harmonious existence at present as well as in the future. (Murove 2007: 181)

In all three quotations, relational concepts of community, love, and harmony are prominent.[2] While these quotations are in the first instance representations of how southern Africans have broadly understood morality, my aim is to draw on them to construct a precise normative principle and to show that it merits belief relative to competitors.

Talk of 'community', 'harmony', and 'love' is ambiguous, and in the rest of the section I work to make it clear and precise. When a number of African thinkers spell out the nature of these relational concepts, they mention two logically distinct features. Consider the following statements:

> Every member is expected to consider him/herself an integral part of the whole and to play an appropriate role towards achieving the good of all. (Gbadegesin 1991: 65)

> Harmony is achieved through close and sympathetic social relations within the group. (Mokgoro 1998: 17)

> We say, 'A person is a person through other persons.' It is not, 'I think therefore I am.' It says rather: 'I am human because I belong. I participate, I share.' (Tutu 1999: 35)

> The fundamental meaning of community is the sharing of an overall way of life, inspired by the notion of the common good. (Gyekye 2004: 16)

[2] For similarly relational views from other African thinkers, see Senghor (1964: 92–4); Aja (1997: 353); Mnyaka and Motlhabi (2005: 218); Taringa (2006: 200); Nze (2007); Mkhize (2008: 35–6); Odimegwu (2008); Ejizu (2011); Tshivhase (2018). In addition, recall the earlier relational statements from Mbiti, Kasenene, Iroegbu, Masolo, and Etieyibo (1.2.3), which I suggested are juxtaposed with some non-relational ones in their work. For claims from social scientists and philosophers of European descent that African peoples have prized harmony or similar as the end in itself, see Krige and Krige (1954: 78); Gelfand (1973: 102, 147–52); Silberbauer (1991: 20); Verhoef and Michel (1997: 397).

> [T]he purpose of our life is community-service and community-belongingness. (Iroegbu 2005a: 442)

> If you asked *ubuntu* advocates and philosophers: What principles inform and organise your life? . . . the answers would express commitment to the good of the community in which their identities were formed, and a need to experience their lives as bound up in that of their community. (Nkondo 2007: 91)

On the one hand, there is considering oneself part of the whole, being close, participating, sharing a way of life, belonging, and thinking of oneself as bound to others, which I often label 'identifying with others' or 'sharing a way of life'. On the other hand, there is achieving the good of all, being sympathetic, sharing, promoting the common good, engaging in service, and being committed to others' good, which I tend to call 'exhibiting solidarity with others' or 'caring for others' quality of life'.

In the following I show that each of these two relational concepts has its own logic and attractiveness, but that when they are encountered together, they form a particularly compelling moral value. As with the prior, welfarist and life-based principles, I interpret elements of the relational approach in secular terms (3.3). While a number of African thinkers have conceived of harmony essentially in terms of a certain relationship between human beings and, say, ancestors living in an imperceptible realm on Earth, I do not, instead analysing it in naturalist terms that could be appreciated by those from a variety of intellectual traditions around the world. Notice that the above characterizations of the nature of harmony, community, *ubuntu*, and related concepts do not mention ancestors or the like, while prima facie offering something substantial to ethical thought.[3]

6.2.2 Identity

When African thinkers advocate relationality, particularly as an end, one thing they tend to have in mind is identifying with others. Léopold Senghor says this of what he calls the 'Negro-African': 'He does not assimilate, he is assimilated. He lives in common life with the Other; he lives in symbiosis' (1964: 73), while Kenneth Kaunda remarks of Africans: 'Our whole life is togetherness and to be cut off from our fellow human beings is to die in the soul' (1966: 35). Although Senghor and Kaunda take themselves to be describing a salient aspect of sub-Saharan cultures, those who think ethically in light of the African tradition often

[3] In addition, recall the point that if there turns out to be strong evidence of the existence of an imperceptible realm with ancestors and other persons, then the relationship I advance in what follows may be understood to apply to them as beings with whom to relate (3.3).

deem a common life or togetherness to be good for its own sake or otherwise to merit pursuit for a non-instrumental reason.

In the following I break down this way of relating into constituent propositional attitudes. That is, I reconstruct identifying with others (or belonging, participating, sharing a life, etc.) in terms of certain kinds of cognition, emotion, volition, and motivation, ones that will be seen to differ from the parallel attitudes constitutive of exhibiting solidarity with others.

First, with regard to cognition, one identifies with others insofar as one thinks of oneself as a common member of a relationship or group with them. Part of considering oneself in relation will involve a tendency to refer to oneself as part of a 'we', and not merely as an 'I'. As one scholar remarks, 'A visitor to Africa is soon struck by the frequent use of the first person plural "we", "ours" in everyday speech' (Andoh 2011: 70; see also Kenyatta 1965: 180). This way of speaking often includes thinking from the perspective of not merely oneself but also everyone with whom one is related. '[T]he unique indigenous social orientation... may be characterized as the "we orientation." In the we orientation life is comprehended not from the perspective of "I" or "they" alone, but from that of both which unite to become "we"' (Dzobo 1992: 229). Such a cognitive orientation need not, and should not, be understood to demand 'group think'. To conceive of oneself as a member of a relationship, and to consider the viewpoints of all those who are party to it, hardly means that one should invariably adopt other people's views. The key point is that cognitively identifying with others means not viewing them as separate from oneself, and instead considering them as members.

Second, turning to emotions, one who identifies with others enjoys a sense of belonging or is glad of the presence of others, in contrast to feeling lonely or isolated. In addition, emotionally identifying with others can mean taking pride in, or conversely feeling embarrassed about, what another person in one's 'we' has done. Even if one is not responsible for an accomplishment or a failure, if one identifies with others who are, then one's emotions will tend to be invested in what they have done. For example, family members will feel ashamed, often to the point of making an apology, when one of their own behaves wickedly.

Third, when it comes to volition, joint activity is the central idea. Practically identifying with others means coordinating one's behaviour with them when pursuing goals, making adjustments to either one's own goals or one's pursuit of them, so that others' goals can also be realized. That could mean adopting their goals as one's own, but it need not, and could merely involve pursuing one's goals in ways that allow or enable others to pursue theirs. For example, such coordinating might involve interacting on a trusting basis where others are allowed to make voluntary and informed choices or, even more intensely, providing encouragement, labour, and resources that would be useful for others to achieve their goals. A salient opposite here would be subordinating others by frustrating the realization of their ends with coercive, deceptive, or exploitive means, ones that undermine trust.

Fourth, identifying with others in respect of one's motivation means that one participates in cooperative endeavours for reasons beyond mere prudence. One advances others' aims not merely so that one's own aims can be advanced in turn. Instead, one is moved to coordinate with others for their sake or perhaps for the sake of the relationship with them, viz., because 'this is who we are'.

The more of these attitudes that one exemplifies, the more one is relating in a way that identifies with others or, as I shall also sometimes put it, shares a way of life with them. Identity comes in degrees, so that the greater the number of these conditions that one exhibits, the greater the extent to which one is identifying with others.

Clubs, churches, schools, firms, and clans are normally clear instances of identity. There is a more substantial shared way of life within these groups, the more that people: think of themselves as a 'we'; view others as members; enjoy a feeling of belonging; take pride or shame in what others do; avoid interfering with others' goals; go out of their way to advance others' goals; interact on the basis of trust rather than threats; and act for the sake of the identity relation itself.

I often call the opposite of identity 'division' or 'divisiveness'. It is roughly a matter of: defining oneself in opposition to others (as in 'us' versus 'them'); feeling distant from them; subordinating them; and acting in relation to them out of fear or hostility. This is one salient feature of a relationship of enmity or discord, the opposite of a communal or harmonious relationship.

In addition, it is worth naming a condition that is one of neither identity nor division. An individual might simply exhibit no substantial other-regard, whether positive or negative. Perhaps she is living as a hermit. In that case, I normally speak of 'alienation'.

Identifying with others is only one major part of what I mean by 'harmony' or 'communal relationship', and I now turn to the other one, which is exhibiting solidarity with others. Only after spelling out solidarity do I consider how identity and solidarity compare and contrast as well as what they amount to when they are conjoined.

6.2.3 Solidarity

When Nelson Mandela is concrete about what *ubuntu* involves, he focuses on the idea that it involves service to others (2012: 147, 155, 2013: 227), which is for me the other major way to relate harmoniously or communally. Serving others or exhibiting solidarity with them involves kinds of cognition, emotion, volition, and motivation different from those constitutive of identifying with others.

First off, exhibiting solidarity with another person includes having a certain kind of awareness of him, one that is attentive to details about him. One not only considers his outward appearance and listens to what he says, but also reflects on what he might be holding back or unable to express. A large part of the knowledge of the other involves empathy, by which I mean taking up the other's standpoint and thinking about what it is like to be him. However, thinking about another's state is not exhausted by empathy, as real solidarity would involve trying to become aware of factors that another might be unaware of himself. Truly understanding someone involves knowing what moves that person and more generally what makes him tick, even if he does not fully recognize it.

Second, a relationship of solidarity characteristically is one in which a person feels a certain way about another consequent to attentive awareness of him. Upon understanding the other, one develops a sympathetic reaction to that condition, a feeling that is of a similar kind and normally of comparable proportion. If one becomes aware that the other is flourishing, then one feels good for him, and if one instead learns that the other is floundering, then one feels bad. John Mbiti remarks of the characteristically African person, 'When he suffers, he does not suffer alone but with the corporate group; when he rejoices, he rejoices not alone but with his kinsmen, his neighbors and his relatives' (1990: 106). That is emotional solidarity.

Third, to exhibit solidarity also means that one acts to improve another's condition. In the first instance, that means meeting another's needs, whether they are biological, psychological, or social, and more generally improving her welfare, which presumably includes pleasure in some respect. However, the human good includes more than well-being, however it is plausibly construed, and, specifically, it also consists of liveliness of the sort described above (5.2) as well as *ubuntu*, that is, human excellence or moral virtue (13.3). Acting in solidarity means not merely striving to make people better off or to advance their self-interest, but also to make others better people or to advance their self-realization. Note that such action does not imply having succeeded in improving another's condition; one might have made an innocent mistake, or the world might have unluckily 'failed to cooperate' or 'gotten in the way'. Although success is not necessary for acting in solidarity, some likelihood of success appears essential; for one is not truly serving another who is drowning if, in order to rescue him, all one does is wave what one thinks is a magic wand.

Fourth, one exhibits motivational solidarity with others insofar as one's helping action is prompted by the prior conditions of roughly empathetic cognition and sympathetic emotion. One is moved by compassion for others, by the thought that they could use one's help and the feeling of what it would be like to receive it or perhaps not to receive it. One's reason for action is altruistic, done simply to advance others' good for their sake, as opposed to, say, one's long-term benefit.

As with identity, the more of these conditions a person exhibits, the more she is in solidarity with others, or, as I shall sometimes say, cares for their quality of life. Charities and the caring professions are typical sites of solidarity. There is a more substantial exhibition of solidarity on the part of donors, nurses, and teachers, the more they: imagine what it is like to be others; are aware of others' needs and contexts; sympathize with them; perform actions expected to enhance others' well-being, liveliness, or virtue; and do so for their sake.

I tend to call the opposite of solidarity 'ill will'. It is roughly a matter of: being unaware of others' good; taking pleasure in the suffering, degeneration, or vice of others; doing what is expected to make them live worse lives; and being moved by self-regarding considerations such as one's own pleasure or power or considerations unrelated to the human good at all such as supporting racial purity or honouring the Roman gods. Enmity or discord, the opposite of a harmonious or communal relationship, is not exhausted by division, but also includes ill will.

Like the neutral correlate of identity, which I labelled 'alienation', there is conceptual space for an orientation that is one of neither solidarity nor ill will. I call it 'indifference', where one is disposed neither to help nor to harm another.

6.2.4 Identity versus Solidarity

Identity and solidarity are distinct ways of relating, both conceptually and practically. One way to see this is to realize that a cooperative endeavour in which people enjoy a sense of togetherness, central to identity, need not be oriented towards anyone's good, which is what solidarity is all about. When one enables others to achieve their aims there is a sense in which one is 'helping' them, but this kind of 'help' is not the sort inherent to solidarity. The latter does not mean doing what is expected to achieve people's ends, whatever they happen to be, but rather doing what enables them to live an objectively better life. If a person's goal for some reason were to gouge out her own eye with a pointy stick, considerations of identity could prescribe giving her a knife that would be useful for whittling, but those of solidarity would not.

For a more everyday example of identity without solidarity, consider the relationship between management and workers in a typical capitalist firm. There is little or no good will there—a union does not tend to sympathize with management, let alone go to work for management's sake. However, workers and managers might be happy to think of themselves as part of a larger group that is involved in a joint project. Consider corporate slogans such as GM's 'Yes, we can!', GE's 'We bring good things to life', and DHL's 'We move the world'. Despite the competitive environment between workers and managers in a labour market, they could to some degree share a sense of self and coordinate their behaviour to produce a service or good for the public.

There are also converse cases, of solidarity without identity, or at least much of the latter. One example is making an anonymous donation to a charity. Here, one is presumably doing what is likely to improve others' lives and doing so for their sake, and so there is real solidarity. However, since one does not even know who the beneficiaries are, some identity is seriously lacking. There is no sense of togetherness with them or motivation to sustain a common life.

Upon getting clear how identity and solidarity are distinct, one sees that neither one on its own would be that attractive compared to the combination of them. Consider, first, identity without solidarity. Identifying with others might ground some duties of loyalty, but it is hard to see how it could exhaust moral considerations. After all, members of the former South African Nationalist Party, which enforced apartheid, enjoyed a sense of togetherness and cooperated amongst each other so as to achieve common aims. Surely, though, one had no duty to promote such a group if one were not a member, and, if one were a member, there was a strong duty to work to dissolve the group, plausibly because of the ill will towards outsiders (not merely because of the lack of identity with them).

Turn now, second, to solidarity without identity. One objection that has been made to the Western ethic of care, which would apply to a pure solidarity principle, is that it permits intuitively objectionable forms of paternalism (Hoagland 1991: 254; Narayan 1995). One who cares for others' quality of life is directed exclusively to another's good, and it is a stock objection to such an approach that it gives insufficient weight to the free and informed decision-making of others. Consider a stereotypical *pater familias* who claims the ultimate authority to make decisions for his wife. Imagine he treats his wife like a child, acting in what is in her best interest, using force and trickery as necessary to improve her lot. Supposing for the sake of argument that the *pater familias* were able to coerce or deceive his wife in ways that would improve her quality of life, it would be wrong for him to do so. However, there would be nothing essentially *uncaring* about his behaviour.

Identity without solidarity is hard-hearted, while solidarity without identity is intrusive. It is more philosophically plausible and also more African to realize them together, so that a moral agent more or less aims to improve others' quality of life and to do so in cooperative ways with them (when they are innocent).

6.2.5 Identity and Solidarity

To see more of the promise of grounding a moral theory on communality understood as including both identity and solidarity, consider some additional everyday glimpses of them together. First off, the combination of those two ways of relating communally captures much about the way that family members intuitively ought to engage with one another. In an ideal family people enjoy a sense of togetherness, participate cooperatively in projects (or at least support one another's aims), strive to make each other better off and also better people, and do so for one another's sake. As Augustine Shutte has noted in an interpretation of the southern African ethic of *ubuntu*, 'The extended family is probably the most common, and also the most fundamental, expression of the African idea of community.... The importance of this idea for ethics is that the family is something that is valued for its own sake' (2001: 29).[4] Familial relationships of the desirable sort tend to have good consequences for those party to them, but the promising idea salient in sub-Saharan morality, which I run with in this book, is that they are to be morally valued in themselves, apart from their long-term results. This approach to morality suggests the broad vision that society should become like an ideal family, which at least some East African philosophers have suggested at times (cf. Nyerere 1968: 12; Oruka 1997: 148–50).[5]

For another way to appreciate the appeal of identity and solidarity as a moral foundation, consider that the combination of them is what many English-speakers mean by 'friendliness' or even a broad sense of 'love'. As David Velleman has pointed out, the standard conception of love in the Anglo-American philosophical literature is to 'care and share' or to 'benefit and be with' (1999: 353). In my terms, benefiting others amounts to exhibiting solidarity with them or caring for their quality of life, while being with others consists of identifying with them or sharing a way of life with them. One way of using the term 'love' that is familiar to Western readers is to understand it as picking out ways of relating, such as enjoying a sense of togetherness, engaging in joint projects, helping others live better lives and become better people, and doing so for their sake, features that are central to the African conception of harmony/communality that I advance.

Now, Velleman rejects this standard account of love as indicating what is inessential to it in favour of the view that love essentially is a matter of experiencing an arresting awareness of another's nature and value that tends to break down emotional barriers. My point is not that Velleman is incorrect about what is necessary and sufficient for love; it is instead that, even if Velleman is correct and the standard view of the nature of love is not essential to it, the standard view captures one (contingent) kind of love that many have found to merit pursuit. What Velleman acknowledges as the standard account of love is a way of interacting with others that is substantially behavioural (and not strictly emotional), that many Western ethicists think is valuable, and that overlaps substantially with the way of relating that some African philosophers believe lies at the heart of morality. One way for those in the Anglo-American tradition to appreciate the relational dimension of African moral thought is to view it through the lens of an influential and powerful conception of love as a kind of interaction.

Although I do think that one frequent use of the word 'love' is captured by relationships of sharing a way of life and caring for others' quality of life, in order

[4] It is not clear to me how this quotation from Shutte squares with other, more vitalist remarks in his book (e.g., 2001: 22–4).

[5] Note that this point differs from saying that society, let alone humanity as a whole, literally is a family or should become one.

to avoid misinterpretation I more often speak of 'friendliness' throughout the book. I expect that such a word will connote less emotional intensity to readers, while capturing the key elements of a sense of togetherness, cooperative interaction, aid, and sympathetic altruism.

However, talk of 'friendliness' might invite its own misreading, which I also need to forestall. Friendliness does not necessarily involve friendship (or being friends), which involves longer and stronger bonds than are essential to the conception of harmony or communality I am advancing. My claim is not that becoming friends with people is alone what matters morally, but rather, roughly, that prizing friendliness is (even more carefully: that one must treat individuals as important because of their capacity to be party to friendly relationships). A friendly way of relating, which may not even amount to a full-blown relationship in a narrow sense,[6] is possible and intuitively desirable between, say, neighbours and colleagues, even where the length of time and closeness that tend to be associated with those who are described as 'friends' are absent.

In sum, the most promising interpretation of the African moral tradition for me is one according to which friendly ways of relating are what ground moral obligations, with 'rightness as friendliness' and 'wrongness as unfriendliness' being rough catchphrases. 'Harmony', 'communal relationship', and 'friendliness' are ultimately equivalent for the purposes of this book; they all refer to ways of relating in which one identifies with others (or shares a way of life with them) and exhibits solidarity with others (or cares for their quality of life).

Each term that I have used to label the way of relating I deem morally important places some obstacles in the way of getting my point across, and yet remains worth using. As just noted, talk of 'friendliness' (and especially 'love') might be thought to imply a kind of ongoing and intimate relationship that I deny has to obtain for people to act morally. Nonetheless, I use the term 'friendliness' because I expect doing so will help Western readers to understand what African relationality involves and why there plausibly can be reason to pursue it as an end.

Speaking of 'harmony' might make it sound as though threats and violence are categorically out of place when it comes to right action, but, as I indicate in the next section, I do not believe that at all. Despite being misleading in that respect, using the word 'harmony' is accurate and useful, insofar as such a value framework centrally concerns balancing, integrating, and aligning (Anedo 2012) or a focus on social relations (Bell and Mo 2014). In addition, the term aptly suggests parallels with other non-Western ethics such as Chinese Confucianism and South American *buen vivir*.

Finally, speaking of 'communal relationship' or 'communality' will suggest to some readers that the community, understood as a group, is more important than the individual, a claim that I emphatically deny, as I instead ascribe dignity to

[6] In the rest of the book I tend to use the word 'relationship' in a broader, looser sense that is not meant to connote a friendship, romance, or other intimate tie.

individual persons. Despite potentially encouraging the unwelcome view that the interests or norms of a community are paramount, I do speak of 'communality', in order to signify continuity with the African tradition that is clearly communitarian in some way. I tend to avoid using the word 'community' in this book, because it indeed invites a collectivist approach (cf. 7.5). Where I do use this word, it is usually meant to express the idea of people entering into community with each other, a way of relating, as opposed to people submitting to what their society wants, expects, or demands.

6.3 The Limits of Extant Communal Principles

As prima facie attractive as harmony, communality, or friendliness is as a moral value, I do not ground my moral theory directly on it as something good for its own sake (or a final end) to be promoted. In this section I indicate why I do not accept principles that would have us at bottom promote relationality in teleological fashion, which African theorists have typically proposed. Basically, I contend that these existing theories cannot capture certain rights that human persons intuitively have. Although I agree with the African tradition that rights are not exhaustive of our duties and also that a focus on rights risks undermining other relational values, I am firm in maintaining that morality includes human rights. I can see no other way to account for the powerful intuitions in this section except by appeal to them. Note that it is only in the next chapter that I advance a principle that resolves the problems facing these rivals.

Consider, first, what Tutu says immediately after having described social harmony as the '*summum bonum*': 'Anything that subverts or undermines this sought-after good is to be avoided like the plague. Anger, resentment, lust for revenge, even success through aggressive competitiveness are corrosive of this good' (1999: 35). A serious problem with this phrasing is that it appears to forbid actions that are discordant or at least not expected to produce harmony down the road. That is, it appears to rule out any discordant division or ill will, unless perhaps it will promote a greater harmony in the long run. However, a plausible moral theory must accommodate the intuition, which is salient in both the African and Western traditions, that sometimes coercion and harm are justified in self- or other-defence, even when such actions will not maximize harmony overall. Consider, for example, the following case:

> You are a peacekeeper who sees three men chasing an innocent, elderly woman with machetes, trying to kill her merely because she has a different ethnicity. You have a machine gun. After firing a warning shot to deter the men, they are not scared off and continue after the woman. You shoot the three aggressors, reasonably judging it to be necessary and sufficient to protect the one innocent. (She lives, and they die.)

The peacekeeper's use of deadly force in this scenario would be permissible. That is true even though it would be an instance of violence (viz., discord or enmity) and would foreseeably result in several more deaths, particularly of younger people capable of a longer span of harmony than the old lady, as well as several more families being distraught upon losing loved ones.

What the case shows is that the right way to respond to relationality is neither always to instantiate it and so never to act discordantly nor to promote it as much as one can. Some non-teleological harmony-based or communal approach, which takes into account decisions others have made, is needed in order to account adequately for the permissibility of violence directed against aggressors to protect innocent lives.

This point is also one reason why I do not accept some principles mentioned above, namely, the formulations that harmony is the 'paramount goal' that is 'the source and justification of all moral obligations' (Paris 1995: 56) and that 'one should always live and behave in a way that maximises harmonious existence at present as well as in the future' (Murove 2007: 181). If harmony were merely a goal to be promoted, then it would be unjustifiable to use a discordant means such as deadly force against aggressors, when doing so would protect their innocent victims but fail to maximize harmony in the long run. In addition to being vulnerable to the previous counterexample, these teleological approaches face an additional problem concerning distributive justice, illustrated by this case:

> A wife has become HIV positive because her husband had cheated on her behind her back and did not use protection when doing so, despite being aware of the risks. You have a single regimen of antiretroviral treatment, and must choose which of them to save. You give the treatment to the wife and not the husband. (She lives, and he dies.)

The case shows that it is both burdens such as deadly force and benefits such as life-saving treatment that should be allocated based on decisions that others have made. In cases of scarcity, where one cannot save the lives of all those who need saving, it would normally be proper to save those who are not responsible for the fact of needing to be saved, at least by virtue of having acted wrongly in the past. Principles that treat harmony merely as a long-term goal to be promoted or direct us to maximize harmonious relationships cannot ground such a position.

Still more, such principles also fall prey to certain damning counterexamples facing Western utilitarianism. Consider the classic organs case:

> You are a doctor who knows that only a handful of people in his country receives the organs they need to survive. You could painlessly euthanize an otherwise healthy, innocent person who has come in complaining of a cold, and then distribute his heart, liver, and lungs to those who would die without them. You elect not to do so. (He lives, and unfortunately they die.)

In this case, the right thing to do is not to kill one innocent person, even supposing that were necessary to save three other innocent lives. Granting for the sake of argument that each person would be capable of a comparable degree of harmony, a principle instructing an agent to protect and create harmonious relationships would entail that one should indeed be killed if that were the only way to save the three. However, that would be wrong.

In addition to forbidding force and harm that are intuitively justified and permitting force and harm that are intuitively unjustified, some extant principles about how to respond to the value of harmony are overly partial. They do not readily admit that human persons generally have a moral status, that is, are owed moral treatment for their own sake. For instance, consider the claim that 'in African societies, immorality is the word or deed which undermines fellowship' (Kasenene 1998: 21). Such a phrasing suggests that wrongness can be done only where there is already fellowship. If I encounter a stranger, there is no fellowship that exists to be undermined, and so a plain reading of the principle entails that the stranger does not count and may be treated however I please. The same point applies to these formulations: 'What strengthens the family, the clan and the tribe or ethnic group is generally morally good' (Kasoma 1996: 108); and 'If you asked *ubuntu* advocates and philosophers: What principles inform and organise your life?... the answers would express commitment to the good of the community in which their identities were formed, and a need to experience their lives as bound up in that of their community' (Nkondo 2007: 91). Only the group in which a person has been reared is mentioned as morally relevant here, which excludes 'outsiders' from the domain of moral consideration and, in particular, entitlement to aid in the face of real need. Although these thinkers, upon reflection, might well reject a strictly parochial or partial ethic as the best expression of African morality, their phrasings suggest such an interpretation. If African morality were just a matter of strengthening bonds with one's family or community, then many human beings would be left out of moral consideration, flouting powerful cosmopolitan or impartial judgements.

6.4 From Highest Good to Basic Duty

In this chapter I have critically explored the suggestion from Paris, Tutu, and others that a harmonious or communal relationship is the highest good for the African tradition, a claim I find promising (even if not precisely correct), at least in comparison to well-being or vital force as candidates. I did not articulate my favoured moral theory yet in any detail, but instead worked to lay the ground for it, by spelling out the nature of the communal relationship that informs it and presenting strong reason to reject rival accounts of how one might morally respond to this way of relating.

I began by noting that when African thinkers are specific about the nature of how people ought to relate, particularly as something good for its own sake, they tend to mention two distinct elements. I specified them in detail, distinguishing identifying with others or sharing a way of life with them from exhibiting solidarity with others or caring for their quality of life. I pointed out that the combination of identity and solidarity amounts to a friendly way of relating with others, so that harmony, communal relationship, and friendliness are equivalent for my purposes and 'rightness as friendliness' is a slogan for my preferred ethic.

I then argued that the right way to respond to harmony/communality or friendliness is not to treat this way of relating merely as a good to be maximized or as a goal to be promoted, for various instantiations of this teleological approach have difficulty accounting for human rights. Key examples were a right that heavy burdens be placed on guilty parties instead of innocent ones, despite long-term costs to harmonious/communal relationship, and a right of an innocent party not to be killed, even when doing so would be the only way to save more innocent lives and thereby foster more harmonious/communal relationship.

In the next chapter, I indicate precisely how an appeal to the sort of relationship articulated in this chapter can anchor an attractive theory of which actions are right and wrong. Instead of deeming relationships of identity and solidarity themselves to be a highest good to be promoted, I take the *capacity* to be party to them to have a superlative non-instrumental value and to warrant *respectful* treatment. Such a deontological principle avoids the problems facing all rivals from Part II of this book, or so I argue in the following chapter.

7

A Relational Moral Theory

7.1 Rightness as Friendliness

This chapter completes Part II of the book, the major aims of which are to spell out my preferred principle of right action and to show that it is the strongest (secular) moral theory from the African tradition. So far I have criticized rival principles that are grounded on well-being (Chapter 4) or vital force (Chapter 5), pointing out respects in which they cannot plausibly account for key intuitions about right and wrong, particularly those salient in African philosophical thought. I have also spelled out an interpretation of communal relationship in terms of identity and solidarity, but argued that the salient approach to relationality from African thinkers, which treats it teleologically as a good or goal to be promoted, also faces serious objections (Chapter 6). In this chapter, I present my favoured relational moral theory, 'rightness as friendliness', note that it avoids objections facing other Afro-relational ethics, and argue that it entails and explains key intuitions better than its African welfarist and vitalist rivals.

It is well known that those who favour relational approaches to morality have tended to eschew the project of a philosopher articulating and defending a theory of right action, preferring particularism or a dialogical orientation (or both). They characteristically maintain that responding to relationships in the right ways is too complex to capture with an abstract principle (1.2.1). Ultimately, my reply to these and other anti-theoretical perspectives is that the proof is in the pudding; let us see whether a principle founded on relational elements can indeed account well for a wide array of moral intuitions and how useful it might be when addressing practical controversies. This chapter begins to execute this plan in earnest.

I start by drawing a contrast between a communal or friendly way of relating and the capacity to be party to it, and advance the principle that a moral agent ought to respect individuals in virtue of their dignified capacity to befriend or be befriended (7.2). After drawing out some corollaries of this principle and showing that they enable it to avoid objections to rival Afro-relational ethics (7.3), I return to the sixteen intuitions that I set down for appraising a moral theory (3.4.3), and argue that my relational theory does better than its welfarist and vitalist competitors with regard to each one (7.4). Next, I show how the relational moral theory easily avoids (and even plausibly explains) prominent criticisms of African morality, such as being collectivist and gendered, concerns often expressed by those

A Relational Moral Theory: African Ethics in and beyond the Continent. Thaddeus Metz, Oxford University Press.
 DOI: 10.1093/oso/9780198748960.003.0007

influenced by Western perspectives (7.5). I conclude Chapter 7 and thereby Part II of the book by preparing the reader to shift direction, away from seeking the best moral theory with an African pedigree and towards seeking the best moral theory, which happens to have an African pedigree (7.6).

7.2 The Capacity to Commune as Foundation

In the previous chapter I argued for a certain interpretation of what it is to relate communally or harmoniously, contending that the combination of identifying with others and exhibiting solidarity with them is not only a plausible way to interpret several African thinkers, but also prima facie morally attractive. It amounts to a friendly way of relating, with one rough slogan for my approach being 'Rightness as friendliness'. However, I also argued that one should not fundamentally treat friendly or communal relationship as a final good or end to be promoted, as this teleological structure has difficulty accounting for rights. In the following, I ascribe a superlative non-instrumental value to our capacity to be party to communal relationship, as distinguished from this way of relating itself (7.2.1). I then begin to spell out my favoured moral theory, according to which one must honour individuals because of their capacity to relate in a communal or friendly way, either as a subject or an object (7.2.2). In the rest of this chapter I defend this deontological moral theory relative to the African principles criticized in previous chapters.[1]

7.2.1 The Capacity to Relate

A communal relationship or way of relating is one thing, while a being's ability to relate in that way is another. I ground my moral theory on the capacity to relate, and not relating itself, since this approach does the best job of accounting for human rights. Here, I spell out the nature of this capacity, which determines moral status in my ethic, i.e., the beings that are owed duties for their own sake. My view is not that communal relationship itself has a moral status or that only those who are in such a relationship have it, but rather that those who in principle could relate in that way have it. Some have sensibly labelled my view 'modal' for this

[1] I have always favoured a deontological interpretation of African morality, though some readers have been misled about that by my first published piece on sub-Saharan ethics (Metz 2007). There, I argued that, of any theoretical interpretation of morality suggested by the literature at the time I was writing, Tutu's view instructing agents to promote harmony was the best. However, even then I indicated that I did not think this principle is adequate and that it needs to be revised to be able to account for rights (Metz 2007: 338).

reason (e.g., Horsthemke 2015: 85–92; Samuel and Fayemi 2020), indicating that it is the possibility of relating, in contrast to actually relating, that matters.

There are two ways to be part of or party to a communal relationship, either as a subject or an object. Being a subject involves identifying with others and exhibiting solidarity with them oneself. A being can be a subject of communal relationship insofar as it can think of itself as a 'we', cooperate with others, help others, and act for their sake out of sympathy. In contrast, a being can be an object of such a relationship insofar as characteristic human beings could think of it as part of a 'we', advance its goals, benefit it, and act for its sake out of sympathy. Note that having the capacity to be an object of such a relationship does not imply that a being would (or even could) respond to any friendly engagement by another, at least not in any way as a subject.

The next concept to analyse is what exactly is involved in being *capable* of being either a subject or object of communality. To be capable of being part of a communal relationship consists of being able in principle, i.e., without changes to a thing's nature. Examples of merely contingent inabilities to be the object of a communal relationship with us, irrelevant to a being's moral status, include the facts that a given person is unaware of the being or is scared of it. While these might hinder a being's actually becoming the object of identity and solidarity with one of us, they are not relevant to determining its moral status, for it nonetheless could become such an object in light of its nature and ours. A being that 'cannot' be the object of a communal relationship in the relevant sense would, for instance, be one that utterly lacks goal-directed behaviour or sentience—say, a rock, shrub, bacterium, or pen. If we have moral reasons to protect these things, it is not because of them, but instead because they are owned by, cared for by, or beneficial to some other being.

Examples of merely contingent inabilities to be the subject of a communal relationship include being asleep, having drunk too much alcohol, electing not to sympathize, being ignorant of what would benefit others, and having been put into solitary confinement. While these might hinder a being's actually becoming the subject of identity and solidarity, they are not relevant to determining its moral status, for it nonetheless could become such a subject in the light of its nature. A being that 'cannot' be the subject of a communal relationship in the relevant sense would be one that, by virtue of its biological constitution, has no concept of a mind distinct from its own or that cannot trade off its own ends or interests for the sake of those of others.

On my account, roughly, the more a being is capable of relating communally, the greater its moral status, where only large differences of degrees count. In the first instance that means that an entity that can be both the subject and object of a communal relationship has a full moral status or a dignity, whereas a being that is capable of being the object but not the subject of such behaviour has a partial moral status. To have a partial moral status means that the being matters for its own sake, but if its urgent interests were to conflict with those of a being with full moral status, it should lose out since it is not as important from a moral point of view.

A principle according moral status based on major gradations of the capacity to commune entails that the overwhelming majority of human persons have a full moral status. They characteristically can by their nature enjoy a sense of togetherness, participate cooperatively with others, help others, and do so out of sympathetic altruism; and, furthermore, we can do so with them. The principle also entails that many animals, such as cows, cats, owls, and mice, have a partial moral status, for although it is unlikely that they can be subjects of communality (at least not to a robust degree required for dignity), they can clearly be objects of it. We characteristically can in principle identify with and exhibit solidarity towards them, even if many of us routinely do not and they can never do so with us.[2]

There are obviously some close connections between the ability to relate communally and the fact of so relating. Normally acquiring the ability to commune as a subject requires having in fact communed, particularly as an object. That is, usually in order for one to be able to identify with and exhibit solidarity towards others, others must have done so with one—which is a fancy way of putting the banality that in order to become a moral agent, other people had to have cared for and socialized you. In addition, one typically maintains one's capacity to commune in the context of communing with others. If one is consistently alienated from and indifferent towards others, one's ability to act in a friendly way is likely to become duller.

However, the capacity to relate is indeed distinct from the fact of relating or even of having related, which makes a moral difference. Just because one was once party to communal relationships does not mean that one still is; one might have been placed in solitary confinement or become shipwrecked on a deserted island. Such individuals could retain a sufficient degree of the capacity to relate communally as subjects and so retain a full moral status, despite the lack of present communion.

And while it might be tempting for some to maintain that it was the fact of having been in communal relationship in the past, e.g., having been cared for by a family, that confers moral status, such an approach cannot make sense of the intuition that a human being who had been cared for matters more from a moral point of view than a dog that had been (on which see 8.4). It also cannot account for the intuition that merely having the capacity to commune is sufficient for a full moral status. Imagine a 'swamp human', a being like the reader in every respect except that it spontaneously arose out of a chemical mixture in a bog. Despite its

[2] I say more about animal moral status below (8.4).

lack of communal history, its present capacity, which includes its ability to be cared for by us and to care for us, seems to make it morally important for its own sake (*contra* the view in Ikuenobe 2016). If for some reason one had to choose between its life and that of a plant, one should save its life, a good explanation of which is that it has a (high) moral status.

There is more to say about which things have a moral status and to what degree, but I reserve further discussion of such matters for a later chapter (8.3–8.5). For now, I have made clear the pertinent issue of what it means for something to be 'capable of being party to a communal relationship', where that is what matters morally for its own sake. There will be debate about which beings in the world satisfy the conditions of in principle being able to be subjects or objects of a friendly relationship. Do ancestors who can be subjects and objects of communality exist? Apes and dolphins exist and can clearly be objects of communality, but can they also be subjects of it? Can we exhibit identity and solidarity with, i.e., be friendly towards, insects? These are principally descriptive questions, and not so much evaluative or prescriptive ones, and so I do not address them in this work, while acknowledging that a complete application of the relational moral theory ultimately requires answers to them.

7.2.2 The Relational Moral Theory

Having spelled out what a communal, harmonious, or friendly relationship is, and indicated what is involved in having the capacity to be part of one, it is now time to present my favoured principle of right action. I do so in part by contrasting it with other prominent Afro-relational principles considered above (6.3).

First, instead of focusing on an actual relationship as the highest or greatest good that is foundational to morality, I deem the capacity for it to be what is superlatively good for its own sake and bestows a moral status. It is not a communal relationship itself towards which we fundamentally have duties; instead, we have them towards individuals capable of it. Furthermore, individuals have a full moral status or a dignity, not because they are in fact members of a communal relationship—say, are part of a family; instead, they have it because they by their nature are able to be subjects and objects of such a relationship. By my account, individual entities are what are ultimately owed moral treatment for their own sake, but they are so in virtue of a modal-relational property, their ability to commune with others, which contrasts with intrinsic properties such as the capacity to feel pleasure or act autonomously (cf. 8.4).

Second, instead of maximizing or otherwise promoting the final good that is basic to right action, I prescribe respecting or honouring it. A moral agent is obligated to avoid degrading or disrespecting what has a moral status, namely, those beings in the world capable of being party to communal relationships.

My morality is therefore deontological as opposed to teleological, in ways I detail below.

Here are comprehensive statements of rightness as friendliness, which use different terms but are meant to express the same principle:

- An act is right if and only if it respects individuals in virtue of their capacity to be party to harmonious ways of relating.
- An act is wrong insofar as it degrades those with the capability of relating communally as subjects or objects.
- An action is permissible if it treats beings as special in accordance with their ability to be friendly or to be befriended.
- An action is impermissible to the extent that it disrespects beings with the ability to be part of relationships of identity and solidarity.

In the rest of this section, I clarify the meanings of these statements, after which I begin to apply and defend the principle they express. To begin, notice that, according to these statements, actions that are right or permissible, i.e., that do not merit negative reactions such as criticism, compensation, or punishment, do not come in degrees, whereas wrong actions do. Intuitively, some kinds of behaviour are morally worse than others, and a moral theory ought to capture that. There is a difference between killing an innocent person for money without her consent and stealing a chocolate bar from her, where the former is (much) more wrong than the latter. It is more wrong, by my account, because it is more degrading of the dignity of a person's communal nature.

Note that the above statements speak of 'individuals' or 'beings', which is appropriate since the principle entails that there are direct duties towards a variety of entities, including not just human persons, but also humans who are not persons as well as many non-human animals (as well as persons who are not humans, if any indeed exist). Depending on the context, sometimes I mention just one sort of being, such as persons and their dignity (as I just did in the previous paragraph), but that is not meant to suggest that I do not believe that, say, many animals have a (partial) moral status. Instead, on those occasions I am just appealing to one salient implication of the more comprehensive principle.

In addition, while some of the above statements are explicit that it is either as subject or as object that one is entitled to respectful treatment, others leave that implicit. When I speak of being able to be 'party to' or 'part of' certain ways of relating, that is not meant to be restricted to being the subject of them; an individual could be party to a harmonious relationship as an object of them, as in the case of human babies.

Finally, to respect or honour a being in virtue of its ability to relate means treating it as the most important non-instrumental value on Earth or expressing the attitude that there is nothing as good for its own sake. I draw on a number of familiar Kantian ideas about the nature of respect and its opposite, but I apply them to our relational nature, as opposed to our rational nature, as what is morally important.

So, for example, treating relational nature as the highest non-instrumental value normally involves not stunting it, especially not for the sake of something worth less than it. It is normally wrong to exhibit unfriendliness, discord, or anti-sociality towards others who have not acted these ways themselves. They are the antipodes of the positive way of relating advanced in the previous chapter, and so consist of division and ill will as opposed to identity and solidarity. They are typically degrading (of innocent parties) since they directly impair the ability for them to be befriended by oneself and for them to befriend oneself or others.

For example, suppose one trips a stranger just for the hilarity of seeing him fall. In the act of doing so, one is viewing him as other, frustrating his end of getting where he is going, doing what is likely to cause him harm, and acting for the sake of one's pleasure as opposed to his good. Such behaviour immediately interferes with the other's ability to relate harmoniously, quite obviously as an object, but also, one sees upon reflection, as a subject. When receiving such treatment, the other is in no, or at least a reduced, position to exhibit identity and solidarity towards oneself or indeed anyone else.

Much immoral behaviour consists of exhibiting such division and ill will towards those who have not done so first and thereby undermining their ability to be communed with and to commune. Instead of a sense of togetherness, considering others part of one's 'we', one thinks in terms of 'us against them', viewing them as separate. Instead of coordinating behaviour with others so that their ends are realized, there is subordination, an active thwarting of their ends. Instead of one helping others, one harms them, doing what is at least likely to reduce their quality of life, whether it is their well-being, liveliness, or moral virtue (*qua* communality, on which see 13.3). Instead of feeling good when others flourish and bad when others flounder, or at least acting consistently with such emotional attunement for the sake of others' good, one acts out of (or consistent with) cruelty, perhaps exhibiting delight in the other's woe. Below I maintain that these kinds of unfriendly or discordant behaviour account well for many of the global intuitions about what is right and wrong.

In addition to negative duties, obligations to avoid treating people in unfriendly or discordant ways, the relational moral theory should be understood to prescribe positive duties, too. One could avoid violating the negative duties simply by remaining aloof, that is, being alienated from people's projects and indifferent towards their good. However, isolating oneself from others would fail to honour sufficiently the dignity of their communal nature, which calls for cohesion. Although division and ill will are normally worse than mere alienation and indifference, the latter are also to be avoided. Treating people's capacity to commune or harmonize as the most important value in the world means participating with them on a cooperative basis and doing what is likely to make them live objectively better lives, which includes enabling them to act in these ways towards others. If what makes people special is their capacity to be party to relationships of identity and solidarity, then one has strong moral reason to identify with others and exhibit solidarity towards them as well as to enable them to do so with still others besides oneself. One not merely must avoid being unfriendly towards others (who are innocent), but also must be friendly with them, part of which could well involve enabling them to be friendly in turn.

Notice how rightness as friendliness differs from the ethic of care, according to which an agent must develop, sustain, and enrich her beneficent relationships. While a number of theorists have suggested understanding African morality in terms of the ethic of care (e.g., Harding 1987; Mangena 2009: 20; Isike and Uzodike 2011: 33, 51–2), my favoured interpretation of the African tradition is distinct from it, in at least three major respects. First, most adherents to the ethic of care eschew the project of developing a general principle of right action, preferring a particularist approach to morality (cf. 1.2.1). Second, the ethic of care is not normally understood to include dignity-based considerations or even any consideration of moral status (as Miller points out in Metz and Miller 2016). While one might suggest an unusual variant of the ethic of care according to which one must honour people's dignified capacity to care, third, that still would not be equivalent to the capacity to be a subject and object of communality. The ability to care may be taken as equivalent to the ability to exhibit solidarity as a subject, while I maintain that what confers dignity on us also includes being able to identify with others as well as being able to have them identify with and exhibit solidarity towards us as objects. In sum, African moral thought tends to include considerations of human dignity and to ascribe moral significance to considering oneself a part of a whole, enjoying close relations, participating with others, enabling others to achieve their goals, choosing because 'this is who we are', and so on. In the following chapters I work to show how a conception of dignity informed by identity does real work in accounting for right and wrong.[3]

In this section I have drawn not so much on the ethic of care to inform the relational moral theory, but more often on Immanuel Kant's philosophy and contemporary Kantian ethics, in which the negative/positive distinction is commonly employed (e.g., Kant 1785: Ak. 429–31). In the next section the reader familiar with Western moral philosophy will notice that I continue to invoke concepts and argumentative strategies made by Kant and his followers. I believe they have taught us a lot about the form of right action,[4] but that the African

[3] I submit that the combination of identity and solidarity best captures what is attractive about a family, and even specifically the mother–child relationship. It is not merely the caring relationship involved, but is also the common sense of self, the liking of one another's presence, the rituals, the trust, the help in becoming a better person, etc.

[4] Even if, as is well known, Kant himself held some immoral, including racist, beliefs.

tradition has much to contribute particularly in regard to its content, i.e., what it is about us that warrants respect, which makes a striking difference in terms of which duties we have and why. For now, I indicate more about what respect for our relational nature involves, saving Part III of the book for consideration of why such a principle is preferable to Kantian respect for our rational nature (and to utilitarianism) regarding many controversies in applied ethics.

7.3 Corollaries of the Principle

In this section, I draw out important implications of the principle of right action sketched in the previous one. I say more about how to respect a being's capacity to be party to harmonious, communal, or friendly ways of relating, in respect of these distinctions: constraints/goals (7.3.1); guilt/innocence (7.3.2); impartiality/partiality (7.3.3); capacity/actuality (7.3.4); and self/other (7.3.5). Along the way, I point out how my dignity-based ethic avoids, and even explains, objections I had made to the rival Afro-relational principles that one finds in the literature (6.3).

7.3.1 Constraints/Goals

In the previous section I drew a distinction between negative duties and positive duties, where the former are requirements not to act in unfriendly ways and the latter are requirements to act in friendly ways towards others, including enabling others to be friendly. As per a standard reading of Kantian ethics, I believe that it is usually the case that negative duties may not be overridden for the sake of fulfilling positive ones. One normally would be wrong to subordinate and harm people either for their own sake, about which Kant (1793: Ak. 291) himself is particularly adamant, or for the sake of others.

In particular, one should usually constrain oneself from acting in very unfriendly ways, or what I often call 'enmity', for the sake of fostering a greater friendliness or some other perceived or actual good. Equivalently, one should restrict oneself from behaving in extremely discordant ways in order to promote a greater harmony or other end. There are degrees to which acts are unfriendly or discordant, with the more subordination and harm involved, the greater the unfriendliness/discord. Actions involving substantial coercion or directly causing immense pain, for example, consist of enmity, and, by the present principle, should normally not be used as a means by which to promote cooperation and aid (or some other value) in the long run. Otherwise, one would be treating others' capacity for friendliness/harmony merely as a means, and not as something good for its own sake, even if to the end of friendliness/harmony down the road.

It is such a deontological corollary of the relational moral theory that enables it to avoid, and also plausibly explain, the wrongness of the organs case above (6.3). Recall that I presumed it would be wrong for a doctor to kill an innocent patient without his consent, harvest his organs, and transplant them into those who would die without them. Although saving lives worth living would be a friendly act or way of communing with persons, it should not be done with such enmity as a means, which would severely degrade the one killed. The relational moral theory entails that an individual has a negative right not to be killed that is characteristically stronger than others' positive rights, even to have their lives saved.

Excluding the use of 'very' unfriendly or discordant ways of relating so as to promote friendliness/harmony would permit doing so by means of some mild unfriendliness/discord. It is not degrading of someone's capacity for harmony to shove him out of the way of an oncoming bus, if necessary to save his life. It does not treat the rich's capacity for communality disrespectfully to force them to give up some of their wealth, if necessary to meet the needs of those who are not responsible for being unable to meet them on their own. One does not dishonour a postgraduate student's capacity for friendliness by breaking a promise to consult with her, if necessary to pick up an unexpectedly sick child from school. Enmity is lacking in these cases, even though there is division or ill will to a minor degree.

There are some rare situations in which it does look justifiable to treat innocent parties in very unfriendly ways or with enmity so as to foster friendliness. A salient case from the literature is that of an 'innocent threat', a situation in which a choice must be made between killing an innocent person who is a deadly threat to oneself or others and letting oneself or them be killed. Perhaps an innocent person has been kidnapped, temporarily drugged, and then manipulated into murdering another innocent person. I am inclined to accept (but am not certain) that deadly force may be used against the one who is non-culpably aggressing.

Some might suggest that, despite not being responsible for his behaviour, he is nonetheless acting in a very unfriendly way or with enmity, in which case my corollary above remains unchallenged. However, I cannot avail myself of that move in the case of a 'redirected threat' or a 'trolley case', a situation in which an impersonal threat such as a runaway train or an incoming meteor will kill a greater number of innocents, unless a third party steers it away towards a smaller number whom it will kill. Redirecting a runaway train towards an innocent party is a very unfriendly means to use in order to be friendly towards a greater number of innocents, and yet this action will seem justified to a very large majority of interlocutors. At this stage, I lack an explanation for this unusual case, beyond noting that it involves an impersonal threat, and I point out that it does not provide much reason to doubt the patent wrongness of many other cases, such as the organs one, in which a very unfriendly means would also foster a greater friendliness.

7.3.2 Guilt/Innocence

So far I have been discussing how to treat innocent parties, who in the context of the relational moral theory are roughly those who have upheld their negative duties not to be unfriendly towards others and their positive duties to be friendly towards others. I have maintained that it is usually degrading of innocent parties' capacity for friendliness to act towards them in very unfriendly ways or with enmity, even when for the sake of a long-term amount of friendliness. However, I argue that, when it comes to very guilty parties, it need not be degrading of their capacity for friendliness to act towards them in very unfriendly ways.

One might have suspected that an ethic prizing people's ability to be subjects and objects of harmonious ways of relating would categorically forbid discordant behaviour. However, mine does not, and, to see why not, consider an analogy with Kantianism. Kantians standardly prize the capacity for autonomy while holding that reducing the autonomy of those who have misused that capacity need not be disrespectful of it. For instance, sometimes they advance the forward-looking (defensive) view that coercion is justified as a way to prevent coercion in the future, while other times they hold the backward-looking (retributive) view that coercion is justified as a proportionate response to coercion that took place in the past (for what appear to be both, see Kant 1797: Ak. 230–3, 331–7). Either way, despite freedom being what must be respected for Kantians, that principle is invariably taken to permit impairing people's freedom roughly when they will impair or have impaired the freedom of other innocents. I similarly maintain that very unfriendly ways of acting towards those who have themselves been very unfriendly (towards innocents) can be respectful of their capacity for friendliness.

More carefully, I submit that it is not disrespectful to act in a very unfriendly way towards someone, if that is the only way to counteract someone's comparable unfriendliness towards an innocent party. This corollary is what accounts for the justifiable use of deadly force in the ethnic cleansing case above (6.3). Recall that it can be permissible to use a machine gun against those trying to kill an innocent person merely because of her heritage. If harmony were a good or a goal to be maximized, it would forbid using deadly force against them, if, say, the one innocent were an elderly woman who would die soon anyway and the aggressors were unlikely to engage in such behaviour again. However, if instead we must treat people's capacity to relate harmoniously with respect, then we can justify acting discordantly towards them when they have misused it and when a comparable discord is necessary to protect their victim from such behaviour. When someone misuses his special ability to harmonize with others, there is no disrespect in using a comparable discord if necessary to get him to stop, while not doing so, letting him subordinate and harm innocents, would fail to respect that special ability in his victims. The relational moral theory entails that there are rights to protect and to be protected.

The fact that the relational moral theory can justify coercion and violence for defensive purposes differentiates it from a plain reading of the Biblical prescription to love one's neighbour as oneself (Mark 12:31; Matthew 22:39; John 13:34–5). Would it be loving of yourself to submit to deadly force? Presumably not, making it wrong ever to submit someone else to it. In the context of being instructed not to resist an evil person, the Christian Bible includes passages appealing to love, saying: 'Love your enemies and pray for those who persecute you' (Matthew 5:44), 'Love your enemies, do good to those who hate you' (Luke 6:27), and '[I]f anyone slaps you on the right cheek, turn to them the other cheek also' (Matthew 5:40; Luke 6:28; see also Romans 12:17, 20–1). Of course, there are ways of interpreting the Christian tradition that would make some sense of why deadly force can be justified. The point is that a principle of respect for our ability to be party to loving (friendly) relationships more straightforwardly justifies deadly force and other defensive threats and harm than does one natural interpretation of an instruction to love one's neighbour.[5]

In addition to justifying defensive force, thereby preventing unfriendliness from occurring, the relational moral theory justifies using force to compensate victims of unfriendliness that has already occurred. Given the corollary that it is not disrespectful to act in a very unfriendly way towards someone when necessary to counteract a comparable unfriendliness towards an innocent party, that could include forcing a guilty party to make reparations to those he has wronged.[6] If a thief will not of his own accord return a stolen item, a court may rightly subordinate him and reduce his quality of life by making him do so. It is on the face of it unfriendly for a court to make someone against his will give another person an object, but it is not necessarily a failure to honour a thief's capacity for friendliness for it to do so to him, since being unfriendly in that way is essential to make up for the thief's initial unfriendly behaviour. Ordering a thief to compensate his victim would express no disrespect towards the guilty party's capacity to relate in a friendly way since he continues to misuse it by keeping the item, while failing to order such compensation would fail to treat the victim's capacity to be related to in a friendly way as important.

Such a rationale plausibly captures the case of the philandering husband who did not use protection when cheating on his wife, acquired HIV despite knowing the risk, passed HIV on to his wife without her having known of that risk, and now wants the sole treatment available (6.3). As he treated her in a very unfriendly way,

[5] The Christian Bible prohibits retributive or vengeful sentiments for human beings and instead reserves them for God (see Matthew 5:38–9; Romans 12:19). Upon seeking out a strictly secular basis for morality, as per the project in this book, it becomes natural to permit human beings to use force against aggressors as essential to protect the innocent and against wrongdoers as needed to compensate their victims.

[6] So, the relational moral theory in the first instance supports a fault-based approach to liability. However, there could be situations in which it is all-things-considered justified to adopt strict liability or to resolve civil cases based on the ability to bear cost.

breaking their vows and infecting her with a life-threatening disease, he ought to compensate her by allowing her to have the treatment. It would be just for the hospital to force him to do so, in effect, by directing the treatment to her. Where someone has acted discordantly towards an innocent party, putting her into a situation in which she needs certain resources to survive that the guilty party also needs because of his discordant behaviour, respect for their capacity to relate harmoniously prescribes providing them to the innocent party. Although there are admittedly strong practical reasons for a hospital not to conduct mini-trials into how people have come to need medical resources, the just outcome would be for the hospital to save the life of the wife if it must choose between them, since the husband's decisions are responsible for her having come to need such aid. The present, deontological corollary can make sense of that position, unlike a principle directing us to promote harmony as much as possible in the future regardless of what has happened in the past.

In short, while my theory instructs agents to treat the capacity for harmony or friendliness as the most important final good, it does not uniformly forbid *acts* of unfriendliness, even enmity. Acting in an extremely discordant or unfriendly way can in fact be respectful of the capacity for harmony or friendliness, roughly if the point is to counter another's initial discord or unfriendliness that is comparable in degree. More carefully, I have suggested that sufficient conditions for it being respectful to be very unfriendly towards someone are that acting that way is no more unfriendly than what he has done and there is no other way to prevent or compensate for his unfriendliness.

7.3.3 Impartiality/Partiality

I believe that, as a matter of description, African ethics has both impartial and partial elements. Regarding impartiality, it is typical for sub-Saharan philosophers to maintain that every human being has a dignity and so is equal from a moral point of view (Wiredu 1996: 157–71; Bujo 2001: 2, 138–9, 142; Deng 2004; Iroegbu 2005b; Gyekye 2010: sec. 6). Traditionally speaking, the view has been that what constitutes our dignity is that we are children of God, i.e., exhibit a divine energy. Such a view well explains the support for hospitality in the African tradition, illustrated by the common practice of a village welcoming visitors with food and shelter (Mnyaka and Motlhabi 2005: 228–31; Mandela 2006; Gathogo 2008).

However, partiality is also salient in the African tradition. According to it, we owe more to those related to us than we do to those who are not (Wiredu 1992: 200; Appiah 1998; Ramose 2003: 385–6; Molefe 2019: 84–6). 'Family first' and 'charity begins at home' are commonly expressed in the field, where amongst indigenous peoples blood ties have often been deemed to provide extra reason to aid.

My relational moral theory provides what I submit is a neat way to integrate these two elements, to view them as complementary rather than contradictory. According to the principle of rightness as friendliness, what gives us a dignity is our capacity to befriend others and to be befriended by them. Any being that by its nature has the ability to relate communally as both a subject and an object enjoys a full moral status, such that a corollary of the relational moral theory is that an agent has some moral reason to fulfil any such being's goals and interests, if she is in a position to do so with ease.

This impartial corollary of the theory makes it different from the problematic extreme partialism of some other Afro-relational principles. Recall that some appeals to relationality were objectionable for apparently restricting the scope of morality to those in one's clan or community, understood as a group that has socialized and cared for one (6.3). Ascribing a dignity to all those capable of communality, regardless of whether one has in fact related communally with them, solves that problem with ease. Everyone on the planet has a claim of *some* weight to be treated in a friendly way by anyone on the planet who can do so. The greater the need, the weightier is that claim.

However, there is also a partial corollary to the theory, such that when an agent has been in a friendly or communal relationship with others, she has some moral reason to maintain and enrich that relationship and hence to participate with and help them more than those with whom she has not so related. One way to honour people in virtue of their capacity for relationship is to honour the actual relationships they have constructed. The longer and stronger the communal relating, the more of a duty to protect and develop it. Here is yet another respect in which the relational moral theory is deontological, as it includes agent-relative duties.

The corollary about partiality enables the theory not only to make sense of characteristically African approaches to morality, but also to capture what look to be strong intuitions about what one owes others. For example, I have somewhat more reason to aid my sons than reason to aid anyone else's sons, for both the African tradition and global ethical thought more broadly, with the present explanation of that being that I have had particularly long and strong ties with my sons. Other people's sons do matter, and if they could not acquire enough food, I could well have the most reason to buy it for them, if at the cost of not buying my sons a video game. However, if I had to choose between providing adequate food to my sons or to someone else's sons who need it to a comparable degree, I would have most moral reason to favour my sons since my ties with them are established and intimate.

Too often, in my view, partial reasons to go out of one's way for those related to an agent have been considered non-moral considerations that are in potential conflict with moral considerations, which are construed strictly impartially. Consider, for example, this way of framing things: '[C]an our obligations to our friends sometimes trump our moral duties, or must we always subordinate our personal relationships to morality?' (Helm 2013: n.p.). According to the relational moral theory, reasons to aid those communally related to us are themselves a species of *moral* reasons.[7] I would be wronging my sons and should feel particularly guilty if, instead of taking care to address their hunger, I were to feed someone else's hungry sons.

In sum, by my approach, it is not divine energy that grounds impartiality and it is not blood ties that ground partiality. Instead, I maintain that these two facets of morality flow from the same source of communality. On the one hand, the capacity to relate communally in a person gives any agent some moral reason to commune with her, while, on the other hand, having related communally with a given person gives a particular agent extra moral reason to continue doing so.

7.3.4 Capacity/Actuality

In the previous sub-section I pointed out that, according to my favoured principle of right action, we have *pro tanto* reason to prioritize those with whom we have communed when it comes to sharing a way of life or caring for others' quality of life. I contended that is so because one way of showing respect for people's capacity to commune is to respect their actualizations of it. Although the capacity for relationship is at bottom what determines the rightness or wrongness of an action by my account, that does not mean relationships themselves, i.e., the actualization of this capacity, are morally irrelevant. Although I do not ascribe a superlative final value to communal ways of relating (and instead do so to the capacity for them) and do not otherwise treat them as goods to be promoted, it does follow from my ethic that we often have reason to pursue communal ways of relating as ends.

To see the difference, again consider the Kantian tradition. There, although what has a dignity is the capacity to set ends, it is standardly believed, following Kant himself (1785: Ak. 430), that one way to respect a being with that capacity is to help it achieve its particular ends. By a Kantian ethic, if a person has made a free decision to collect coins, respect for her (in part) means taking care not to prevent her from collecting more as well as giving her some coins she does not already have. Such an approach means a moral agent has reason to realize others' ends as ways of expressing respect for her end-setting capacity.

My approach is similar, in that a moral agent is to respect actual relationships as a way of ultimately respecting the beings capable of them. Above I noted that one has some reason to sustain and enrich the communal relationships of which one is

[7] There have been others who have deemed 'obligations to our friends' to be a subset of morality—although they focus more on virtue and less on rightness than I do. See, e.g., Blum (1980: 67–83), Kekes (1981), and Cottingham (1983).

a part, relative to starting up a comparable degree of communality with strangers. Now I also suggest that one has some reason to enable others to sustain and enrich their communal relationships, even if one is not party to them.

Here are some examples in which the relational moral theory entails specific duties to protect and develop communality that does not include the agent. To start, consider that an individual has a duty of some weight not to interfere with other people's romantic relationships. If a couple is reasonably happily married, one ought not try to woo one of the spouses away. In addition, the dean of a university faculty has some obligation to try to foster collegiality amongst its members. Of course, people are more likely to get work done if they feel a sense of togetherness, participate on a cooperative basis, engage in mutual aid, and do so for one another's sake, but the suggestion here is that such communal relating is also worth cultivating as an end. At the level of government, it has some moral reason to do what it can to support cohesive relationships amongst citizens. For instance, it should offer couples counselling and parenting classes in its public clinics and require private healthcare insurers to pay for them. Also in a medical setting, it is apt for a state hospital to treat those who have sex with the dead or those who are 'intimate' primarily with lifelike dolls. There would be good reason for the state to treat them for mental illness, naturally conceived at least in part as a matter of being unable to have healthy relationships with others (see 9.2).

In these cases and a range of others (some of which I address in Part III), respect for others' capacity to relate communally can mean helping them to do so, even if one is not or will not be party to that relationship. The last major issue that I now explore in articulating the relational moral theory is roughly how much an individual is obligated to do so.

7.3.5 Self/Other

Recall that the relational moral theory speaks of treating 'individuals' and 'beings' with respect in virtue of their ability to be part of communal relationships, and that it does so to include certain non-persons, such as babies and animals, in the light of their capacity to be objects of such relationships. A further question, though, is whether it is only others, whether human persons, non-personal humans, or non-human animals, who are owed such respect, or whether the agent also owes such respect to herself. The question of whether there are duties to oneself is closely related to the question of whether one is morally permitted to do less than all one could to support others' ends and foster their good.

There has not been much discussion of whether there are moral 'options' to do less than the best one could for other people and animals, as one African ethical theorist has pointed out (Molefe 2019: 93). However, to the extent it has been addressed, the suggestion has usually been that there is no category of supererogation—that is, no ability to go beyond the call of duty for others—since one's duty is to do all that is possible for them. Such an approach is explicit in the work of Kwame Gyekye (1997: 70–5, 2004: 105–11), and implicit in the views of Kwasi Wiredu, insofar as he supports the Golden Rule. Regarding the latter, if I ask how I would want to be treated by an agent, I would naturally want her to do all she can to realize my ends and improve my quality of life.

Although it might make my theory even 'less African' than it already is (for not essentially including imperceptible agents, and perhaps for its theoretical structure), I am at this stage inclined to accept a category of duties to oneself.[8] That is, when the relational moral theory prescribes respecting beings that are capable of relating communally, I suggest reading that as including one's own such capability. One way to account for the category of supererogation, or the existence of options to do less than all one could for others, is to contend that one also owes oneself certain kinds of consideration.[9] Duties in respect of one's own dignity need to be balanced with those in respect of the dignity (or moral status) of others, or so currently appears plausible to me.

Again, my approach to what is owed respect and how it is to be manifested accords with a familiar kind of Kantianism. Following Kant himself (1785: Ak. 429–30, 1797: Ak. 373–473), contemporary Kantians standardly divide duties into those that are self-regarding and those that are other-regarding. Up to now, I have aimed to account for other-regarding duties, that is, duties towards other animals and persons. While the existence of a category of self-regarding duties is more controversial, and hence I included no intuitions about them amongst the key sixteen by which to appraise a moral theory in the first instance (3.4.3), one may read the relational moral theory as entailing them. Whatever it is about the capacity of others to relate communally that demands respect can also be found in oneself and presumably likewise merits respect. For those who firmly deny that there are any duties to oneself, they will find more attractive a cousin of the present ethic that would talk of honouring 'other individuals' instead of simply 'individuals'.

There are two different ways to make sense of the category of self-regarding duties, given the idea that our relational nature is what must be honoured. A first way would be to contend that we have obligations to actualize and perfect our capacity for communality with others. Perhaps we do ourselves wrong if we do not enter into communal relationships with others; we might owe it to ourselves not to remain isolated and instead to seek out a romantic partner, say. And where our capacity for communality is weak, we might have duties to strengthen it. For

[8] For one in the African tradition who would be sympathetic to the point, see Kayange (2018: 131–42).

[9] For a quite different approach to making sense of supererogation in the context of African ethics, see Molefe (2019: 93–116).

example, perhaps one currently has a tendency to interrupt people when they speak, or does a poor job of sympathizing with others. These are imperfections in one's ability to be a subject of communal relationship that one might have some obligation to oneself, not merely to others, to correct. Relatedly, one might have imperfections in one's ability to be an object of communal relationship. For instance, consider those who are uncomfortable with interdependence and are reluctant to ask for help from others. Distancing oneself from others in that way is plausibly viewed as wrongful, in part because one owes it to oneself to let others advance one's ends and good.

A second strategy by which to make sense of the category of self-regarding duties, given the dignity of our relational nature, would be to contend that we have obligations to 'relate' to ourselves that parallel the ways we ought to treat others. Such an approach would stretch the normal sense of what talk of 'relationality' involves (or at least has involved so far in this book), but there is prima facie reason to take it seriously. For instance, perhaps one has a duty not to be unfriendly towards oneself. One ought above all not exhibit full-blown enmity towards oneself, which captures intuitions that there is something wrong with hating oneself or doing what one knows to be harmful to oneself. For another example, perhaps there are also more positive obligations in respect of oneself—say, to be neither alienated from one's projects nor indifferent towards one's good. Being friendly towards those capable of friendliness appears to entail a duty to be friendly towards oneself, that is, to enjoy a sense of cohesion, to coherently carry out projects, to do things that are good for oneself, and to be compassionate towards oneself.

Somewhat surprisingly, I have suggested that communality is one promising theoretical resource in the African tradition by which to make sense of why our obligations towards others might be limited. In a nutshell, since we ourselves have the same capacity that gives others a dignity, we also have a dignity, which, in turn, plausibly grounds obligations to ourselves that must be balanced in some way with obligations to others. Duties to ourselves could consist of exercising and developing our ability to befriend and to be befriended by others, or they might be a matter of not treating ourselves in unfriendly ways and instead acting in friendly ways towards ourselves.

To sum up this important section, in it I have worked to bring out more of what it means to treat the dignity of people's communal nature with respect and, conversely, to degrade their capacity to be party to friendly relationships. Much of this consisted of highlighting various respects in which my relational moral theory is deontological. For example, I pointed out that it is normally degrading to use a very unfriendly means to realize an end, even the end of friendliness, i.e., that people have the right not to have their capacity for friendliness stunted, let alone eradicated, for the greater good. I argued that facts about the past decisions people have made can provide principled reasons for treating them in certain ways now, such that people have the right to use deadly force against aggressors as necessary to protect innocents, who probably also have a right to be so protected. And I contended that some moral reasons are agent-relative, whereby an agent has somewhat greater reason to relate communally with those who have already been party to communal relationships with her than with those to whom she has not so related. In all these respects, the relational moral theory is distinct from a teleological principle that instructs one to do whatever it takes to produce goodness and reduce badness in the future, wherever it may be located in the world.

Although rightness as friendliness is deontological in the above ways, it has some implications that overlap with salient teleological theories. For instance, recall that since everyone has a dignity, the principle entails that there are impartial reasons to commune with anyone, directing an agent to be particularly concerned to do so with the worst off regardless of whether they are related to herself. In addition, recall that since respecting people's capacity for communality means respecting their actualization of it, an agent can have some obligation to create and protect communal ways of relating on the part of others.

With this description of how to understand rightness as friendliness, I am finally ready to apply it to the sixteen key intuitions about right and wrong. I now work to show that the relational moral theory can more easily entail and powerfully explain all sixteen compared to African principles that take either well-being or vital force as foundational.

7.4 Accounting for the Key Intuitions

This section completes the major task of Part II of this book, which has been to distinguish sharply between three broad candidates for a moral theory suggested by the English-speaking African philosophical literature and to argue that one is more justified than the other two. In catchwords, I have distinguished between moral theories grounded on well-being, vital force, and communal relationship, contending that these values have their own logics and implications for right and wrong. Recall that my principal way of choosing an African moral theory to the exclusion of others is to show that it best accounts for two kinds of intuitions about right and wrong. Half of these intuitions about morality are 'global' in the sense of being held by ethicists and people more generally from a wide array of intellectual traditions, including the Western above all. The other intuitions are 'African' in the sense of having been recurrent amongst contemporary sub-Saharan ethicists and their peoples to a much greater degree than amongst ethicists and their societies in most other parts of the world.

I now indicate how the relational moral theory, prescribing respect for individuals' capacity to be party to relationships of identity and solidarity, accounts for the intuitions better than rival principles. Communality, rather than utility or vitality, is the foundation for a basic and comprehensive moral duty that can appeal to both an African and global audience of moral philosophers. I do not try to show that communality does better than rivals for *each* of the following sixteen intuitions, instead seeking the weaker claim that it does better than rivals on balance, taking the intuitions as an aggregate. Where I did not contend that an appeal to well-being or vital force could not account well for a given intuition, below I merely point out how communal relationship can (also) account well for it. However, where I did contend that a rival principle could not account well for a given intuition, I argue that rightness as friendliness can account for it better.

First off, recall that for most ethicists one would usually be violating a duty of some strength if one were (a) to kill innocent people without their consent for money. Such an action is characteristically a patent case of enmity or great unfriendliness, which may almost never be directed against an innocent party (7.2.2–7.3.2). It degrades the person's capacity to commune as a subject by eradicating the ability to exhibit identity and solidarity for the sake of something worth much less than it. It also degrades the person's capacity to commune as an object, centrally by subordinating him instead of coordinating, harming him instead of helping, and doing both to an extreme extent.

Note that the action would be degrading regardless of whether the money was used for a holiday in the Bahamas or to purchase medical equipment needed to save others' lives. Either way, the individual's capacity to relate communally would not be treated as the superlative non-instrumental good, and would instead be treated merely as a means to an end.

Consider now the widely held intuition that it is wrong (b) to have sex with someone against her will so as to feel pleasure or a sense of power. Like murder, rape is degrading because it is an instance of enmity done when unnecessary to rebut a comparable enmity on the other's part and instead done for the sake of something worth much less than her dignified communal nature. Rape is an instance of extreme unfriendliness, characteristically being done out of a sense of otherness, subordinating another person to an intense degree, harming her to the same degree, and being done out of cruelty or at least indifference with respect to her good.

These forms of division and ill will not merely degrade the other person's ability to be befriended, but also disrespect her ability to befriend, for no justifying end. The specific nature of the harm involved concerns not merely the victim's physical and emotional well-being, but also her own special capacity to relate communally or to harmonize with others. As is well known, those subjected to rape and similar kinds of sexual assault can expect to have difficulty being romantically intimate, potentially one of the most intense ways of harmonizing with another as a subject. In short, trusting, loving, and sexual relationships are central to an explanation of why rape is such a serious wrong, by the relational moral theory.

Next, it is commonly held that it is normally at least somewhat wrong (c) to deceive a person, at least when not done in self- or other-defence. Although deception of those who are not aggressing need not involve full-blown enmity towards them, it still typically involves unfriendliness. In particular, deception of others can involve ill will and so be expected to harm them. Asking for a loan while never intending to pay it back and cheating on a romantic partner risk reducing the quality of life of those deceived.

There are of course times when deception is not in fact likely to make others worse off, but still seems wrong, a problem that I raised for a vitalist ethic (5.3). Recall the scenario in which there really is no way that one's romantic partner would find out about one's cheating. Furthermore, there are cases of paternalism in which deception is done precisely to make others better off. There is some real debate about when paternalism might be justified, but I presume readers will agree that it is unjustified at least when the same good (of well-being or liveliness) could be promoted without using a deceptive means. Having the intuition that deception is unjustified as a way to improve other's quality of life when it is unnecessary for that end is best explained by the idea that there is something morally undesirable about the deception 'in itself', apart from its consequences.

My suggestion is therefore that division is more integral to why deception is characteristically wrong than is ill will. Deceiving another person is essentially a way of stunting another's ability to participate on a cooperative basis. When you lie to a person, or otherwise get him to believe what you know to be false, you are not merely failing to share a way of life together when you could, but also directly impeding the other person's capacity for that with you. For instance, when you deceive your romantic partner into thinking you are not cheating, you are not only likely hindering the other person from achieving his goals, but also, as Kantians have noted (e.g., O'Neill 1989: 112–7), invariably preventing the other person from adopting yours. If you act in such an unfriendly, because subordinating, way for a purpose other than counteracting an unjustified instance of unfriendliness, such as misdirecting the proverbial axe murderer at your doorstep, then you are, in most cases, treating the capacity for friendliness as less than the superlative non-instrumental good.

A fourth intuition widely held by ethicists around the world is that it is wrong (d) to discriminate on a racial or gendered basis when allocating opportunities, at least when not redressing a previous comparable discrimination. Recall that I argued that it is difficult for a vitalist ethic to explain why, if the state is going to give people the opportunity to marry, it must do so in a way that permits them to marry persons of another race (5.3). Even if there would be some inhibition and depression and hence reduction in liveliness upon being unable to marry interracially, such would not obtain if the state succeeded in keeping races sufficiently far apart and did so without expressing the attitude that one is inferior to the other. A more promising explanation of why the failure to recognize interracial marriages would be wrong is that it would be a serious degradation of the individual's capacity for the most intense kind of harmonious or communal relationship possible—romantic love. Placing restrictions on people's ability to marry to advance some (bizarre) notion of cultural purity or religious ideal would disrespectfully treat the latter as more important than people's capacity to come close to each other.

Similar explanations apply to other forms of discrimination, for instance, gendered ways of allocating jobs. Where institutions have a substantial influence on the course of people's lives in a society, they must operate according to a principle of equal opportunity, roughly awarding jobs and related goods, such as admissions into higher degree programmes, on the basis of qualifications (unless seeking to redress a previous unequal opportunity). Doing so is the only way to treat everyone as having an equal dignity, particularly when it comes to their capacity to be party to caring relationships. Consider an employer who refuses to let certain people become firefighters merely because they are women, where the employer believes that God has forbidden such a practice or that women are uniformly incapable of doing such a job well. Such a policy would fail to honour women's equally valuable ability to be an object of care, insofar as receiving jobs would foster goods such as productivity, self-esteem, and wealth for those who hold them. In addition, and more deeply, such an approach would fail to honour women's equally valuable ability to be subjects of caring ways of relating, insofar as those who could indeed do the job well would not have the chance to actualize their own, special capacity to help others.

Next, return to the intuition that it is wrong (e) to express ethnic, sexual, or similar epithets towards others. I suggested above that a focus on the common good has difficulty explaining why slurs and related insults are wrong, in that it does not appear to be a basic need not to be targeted by them (4.3). Advocates of that approach could broaden their notion of the common good to include well-being that is not the meeting of a basic need and then point out that it is hardly pleasant to be called slurs. In addition, Gyekye in particular could say more about his conception of human dignity in order to ground the claim that slurs are disrespectful.

However, a principle of respect for our capacity to identify with and exhibit solidarity towards others already includes these kinds of considerations. On the one hand, a slur is often an instance of unfriendly behaviour for conveying the attitude that a person is separate and other, reducing her self-esteem and hence ability to achieve her goals, causing her psychological pain, and being used out of cruelty or at least indifference to the other's good. Many of these behaviours are causal in the sense that they impinge on another person's ability to pursue ends and live well.

However, I believe that another part of what makes slurs wrong, and specifically disrespectful, is a purely symbolic element to them. So, on the other hand, a slur is also degrading simply because of what it expresses, even if the target of the slur luckily does not become aware of it and so is not physically affected by it.

A dignity-based theory can easily capture symbolic wrongness. If our basic duty is to express respect for beings with a superlative non-instrumental value, then we ought not try to tell them or others that they lack such a value.

One advantage of these explanations of the wrongness of slurs and the like is that they can make good sense of situations in which slurs are not degrading, neither causally nor symbolically. That is, my claim is not that ethnic and sexual slurs are inherently unfriendly and degrading, but is instead that, *when* they are wrong, they are so in virtue of that. There are times when slurs can be permissible to express, e.g., when one is recognized as part of an in-group (a member of a 'we') and has 'appropriated' the slur to express closeness. The relational moral theory provides a straightforward explanation of why slurring in such a particular context would not be wrong: the slur would not be used to express that the person lacks value and would not be unfriendly, e.g., would not threaten self-esteem or cause mental anguish. Indeed, using it in that way could well be something that is to be encouraged for prizing the capacity for friendliness, viz., for bringing people closer together and meeting psychological needs.

I consider the next two global intuitions at the same time—namely, the judgements that it is wrong (f) never to fight hunger, poverty, displacement, or the like suffered by those outside one's in-group, when one could do so at little cost to oneself, and also wrong (g) never to prevent serious crimes done to others, when one could do so at little cost to oneself. What these two intuitions have in common is that they involve positive duties to advance other people's goals and to improve their quality of life (7.2–7.3.2). By the relational moral theory, human persons have a dignity by virtue of their capacity to be party to relationships of identity and solidarity, and it is not enough merely to avoid subordinating, harming, or insulting them. Instead, since they have the highest non-instrumental value in the world because of their ability to relate communally, we are obligated to go out of our way to relate to people in that way and often to enable them to do so with others. When we prevent crimes such as killing, assault, and theft, we are preventing division and ill will and thereby treating the other's capacity for communality as important. Similar remarks apply to supporting charities and social welfare programmes.

One naturally would like some specification of how much support and aid is too much to expect of a moral agent. Like most of the field, I lack a sophisticated account of that. However, one salient theoretical resource is the distinction drawn earlier between duties to others and duties to oneself (7.3.5). If one interprets the relational moral theory to say that one is obligated to treat oneself with the sort of respect that one must show others, then there is the start of a powerful answer to the question of how much one owes others. One may not commune with others or enable them to commune in ways that would involve treating oneself in unfriendly ways or would otherwise be degrading of oneself. Presumably, if one were to be so self-abnegating as never to use one's time, money, and other resources in support of one's own projects in favour of invariably helping other people to pursue theirs, one would fail to honour oneself.

The last global intuition is not about human persons, but rather animals, and it is the belief that it is wrong (h) to torture an animal merely for the fun of it. According to the relational moral theory, nearly all human persons have a full moral status because they can be both subjects and objects of communal relationships. Roughly speaking, we are capable of other-regard in a way that at least pigs, rabbits, and parakeets are not. While these animals lack a dignity, they nonetheless have a partial moral status because they can be objects of communal relationship with us. We can enjoy a sense of togetherness with them, support their goals, improve their well-being, and do so out of sympathy and for their sake. Torture is a matter of both imposing intense control over another being and inflicting great pain on it, and hence is an instance of enmity. When done to an innocent animal for the sake of the mere thrill, it is degrading of its capacity to be part of a communal relationship with us as an object, trading off that special ability for something worth much less than it.

I pointed out that Gyekye's and others' welfarist theories in the African tradition have been anthropocentric (4.3), taking human well-being as the sole end of moral action. Admittedly, these views could be broadened, including animal welfare as an end, or perhaps including the avoidance of animal woe as a constraint on the pursuit of human well-being. One advantage of the relational moral theory relative to these accounts is that it can capture the sense in which it is possible to degrade an animal, not merely cause it harm. The prima facie problem with keeping birds caged for the pleasure of looking at them or repeatedly tricking animals for one's amusement does not have to do essentially with pain or suffering. According to rightness as friendliness, these creatures are important; they have a moral status that merits respect (even if they lack a dignity). While the relational theory does not forbid all contact with animals, and in fact probably provides some support for domesticating them under certain circumstances (8.4.1), it does entail that certain ways of interacting with them can be disrespectful and not merely because of the harm done to them; subordination, too, can be a form of degradation.

I have now completed my discussion of how the relational moral theory, developed in the light of African communal values, seems easily to entail and powerfully to explain the 'global' ethical intuitions, ones that have been recurrent not merely in the African philosophical tradition, but also in a wide array of other traditions around the world. I have not yet argued systematically that rightness as friendliness is more justified than the competing moral theories suggested by the work of contemporary African philosophers, which focus on the common good and vital force. Although I suggested that the competitors have difficulty here and there, for instance when it comes to capturing the wrongness of discrimination and slurs, I have not really shown that rightness as friendliness best captures the global intuitions on balance. Instead, the central reason I offer for preferring the relational moral theory over competitors from the African tradition is, to put it roughly, that it is more African. I now argue that communal relationship, better than the common good or vital force, captures moral intuitions that are prominent in the African philosophical tradition but not in many other traditions. These moral judgements are not, I repeat, utterly unique to sub-Saharan moral thought, but are much more common in it than they are in, say, Western, Islamic, Confucian, Buddhist, or Hindu thinking.

I again proceed one by one. Recall that, more often for African philosophers and their indigenous societies than for non-African ones, it is wrong to some degree (i) to resolve political conflicts in the face of continued dissent, rather than seeking consensus. I argued above that a standard vitalist ethic has difficulty accounting for this intuition, which in effect would accord law- or policy-makers equal political power, since either a supermajority (seeking somewhat less than unanimity) or plural voting (giving more votes to the educated) seems likely to foster liveliness to a comparable or even greater degree. The deep problem with vitalism is that it makes the justification of consensual democracy contingent on its outcomes in respect of liveliness, and it is implausible to think such a procedure will invariably produce the best such outcomes, no matter what else is going on in a society.

In short, what is needed is a principled justification for consensual democracy, by which I mean one that accounts for its rightness in terms of something inherent to its procedure. Even if a supermajority or plural voting had better outcomes, whether for liveliness or some other value such as welfare, why might these ways of allocating political power be unjustified relative to consensus? A plausible answer is that each individual has a dignity in virtue of her capacity to be party to communal relationships, which, in turn, means that the default position should be to get each person on board with whichever laws or policies will govern her. If what is special about us includes our capacity to share a way of life with others, then that is going to require sharing political power. Our ability to enjoy a sense of togetherness and cooperate with each other is best honoured when what happens in a state's territory has been ratified by each competent adult who lives there (or at least by her representative).[10] It seems clear that such a capacity would be

[10] Notice that my argument does not turn on everyone coming to hold the same beliefs about what should be done and why, in the way another scholar's does when he remarks, 'Discussion must continue until unanimity is achieved, a really common mind and heart. This is the only adequate sign that the truth of the matter has been discovered. But it is also a valuable achievement in its own right. Achieving a common mind and heart on a specific issue builds up the community as such, intensifying the spirit of solidarity of its members' (Shutte 2001: 29). For me, what principally matters is not coming to share the same judgement, i.e., adopting the same policy for the same reasons. Instead, togetherness, cooperation, and decisions likely to be good enough for all are advanced when no one has such serious problems with a policy to prevent it from going ahead.

degraded by authoritarianism, where a monarch or a single party controls the state and determines unilaterally how those in its territory shall live. That would be subordination instead of coordination.

However, a similar point applies to majoritarian democracy, which is a sharing of power but only in a weak sense. That system gives to minorities a degree of power according to the number of votes they have acquired, along with the opportunity to become majorities in elections scheduled every few years. A more intense sharing of power would accord every citizen not merely the equal ability to become the ones who largely determine law and policy, but also 'the right of representation with respect to every particular decision', in Kwasi Wiredu's (1996: 173) influential terms, that is, the right not to be marginalized when major laws and policies are formulated and adopted. And if we are *equally* special by virtue of having the requisite capacity to share a way of life, that means according people equal representation with regard to each decision, which consensus facilitates. The deep reason why a supermajority and plural voting are plausibly unjustified compared to consensus is that those decision-making procedures would be degrading of our dignified ability to share a way of life with each other. They would insufficiently honour our equally valuable ability to enjoy a sense of togetherness and cooperate with one another, even if their results would be marginally more favourable for the promotion of vitality or some other good.[11]

Another moral judgement that is prominent amongst African philosophers is that it is wrong (j) to fail to do what is likely to make people's lives go better, if one is politically in charge. The dominant theme in the African tradition is that the state or other political organization ought to be employed neither to satisfy monarchical whim nor merely to protect liberal rights to pursue one's conception of the good life. The proper aim of a state or some other form of political organization is to improve people's objective quality of life, which welfarism and vitalism can capture well on the face of it. I point out here that communalism can also do so, while avoiding concerns about paternalism with comparative ease.

I believe that the state is plausibly viewed as a moral agent distinct from the individual people who compose it at a given time, such that it has positive duties of its own to commune with its citizens. However, if one rejects the idea the state can bear duties, a parallel point is plausibly true of a state's officials in their public capacity; respect for citizens' capacity to commune requires them to relate communally with citizens. A substantial part of communing is of course exhibiting solidarity with or caring for others, i.e., doing what is expected to advance people's good and doing so for their sake. I have suggested a broad understanding

[11] There are of course important objections that have been raised to consensual democracy, but those are not pertinent here. I take the characteristically African intuition that it is justified for granted, in order to seek the best explanation of it; the ultimate aim is to support a relational moral theory as African and plausible. In a later work, *A Relational Theory of Justice*, I intend to address objections to a unanimitarian approach to allocating political power (see 13.4).

of what constitutes people's good, including well-being, liveliness, and also moral virtue (6.2, 7.2). Hence, whatever advantage a rival African principle gains in respect of the present intuition about the proper final end of a political organization, the relational moral theory can obtain it to the same extent.

However, one difference between the relational theory and some of its African rivals, particularly the vitalist principle and a welfarism without a dignity constraint, is that they are going to justify a paternalist state much more readily than it will. If a state must do whatever is expected to promote liveliness, then people's decision-making can have a merely contingent bearing on its policies. However, if a state is obligated not merely to exhibit solidarity with citizens, but also to identify with them, i.e., to coordinate behaviour with them, then it has principled reason normally to *enable* people to live better lives should they so choose, and not to do whatever will in fact make them live better lives against their will. Forcing innocent people to live well would usually be an instance of unfriendliness or anti-sociality, a failure to pursue positive duties to improve others' lives in ways that do not violate negative ones against subordinating them (6.2.4, 7.3.1).

Let us turn to the intuition the state would be wrong (k) to make retribution the fundamental aim of criminal justice, in contrast to seeking reconciliation. Above I pointed out that vitalist theories, and related principles that prescribe promoting a final good such as well-being, can easily entail the impropriety of retributivism. By definition, that approach to punishment is the view that it is justified merely because it is a proportionate response to a crime committed in the past, regardless of whether the penalty is expected to produce anything desirable in the future. Forward-looking moral principles, prescribing the promotion of a final good in the future, straightforwardly exclude such a backward-looking rationale for punishment.

However, I also suggested that welfarism and vitalism have difficulty capturing the precise nature of the good that the African tradition characteristically prescribes in the context of criminal justice, namely the mending of a broken relationship. The dominant theme in sub-Saharan philosophical approaches to dealing with crime and other wrongdoing has been reconciliation, with recurrent mention of offenders hearing out victims, making apologies to them, effecting compensation for wrongful harm done, undertaking moral reform, eventually becoming reintegrated into society, and perhaps even being forgiven by their victims. Insofar as these reconciliatory approaches to crime are unlikely to do more long-term good than, say, deterrence and incapacitation, the former obtain no unique justification from vitalist and welfarist principles relative to the latter. Furthermore, it is on the face of it difficult for vitalism and welfarism to draw a principled distinction between the guilty and the innocent, since they instruct an agent to do whatever will promote liveliness or well-being, respectively. As is well known, such a teleological structure entails that it is justifiable to punish innocent parties for the greater good in cases where it does not seem to be justified.

In contrast, the relational moral theory provides a strong explanation of why criminal justice in the first instance consists of reconciling wrongdoers with their victims and the broader society: the state must respect people's capacity to relate communally. After all, reconciliation is the ending and mending of discordant relationships, so that it is natural for a theory instructing an agent to prize people in virtue of their capacity for harmonious relationship to prescribe fixing ones that have been wrongfully broken.

More carefully, consider that if we must treat people's ability to commune with respect, then we must hold them accountable when they misuse that capacity (7.3.2). Failing to base our treatment of others in the light of how they have exercised their capacity for friendliness would fail to honour that capacity. It is therefore roughly those who have initially failed to be friendly, and not innocent parties, who merit unfriendly treatment, even if punishing the innocent would bring about the most long-term good.

In addition, the kind of unfriendliness imposed on the guilty should normally be expected to perform the function of counteracting their initial anti-sociality or unfriendliness (7.3.2). Concretely, state punishment should typically consist of burdensome forms of compensation and rehabilitation. For a court to force an offender to undertake labour or undergo some other hardship that will make up for harm done to his victim would express the judgement that the offender should not have treated her in an unfriendly way and also that he can and should treat her in a friendly way now. In addition, for a court to force an offender to undergo therapy and related kinds of moral reform would similarly express the judgement that the offender should not have failed to treat his victim in a friendly way and also that his capacity for friendly behaviour should be strengthened. While deterrence and incapacitation can protect the broader society from unfriendly behaviour, neither approach addresses the relationship between offenders, victims, and the broader society. In contrast, punishment that makes up for harm done to victims and rehabilitates offenders expresses disapproval of how offenders misused their capacity for communality, shows concern at how victims were treated in an anti-social way, and makes it reasonable for society, if not also victims, to relate communally with offenders again.

When it comes to the economic sphere, recall that it is a characteristically African view that it is wrong (l) to create wealth largely on a competitive basis, instead of a cooperative one. Remember Steve Biko's remark that Africans tend to think that life does not warrant 'endless competition' and instead that people should engage in 'joint community oriented action rather than the individualism which is the hallmark of the capitalist approach' (2004: 46). I argued that an appeal to welfarism or vitalism has difficulty capturing the intuition that even if a firm's profit maximization is best for everyone in the long run, there is something morally problematic about it relative to, say, cooperatives. Specifically, I suggested that what is plausibly *pro tanto* wrong with producing goods and services with the aim of maximizing self-interest is that one is not *aiming* to make others better off.

A theory prescribing respect for our ability to relate communally can make sense of why, even if a competitive system of production were on balance justified because it had better outcomes than a cooperative one, there would be something missing from the former relative to the latter. Engaging with other economic agents in a self-interested manner infringes, if not flouts, communal values such as enjoying a sense of togetherness, doing what one can to advance others' goals, and acting for the sake of others. Even if by acting in a competitive manner one indirectly benefits people in the long run, the means taken to that end involve behaviour that is unfriendly to some degree.

Turning from production to consumption, it is typical for African moralists to find it wrong (m) to distribute wealth in a greatly unequal way and to fail to meet everyone's needs. Above I noted that welfarism and vitalism can account for this intuition when it is the inequality that is responsible for the lack of meeting needs, but that they cannot do so when inequality is consistent with meeting the needs of all or otherwise promoting well-being or liveliness. As John Rawls (1999) is particularly well known for having reminded political philosophers, it is possible for substantial inequalities of wealth and related resources to be better for the worst off than more equal distributions of them. For instance, it could be that offering those with talents extra income in exchange for using them on the job could produce more wealth to be allocated to those who are not as well off than would avoiding economic stratification. An exclusive focus on outcomes in respect of well-being or liveliness lacks the theoretical ability to question great inequality in such a case; it cannot entail that there is something morally problematic about the means when the end produced is desirable.

In contrast, a relational approach to morality can say that great inequality is likely to inhibit harmonious relationships in ways that are probably worth avoiding at *some* cost to well-being, liveliness, or other benefits. African philosophers have rejected economic inequality on the ground that it would foster 'disharmony' (Magesa 1997: 278; Oruka 1997: 120), and here are four distinct reasons for thinking that it would undermine harmony as conceived in this book (6.2, 7.2.2). First off, it is difficult for people to experience a sense of togetherness, one part of identifying with others, when there is substantial economic stratification, with it instead prompting envy and distrust (Wilkinson and Pickett 2009). Second, the other major dimension of identity, participating with others on a cooperative basis, is also threatened by substantial economic inequality, for with enormous wealth usually comes the ability to subordinate others, whether in the workplace or the political process. Third, considerations of solidarity provide reason to temper significantly unequal distributions of wealth insofar as they are thought by sociologists to foster crimes attended by violence such as armed robbery (Kelly 2000). Fourth, recall that another element of solidarity includes seeing others as meriting help for their own sake as well as tending to be moved by sympathy, where work by psychologists indicates that those who acquire wealth are on average less moved by the plight of others who are worse off than they

(Grewal 2012; Goleman 2013). All four of the key elements of harmonious or communal relationships would be threatened by great inequalities in holdings, providing the state some reason to reduce them if it must treat our capacity for such relationships with respect.

Moving from institutional considerations to more interpersonal ones, it is a characteristically African intuition to deem it wrong (n) to avoid greeting people, especially elders, upon encountering them. I argued that welfarism has difficulty accounting for this judgement in that greetings do not appear to meet a need or even to be justified merely on grounds of well-being more broadly construed. Instead, I suggested that they are at least partially prescribed on grounds of respect. Now, in the case of slurs, I contended that part of their wrongness is their purely symbolic dimension—the attempt to communicate that a person lacks a dignity. Failing to greet is similar; it is likewise wrong principally because of what it means. A greeting is straightforwardly understood to be a symbolic acknowledgement of another's presence; in greeting one is expressing the attitude that the other is important enough to warrant one's attention. When one does not make the effort to greet, one is thereby expressing the judgement that the other is not worth the effort (cf. Onwuanibe 1984: 185).

One might object that meanings are conventional, that symbols vary from society to society, so that failing to greet need not be disrespectful. While it is of course true that the content of linguistic expressions depends on conventions, adherents to a respect-based ethic are probably committed to denying that all expressions are conventional (cf. Metz 2002). Making a false promise for money expresses the judgement that the other exists merely as a means to one's ends, regardless of the society in which such an action is performed. Similarly, if one comes upon a person but acts no differently from the way one normally does when engaging with things, one plausibly expresses the attitude that she is worth no more than a thing. Of course, the content of a greeting's words, such as the meaning of 'hello', depends on convention, but the aptness of greeting in some way or other, perhaps without words at all but instead a nod, could be universally applicable.

Next, consider the intuition that it is usually wrong to some degree (o) to remain isolated or to flout long-standing norms central to a people's self-conception, as opposed to partaking in customs. Against both welfarism and vitalism, I pointed out that, for many African thinkers, ways of life can merit protection even when they come at *some* cost to well-being and liveliness. While the solidarity element of a communal relationship similarly cannot account for the rightness of participating in rituals, celebrations, and related traditions, the identity element can. Recall the corollaries to the relational moral theory that upon having communed with certain people, one has extra reason to continue doing so (7.3.3) and that one has some reason to respect the way people have actualized their capacity to commune with one another (7.3.4). The former corollary entails that having shared a way of life in the context of a certain culture provides some reason to continue doing so, while the latter entails that even if one has not been part of a certain culture, one has some reason to avoid undermining it and might further have reason to begin participating in it if one can do so at little cost to oneself.

Note that since my conception of communal relationship includes cooperation, it is only practices that have been voluntarily adopted that merit moral consideration. So, for example, clitoridectomy imposed on girls is a tradition that does not merit respect insofar as minors are not competent to make free and informed decisions to undergo the procedure. Furthermore, the relational moral theory does not entail that voluntarily adopted customs should never change—for the solidarity element can sometimes provide all-things-considered reason not to do what identity would prescribe. Since, for all we can tell, killing innocent people did not in fact serve the function of appeasing the gods, considerations of communality on balance entail that the practice was right to challenge and overturn, even if everyone had been accepting of it for a long while.

Finally, let me show that the relational moral theory can account for the more African than Western intuition that it is somewhat wrong (p) to fail to marry and rear children, as opposed to creating a family. When construing this intuition in procreative terms, I pointed out that a prescription to promote the common good, understood as meeting the needs of all, entails that normally one should not increase the number of needy beings (and that a related welfarist principle of maximizing average well-being forbids procreating when these beings would live only marginally worse lives relative to those who already exist). I accepted that a principle to promote liveliness could entail making more children, i.e., more sites of vitality that are also healthy, productive, and the like, where families are instrumentally useful for producing such lives.

Another plausible way to justify marriage and procreation, however, is relationally. In terms of procreation, consider that if people have a dignity, then there is some moral reason to create them. It does not follow that one should maximize the number of people in the world or ignore whether they would have lives worth living. However, in the way that respecting the capacity for communal relationship means actualizing that capacity and enabling others to do so to some degree (7.2.2, 7.3.4), so respecting it means creating it in the first place to some degree (that is naturally difficult to specify). If the final value of an artwork can provide some reason to make one, so can that of a person.

One might baulk at the suggestion that there is some moral reason to procreate, and instead believe there is merely a *pro tanto* duty to look after children who may already exist. If so, the relational theory would account for the duty as one manifestation of the obligation to come closer to others and in particularly intense ways. A similar point applies to marriage, which is plausible to view not as a mere means to fostering liveliness, but instead as a relationship that is worth pursuing as an end. Marriage is one of the most extreme ways to relate harmoniously or communally, and is within reach of most people. It is possible to have greater reason not to sustain a marriage, for instance if one were like Nelson Mandela and able to improve the lives of the public to a noticeable degree. For typical people, though, whose influence cannot extend so far, a relational moral theory counsels them to do a lot in respect of a few. The claim is not that family is a final good that should be promoted, but rather that honouring the capacity to commune provides strong reason for most of us to seek out marriage and the rearing of children as ends.

In sum, I submit that the relational moral theory, in the light of its corollaries, at the very least provides plausible rationales for all sixteen intuitions. In addition, in the case of many of these intuitions, it more easily entails and more powerfully explains them compared to moral theories ascribing basic value to either well-being or vital force. Of course, there could be still other intuitions I have not addressed where these rival theories do much better than the relational moral theory. However, in the absence of such considerations, which I invite other philosophers to present, at this stage I submit there is a strong case for taking a principle of respect for our communal nature to be the best secular and theoretical interpretation of the African tradition. Supposing one wants a principled understanding of sub-Saharan mores that could appeal to a multicultural audience, I conclude that the relational moral theory merits the most consideration.

7.5 Avoiding Common Objections to African Morality

In this last major section of Chapter 7 I begin to turn my attention towards the West, by rebutting objections to African ethics that are frequently made by those who are sympathetic to contemporary Western moral theories. Supposing that the relational moral theory counts as 'African', at least in virtue of capturing the intuitions that are more recurrently held by sub-Saharan philosophers and their peoples than by those in other traditions, I am able to show that it is not African morality as such that is vulnerable to familiar Western criticisms. My point will not be that the criticisms are unfounded, but rather that they need not be viewed as particularly Western; an African ethic can not only avoid these criticisms, but also make good sense of them. In particular, I now demonstrate how rightness as friendliness easily deals with objections pertaining to relativism (7.5.1), corporatism (7.5.2), traditionalism (7.5.3), and hetero/sexism (7.5.4).[12]

[12] Another salient objection to African ethics has been extreme partialism, restricting moral standing to members of one's in-group, but that was already directly addressed above (6.3, 7.3.3). The relational moral theory ascribes a dignity to all those with the capacity to be subjects and objects of communality, meaning the objection does not apply to it.

7.5.1 Concerns about Relativism

Sometimes the communitarianism of the African tradition has been interpreted to mean that a given community's standards constitute what is right or wrong for its members, where different communities have different standards, some of which are intuitively wrong for most twenty-first-century moral philosophers. Some African philosophers have indeed made remarks suggesting that right action or good character is to be identified with behaviour that conforms to a society's norms. For instance, in one place John Mbiti suggests that, according to an African perspective, a person 'acts in ways which are "good" when they conform to the customs and regulations of his community, or "bad" when they do not' (1990: 208). Similarly, a scholar of Shona morality says at one point: 'To become truly human is measured by the acquisition of virtues of character and qualities of personhood that are considered appropriate by the community' (Mungwini 2019: 145; see also Ogbujah 2007: 133–5). Probably most familiar to African philosophers, Ifeanyi Menkiti's (1984) first statement on personhood, i.e., on human excellence or virtue, is often read as saying that developing it is contingent on, if not consists of, one becoming initiated into and supporting the way of life of one's society (e.g., Oyowe 2013; Oyowe and Yurkivska 2014; Manzini 2018).

These remarks suggest the view that right action or good character is relative to different socially held beliefs about how to live, but that differs from my principle that makes a certain way of relating central to right action (7.2–7.3). The former, relativist approach entails that morality is thoroughly subjective and variable, i.e., that there are no (substantive) universally binding ethical norms, insofar as different societies have different beliefs about how to behave. As is well known, relativism has counterintuitive implications, such as that slavery was morally right for nineteenth-century America insofar as a large majority of people in that society had accepted it. However, most contemporary philosophers are inclined to say that slavery was wrong even then, that Americans at that time were mistaken about morality, and that believing something to be right is not sufficient to make it so.

A relativist ethic differs from the relational ethic I advance, which I put forth as an objective principle prescribing respectful treatment of a certain kind regardless of the society in which one lives. By my approach, a given community—that is, a group—would be mistaken about what is right and wrong if it did not conceive of them in terms of communality and anti-sociality, respectively. Just as utilitarians and Kantians nearly always advance their theories as true for everyone, regardless of whether others recognize it or not, so I defend the relational moral theory as having a similar standing, providing a vantage point from which to appraise a given society's standards.

The relational moral theory might seem to include some subjective and variable elements in it, insofar as sharing a way of life, which is part of a communal or harmonious relationship, does of course vary from society to society. However, such contextualism is not relativist. For one, recall that by 'sharing a way of life' or 'identifying with others' I mean particular kinds of interaction, ones that include, amongst other conditions, thinking of oneself as a 'we' and participating with others on the basis of trust and cooperation as opposed to coercion and deception. I do not mean just any custom or tradition. For another, the relevant customs and traditions involved are not deemed to be right simply because a certain society believes them to be; instead, my claim is that they can merit observance and protection when doing so is a way to abide by the objective principle that one must treat people's capacity to commune with respect (7.3–7.4).

7.5.2 Concerns about Corporatism

An approach to morality might not be relativist, but might be collectivist in another problematic way, namely by ascribing moral status only or primarily to groups. Sometimes African communitarianism has been understood to mean that it is a community, for instance a family or clan considered a whole, that alone is owed moral treatment for its own sake or at least to a much greater degree than an individual. Claude Ake seems to hold such a corporatist account of African morality:

> [I]n most of Africa . . . people are still locked into natural economies and have a sense of belonging to an organic whole, be it a family, a clan, a lineage or an ethnic group . . . . All this means that abstract legal rights attributed to individuals will not make much sense for most of our people . . . . Our people still think largely in terms of collective rights and express their commitment to it constantly in their behavior. This disposition underlies the zeal for community development and the enormous sacrifices which poor people readily make for it.
>
> (1987: 9; similar views are suggested by Gbadegesin 1991: 66–7; Kigongo 2002; Nkondo 2007: 90)

Ake believes that individual rights might be appropriate for 'atomized' Western societies, in which people have a sense of their identity as separate from groups, but that they are inappropriate in a context where characteristically African conceptions of the self and of the human good predominate. According to Ake, African peoples 'do not allow that the individual has any claims which may override that of the society' (1987: 5), in contrast to Western ones. An adherent to corporatism could, however, take an even stronger view, namely that individual rights are inappropriate for any society because, objectively speaking, only wholes such as families have the sort of final value that merits respect or promotion from a moral point of view.

I believe that corporatism cannot make any sense of the widespread African belief in human dignity (see 7.3.3), and I have also implicitly argued against corporatism on substantive philosophical grounds when I noted widely shared intuitions about the existence of individual rights not to be used merely as a means for the greater good (6.3, 7.3). In any event, my interpretation of African morality maintains that it is only individuals, such as human beings and certain animals, that are owed moral treatment for their own sake and that such treatment sometimes involves upholding their rights in ways that might come at some cost to family, ethnic group, or culture. It is one thing to believe that morality is a matter of acting for the sake of the community, understood as a given group, and another to hold that it consists of relating to other individuals communally. Killing one innocent without her consent, harvesting her organs, and thereby saving three more lives could well assist the community *qua* group, but it would be a gravely wrongful failure to relate communally towards the one killed.

It is important to see that my relational approach remains consistent with many other characteristic features of African morality. It is not merely a Western ethic clothed in a dashiki, as it were. First, considering individuals to have a moral status is compatible with rejecting individualism of a sort prominent in Western ethics. Although I address this more below (8.3–8.4), above I have said enough to make it clear that relational properties are what ground moral status, for me. Although individuals are owed duties for their own sake, they are so in virtue of their capacity to be a subject and object of a harmonious relationship, which contrasts with an appeal to intrinsic properties such as the ability to reason or to feel pleasure, prominent in Euro-American-Australasian philosophy.

Second, ascribing rights to individuals coheres with maintaining that the correct morality is duty-based as opposed to rights-based. Rights, by my account, simply are duties on the part of agents to treat individuals in certain ways (cf. Metz 2014a), but they do not exhaust our duties, with some duties not being correlated with any rights. For example, one has a duty to give to charity, but no particular charity has a right to one's aid (in the absence of some prior engagement with it).

Third, there is no tension between deeming individuals to have the rights, roughly, not to be treated in very unfriendly ways (unless doing so would counteract their own comparable unfriendliness) and positing strong duties to exhibit solidarity with others. The fact that others may not subordinate or harm an individual whenever it would benefit the group is perfectly consistent with the individual having weighty obligations to go out of her way to aid members of the group.

Fourth, there is similarly no tension between deeming individuals to have rights not to be treated in very unfriendly ways and holding that they have obligations to identify with others. The fact that others may not subordinate or harm an individual whenever it would sustain the integrity of a group is perfectly consistent with the individual having weighty obligations to prize sharing a way of life with others. A principle of respect for the capacity to commune entails that one has moral reason not only to create communal relationships for oneself (7.2) and to sustain them (7.3.3), but also to enable others to create, maintain, and develop theirs (7.3.4), including their cultures (7.4).

7.5.3 Concerns about Traditionalism

Even if an approach to morality is neither relativist nor corporatist, it might be thought to give too much weight to long-standing beliefs and practices, to the detriment of individualist interests in, say, independent judgement or authenticity. Mbiti again appears to be vulnerable to such a criticism when he lists norms that he takes to be central to African cultures:

> [B]e kind, help those who cry to you for help, show hospitality, be faithful in marriage, respect the elders, keep justice, behave in a humble way toward those senior to you, greet people especially those you know, keep your word given under oath, compensate when you hurt someone or damage his property, follow the customs and traditions of your society. (1990: 208–9)

Similarly, note that Yvonne Mokgoro, a South African jurist who has championed the ideal of *ubuntu*, says: 'Group solidarity, conformity, compassion, respect, human dignity, humanistic orientation and collective unity have, among others been defined as key social values of *ubuntu*' (1998: 17). There is little in these quotations suggesting that realizing one's deepest desires or living in a unique way are permitted, let alone that they morally merit pursuit in any respect. Instead, the focus is on the interests and expectations of others, especially those of a certain age, with talk of 'customs', 'traditions', 'conformity', and 'unity' suggesting there is little space for idiosyncratic belief, expression, and association. One philosopher speaking about African communitarianism puts the point starkly indeed: 'The primary requirement of tradition on the part of the individual is total compliance with the specific beliefs and customs prevalent in the community' (Ogbujah 2007: 133; less stark are comments from Masolo 2010: 96, 154, 206, 243). Such an approach would make it compulsory for girls to submit to clitoridectomy, for just one example.

While these and some other interpretations of African morality have been rather traditionalist, mine is not. According to rightness as friendliness, one is more or less obligated to act in friendly ways towards others and enable them to do so, without using extreme unfriendliness as a means (unless to counteract their unfriendliness). That, in turn, at the core amounts to saying that one should coordinate with the ends of innocent parties and strive to improve their objective quality of life, without greatly subordinating or harming anyone in the process. There is nothing in such a prescription that by default requires deference to the judgement or will of elders or to anything traditional more generally. Instead, one is obligated to support others' ends and do what is likely to meet their needs, both of which could be inconsistent with long-standing mores.

To be sure, the relational moral theory does ascribe some moral weight to extant cultures, the thought being that respect for others' capacity to commune means giving some consideration to the way they have actualized that capacity (7.3.4). Concretely, that will mean, amongst other things, giving some priority to local ways of life when teaching the young about matters of culture (see 11.2 below). However, the ways of life for which there is *pro tanto* reason to sustain are only those that have been adopted voluntarily and on an informed basis, not ones imposed by force or by censoring awareness of other ways of life. Individuals must have genuinely *shared* a way of life, in the sense of cooperatively chosen it for themselves, in order for it to merit respect as an expression of their communal nature. Still more, where people have indeed identified with one another, and so chosen lifestyles by coordinating their ends, but these lifestyles are seriously harmful, the other major element of the ethic, solidarity, provides grounds for criticism and revision as insufficiently communal.

7.5.4 Concerns about Heterosexism

Finally, it has been common for those influenced by the West to cast doubt on African morality as it has appeared to have been gendered and homophobic. It does seem as though education and jobs have often been allocated on a sexist basis in 'traditional' African societies. As some African theorists of indigenous education have (apparently approvingly!) pointed out, women have been brought up to look after the home, by cooking and rearing children, while men have been socialized to farm or hunt, defend the clan, and become rulers (Adeyinka and Ndwapi 2002: 18, 21; Adeyemi and Adeyinka 2003: 431–2). In addition, many African politicians and thinkers continue to maintain that homosexuality is 'unAfrican'. Here is an influential expression of this point:

> Homosexuality and lesbianism are deviations from Afrocentric thought because they often make the person evaluate his or her own physical needs above the teachings of national consciousness.... An Afrocentric perspective recognizes its existence but homosexuality cannot be condoned or accepted as good for the national development of a strong people. (Asante 2003: 72, 73)

Needless to say, contemporary Western ethicists tend to reject such heterosexism firmly, as do many other moral philosophers in the twenty-first-century.

Even if it is true that many indigenous African peoples have favoured gendered allocations of opportunities and have censured homosexuality, such practices do not accord with their deepest values. Or at least such practices do not accord with the philosophical interpretation of their morality advanced here, which is focused on respecting human dignity and prizing communality.

Regarding sexism, recall the explanation given above of why it would be unjust not to allow a woman to become a firefighter, supposing she were able to do the job (7.4). Her special capacity to exhibit solidarity with others would be degraded if she was not allowed to help others by fighting fires, while her capacity to be the object of others' solidarity would also be degraded if she was unable to obtain the remuneration, confidence, and other perks of such a job.

Regarding homophobia, those who have gay romantic relationships are not thereby being unfriendly or otherwise failing to relate communally. Those party to such relationships are not thereby viewing anyone in 'us versus them' terms, subordinating others, harming them, or acting out of cruelty. There is simply nothing immoral with homosexuality, if rightness is friendliness. If anything, insofar as romance is an intense realization of communality, there is good moral reason to support gay relationships as they suit people's needs.

In sum, insofar as this section has been successful, it has demonstrated that African philosophers need not appeal to values from other intellectual traditions in order to criticize belief systems and practices that, say, prescribe oppressive or discriminatory norms in the name of community. A principle of respect for people's capacity for relating communally, which is African at least insofar as it best accounts for many mores defended particularly by sub-Saharan philosophers and lived by their peoples, is sufficient to ground duties not to suppress or discriminate against others, without falling into the Western individualism of taking pleasure, autonomy, self-ownership, desert, or the like to be basic.

7.6 Turning to Friendly Competition with the West

My aim in this chapter has been to complete my support for the claim that rightness as friendliness is the most defensible principled and secular interpretation of the African moral tradition. I have supposed that readers share with me the desirability of ascertaining which principle of right action could be found particularly attractive, not only by those steeped in a sub-Saharan culture, but also by a multicultural audience of twenty-first-century philosophers. Although African moralities are characteristically communitarian, Part II has demonstrated that an appeal to community has taken a variety of forms. The most important distinction has been between theories that take communal relationship of some kind to be a mere means to the production of a final value such as well-being or vital force, on the one hand, and those that take it to merit pursuit as an end, on the other. In this last chapter of Part II, I have sought to defend the latter approach, arguing in favour of a certain relational moral theory prescribing respect for our communal nature.

I began by drawing on the interpretation of communal, harmonious, or friendly relationship articulated in Chapter 6, in terms of the combination of identity and solidarity, to propose the idea that moral status is a function of a being's ability to so relate (7.2). If a being can by its nature exhibit identity and solidarity with others and others can do so with it, or, equivalently, if it can befriend and be befriended, as a very large majority of human beings can, then it has a full moral status or dignity. If a being in principle cannot be a subject of such a way of relating, but instead can be related to in that way, in the way many animals can, then it has a partial moral status.

Whatever degree of ability to be party to communal, harmonious, or friendly ways of relating a being essentially has, it is to be respected in virtue of that. I then argued that such a principle of right action entails a number of corollaries, such as that one generally ought not to promote harmony by means of substantial discord directed towards innocent parties, and that, supposing one has already related communally with someone, there is extra moral reason to continue to do so relative to, say, helping strangers with a comparable degree of need (7.3). Next, I routinely appealed to the corollaries in order to argue that the relational moral theory does better at accounting for the key intuitions about right/wrong than rival welfarist and vitalist principles that have been suggested by African philosophers (7.4). Half of these intuitions tend to be held by moral philosophers and the like around the world, while the other half are more often held by those working in the African tradition. If the relational moral theory indeed captures both sets of intuitions best, then there is strong reason to take it to be the principle that is most justified in respect of both an African and global audience. I finally maintained that an additional respect in which rightness as friendliness is strong is that it neatly avoids—and also explains in African terms—stock objections to African morality, such as being collectivist or gendered, which have been made particularly by those influenced by Western values (7.5).

Of principles with a sub-Saharan pedigree, then, the relational moral theory is the one to weigh up against rival Western theories in the rest of the book. In the last major part of it, my aims are to show that the principle of respect for relationality is distinct from the principles of respect for rationality and of utility promotion and, furthermore, is a plausible alternative to, if not an improvement on, them in regard to several controversies in applied ethics.

Here is one broad way to put some of the difference between the moral theory I defend and salient rivals in the Western tradition. The latter would typically instruct friends or family members to treat each other morally, whereas the former would say that morality is roughly a matter of being friendly or familial. Most recent Anglo-American-Australasian philosophical discussion of friendship in relation to morality has viewed the two as distinct values and explored the extent to which they are consistent. For example, there has been debate about whether a moral agent can be a true friend (Badhwar 1991; Friedman 1993) and whether reasons of friendship can outweigh those of morality (Wolf 1982; LaFollette 1995). In contrast to these discussions, the present claim inspired by the African tradition, according to which 'the family is something that is valued for its own sake' (Shutte 2001: 29), is that morality itself is well understood in terms of honouring the capacity to befriend and to be befriended. The African perspective suggests that insofar as two individuals we would call 'friends' or 'family' are wronging one another, then they are not truly being friends to, or familial with, each other. The intuitive way that friends and family members ought to treat each other is a model for all moral relationships, even if the intensity of such bonds is not a realistic or even proper aim when relating to strangers. In Part III of the book I work to show that such a conception of right and wrong is a real contender against familiar Kantian and utilitarian approaches.

PART III

APPLIED ETHICS

Communality as the Ground of Morality *Simpliciter*

8

Environmental Ethics

8.1 Interacting with Nature

In Part II of the book I distinguished between three major principles of right action suggested by the works of literate African philosophers and argued that one is preferable to the other two. In particular, I maintained that when each of the values of well-being, vital force, and communal relationship is construed in secular terms and taken as basic, it has its own logic and implications for morality. I argued that, of these three, a principle grounded on communal relationship is the most justified for being able to capture several moral intuitions, some that are salient amongst thinkers from African cultures and some with global resonance. By my account, a moral agent must respect individuals in virtue of their capacity to be party to relationships of identity and solidarity, with the aim of Part III being to show that this principle is also preferable to dominant Western moral theories in several respects. That is, I now move from arguing that a relational moral theory is the best interpretation of the African tradition to arguing that it is the best moral theory, which happens to be informed by relational ideas salient in the African tradition.

Typically appealing to intuitions that I expect many adherents to the principle of utility or the Kantian principle of respect for autonomy themselves hold, I argue in Chapters 8–12 that rightness as friendliness does better at making sense of right and wrong in a variety of applied contexts. Where it does not clearly do better, I submit that the relational moral theory at least offers an under-appreciated perspective that merits consideration.

The present chapter addresses environmental ethical matters and especially the moral status of animals. Modern Western philosophical accounts of moral status characteristically accord animals either no moral status, as per Immanuel Kant's and many neo-Kantian accounts, or a full moral status, as utilitarianism and related welfarist views straightforwardly do. In contrast, I believe our intuitions clearly indicate that animals have a partial moral status, meaning that they matter for their own sake (*contra* anthropocentrism), but not as much as we do. I argue that the relational moral theory is a more promising way to make sense of such a position than Kantianism and utilitarianism. I do not deny that there might be idiosyncratic variants of the Western principles that can do better than the standard versions I address. My point is that rightness as friendliness can avoid

A Relational Moral Theory: African Ethics in and beyond the Continent. Thaddeus Metz, Oxford University Press.
 DOI: 10.1093/oso/9780198748960.003.0008

ad hoc manoeuvres and ground an under-considered, plausible account of the standing of animals in relation to us, and moreover do so as part of a comprehensive picture of right and wrong.

What Kantianism and utilitarianism have in common is individualism, which in the present context is the view that moral status is constituted by properties intrinsic to an individual, such as her capacity for reason or pleasure. In contrast, I advance a relational account of moral status, which, I argue, easily accords many animals a partial standing, while also promising to solve other long-standing conundrums that plague Anglo-American-Australasian discussions of moral status. Beyond arguing that the relational moral theory provides a novel, attractive explanation of why animals and humans both have moral status that is of the same kind but different in degree, I also contend that it promises to account for additional intuitions that have been difficult to explain in the light of intrinsic properties. For instance, the relational moral theory can explain why a severely mentally incapacitated human being might have a greater moral status than an animal with identical internal features and why a newborn infant plausibly has a greater moral status than a mid- to late-stage foetus.

I begin by saying more than I have up to now about what I mean by 'moral status', noting how this concept affects a variety of issues in environmental ethics, and differentiating between individualist, holist, and relational accounts of it (8.2). In the next section, I return to my initial discussion of moral status (7.2.1), according to which the (markedly) more a being is capable of being party to a communal relationship, the greater its moral status, where I am now a bit more careful and thorough about what this account involves (8.3). Then, I apply the account to many cases, noting respects in which it easily entails and plausibly explains a variety of firm judgements, including about differential standing between human beings and animals, that have evaded theoretical capture up to now by familiar versions of Kantianism and utilitarianism (8.4). Then I address cases pertaining to plants, species, and ecosystems, which are admittedly harder for my theory to accommodate, but for which I contend it has the resources to ground reasonable positions (8.5). I conclude that, in the light of the relational ethic's ability to make sense of many comparatively uncontroversial judgements about how to interact with various parts of nature, it warrants attention as a new and promising form of monism about moral status.

8.2 Neither Individualist nor Holist

A *conception* of moral status is a theory of it, i.e., a comprehensive and basic principle that purports to entail that, and explain in virtue of what, things either have a moral status or lack one. A conception of moral status aims to account for the 'underlying structure' of the myriad things with a moral status by invoking as few properties as possible. Individualism, holism, and relationalism are (abstract) conceptions of moral status, expounded below.

In contrast, the *concept* of moral status is what all these competing conceptions are about; it is that which makes a given theory one of moral status as opposed to something else such as good character or final value. Substantively, the concept of moral status is the idea of us having direct duties towards something for its own sake, i.e., it being owed a duty in its own right. It is also the idea of something that can be wronged by us and hence that can merit guilt on the part of the wrongdoer and compensatory responses from him.

Contrast this idea with us having indirect duties towards something, where we have a moral reason to treat it a certain way but not ultimately because of facts about it. For a standard illustration of the difference, I could have a duty not to break a pen in two, where this duty would be indirect, something owed not to the pen, which cannot be wronged, but instead to its owner. There would be no reason to feel guilt in respect of the pen, but rather for how one treated the owner, with a replacement or restitution being in order.

The way I understand moral status, it in principle admits of degrees. I have two major reasons for thinking of moral standing in gradient terms. First, the existence of degrees of moral status best explains many intuitions about forced trade-offs amongst the urgent interests of different beings. Suppose, for example, that you are driving a bus and have no alternative but to run over either a mouse or a normal, adult human being (who is not seriously threatening anyone). The right thing to do would be to run over the mouse, which seems best explained by the idea that its moral status is not as great. Or if the reader and I were starving along with a pig, and if I had a gun, it would be permissible for me to shoot the pig to feed us, but impermissible for me to shoot the reader to feed myself and the pig. The best explanation of such a judgement is that pigs have a lower standing than persons.

Mice and pigs plausibly matter and do so for their own sake—for instance, if one had to choose between running over a mouse or a blade of grass, one should run over the grass, which is, in turn, best explained by the idea that the standing of the mouse is higher than the grass (which might in fact have no standing). However, if the choice is between the life of a mouse and a person, the reason not to flip a coin and instead to strike the mouse is that, while it might matter morally, its status is not as great as that of a person. Such unavoidable conflicts amongst urgent interests are rare, but thinking about what it would be right to do in such cases and why reveals much about our views of moral standing between certain animals and persons as unequal.

A second reason for thinking in terms of gradations of moral status concerns cases in which we have to decide how to treat beings that have already been killed. If a goat has been accidentally killed, many sympathetic towards the plight of animals would find it permissible not to let it go to waste and would eat it (sometimes called 'roadkill vegetarianism'). Even many vegans/vegetarians will find something respectful in the stereotypical Native American practice of using every part of a buffalo that has been intentionally killed. However, such a practice applied to us would be horrific. The best explanation of the intuitive difference in how we ought to treat goats and buffaloes that have been killed, on the one hand, and human persons who have been killed, on the other, is that the latter have a higher status than the former.

In any event, I work with an understanding of moral status that is not an all-or-nothing matter. I suppose that something can have either a full moral status, which most ethicists around the world ascribe to normal, adult human beings, or a partial moral status, which could also come in further degrees—consider an elephant versus a mollusc. Much environmental ethical reflection about how to treat non-human parts of nature is crucially influenced by what is judged to have a moral status and to what degree.

An individualist account of moral status is the view that properties intrinsic to an entity ground the capacity to be wronged or to be the object of a direct duty. An intrinsic property is one that is internal to an individual and includes no essential positive relation with any other being. Influential forms of individualism include the views that moral status is solely a function of: being the agent (egoism), possessing a soul (monotheism), being alive (vitalism), being an organism (biocentrism), exhibiting the capacity for autonomy or rationality (Kantianism), being able to recollect the past and satisfy desires for future states of affairs (subject of a life theory), and having the capacity for preference realization/frustration or for pleasure/pain (welfarism). Although these properties could exhibit some kind of connection with others, they do not necessarily do so, and hence are intrinsic.

Although a large majority of Western environmental ethical reflection has been individualist, lately there has arisen a holist or corporatist account of moral status. This is the view that the bearers of moral status are groups, where a group is a discrete collection of entities that are near to, similar to, or interdependent with one another. Aldo Leopold's (1968) land ethic is a clear version of holism, as are related views ascribing a standing to ecosystems. From this standpoint, wholes are what ultimately matter and merit moral treatment for their own sake, and not their parts as distinct from them.

Much of the contemporary debate about moral status in Western philosophy has been about whether it is adequately captured by either individualism, holism, or some combination of them, and also about which specific versions of these general perspectives are most attractive. However, there is a third alternative that is under-explored and that is suggested by the African tradition, namely relationalism.

A relational account of moral status is the view that it is constituted by some kind of interactive property between one entity and another. It therefore stands 'in between' individualism and holism. Similar to individualism, a relational account implies that moral status can inhere in things as they exist apart from their membership in groups. A relational approach implies that something can warrant moral consideration even if it is not a member of a group, or at least for a reason other than the fact that it is a member. Similar to holism, though, a relational account accords no moral status to organisms on the basis of their intrinsic properties such as their capacity to reason or to feel pain. A relational theory implies that a being warrants moral consideration only if, and because, it exhibits some kind of intensional (attitudinal) or causal (behavioural) property with regard to another being. It is a being's extrinsic properties that make it count from the moral point of view.

One might reasonably wonder what the difference is between holism and relationalism: is not a group just a kind of relationship? As I understand the meaning of the word 'group', something could constitute a group without it being a 'relationship' in the relevant sense. For example, the species of elephants is a group, but there is not any interaction between elephants in Kenya and those in India and hence no relating. Furthermore, beings could interact with each other in ways that do not constitute a group—say, tourists paying to ride on an elephant for ten minutes. In short, ways of relating essentially involve interaction of some kind between organisms, while groups do not; in addition, groups require some kind of discreteness amongst several parts, while relationships do not. To be sure, there are some groups that are constituted by relationships—say, an ecosystem—but a group's properties and an individual's relational properties are distinct and ground differing accounts of moral status.

It is typical of sub-Saharan philosophers to conceive of morality in terms of community in some way, where holism is one form that communitarianism has taken in respect of moral status. For instance, some believe that groups such as a family or clan have moral rights distinct from those of the individuals who compose them (Ake 1987: 9), while others accord moral status to an animal species as a whole beyond its members (Samuel and Fayemi 2020). A purely holist view faces the problem that it cannot account for the dignity and rights of any individuals (6.3, 7.2–7.3, 7.5.2).

Another form of communitarianism in respect of moral status has been actual relationalism, with those African philosophers who describe harmony and similar relationships as the greatest or highest good (e.g., Tutu 1999: 35) occasioning awareness of the view that it is a relationship itself, not the members of it, that bears moral status.[1] Like holism, such a view cannot account for the strong intuition that we owe duties to certain individuals, such as those not in relation for whatever reason.

[1] In my first paper on African ethics, I myself spoke in a way that suggested this view, but do not recall having done so since then; see Metz (2007: 333, 340).

Finally, there has been a more plausible kind of actual relationalism, which is that an individual has a moral status in virtue of having interacted with other beings in a certain way (e.g., Ikuenobe 2016; Menkiti 2017). However, such a view has the counterintuitive implications that individuals utterly lack a moral status if they for whatever reason have not been subjects of the relevant relationship and that animals and persons would have the same moral status if they had been the objects of the same (say, caring) relationships (7.2.1).

To avoid these concerns, amongst other reasons, I advance a modal relational view, according to which moral status is constituted by an individual's capacity to relate to others communally, regardless of whether the individual has in fact so related. After spelling it out in the next section, I apply it to a range of beings and argue that its implications are attractive.

8.3 The Capacity to Commune as Foundation Redux

When I introduced my account of moral status above (7.2.1) I put it roughly as the view that the more a being is by its nature capable of being party to communal relationships, the greater its moral status. One way to understand this approach is that those beings that in principle can be friendly and be befriended have a dignity, while those that in principle cannot be friendly but can be befriended have a standing, albeit one less than a dignity. In this section I address some unclarities and controversies pertaining to this account of moral status. Specifically, I discuss what is involved in thinking in terms of degrees of moral status (8.3.1), why it is the capacity and not potentiality for communality that matters (8.3.2), when such a capacity is part of a being's nature (8.3.3), and whether this capacity should be construed as essentially tied to characteristic human persons (8.3.4). Often I note that the modal relational approach to moral status could be plausibly understood in different ways and with varying implications for the standing of beings that are quite unlike persons and animals of the sort we find on Earth. Like my earlier discussion of duties to oneself, the following analyses of duties to, say, God and intelligent aliens are more tentative and exploratory. The modal relational approach to moral status is under-developed, and will take time to spell out along a variety of tracks in order to see which approaches are particularly defensible. It is too soon to draw firm conclusions here.

8.3.1 Degrees of Status

A long-standing feature of African moral thought is the idea that there is a 'great chain of being' in the universe, such that different entities have different degrees of final value or moral standing. Traditionally, gradations of moral status have been conceived in terms of quantity (or quality) of vital force, with animals having some and so mattering for their own sake, but humans having a greater vital force and so mattering more (for a recent statement, see Etieyibo 2017).[2] In contrast, I conceive of the hierarchy in terms of capacity to be party to communal relationships.

I mean two things when I say that the 'greater' the capacity to be part of relationships of identity and solidarity, the 'greater' a being's moral status. In the first place, I am indicating, as I have said (7.2), that full moral status goes to those who can be subjects and objects of such a friendly way of relating and partial moral status goes to those that can be merely objects of it. In particular, if an entity by its nature has the ability to identify with others and to exhibit solidarity with them, as well as the ability for us to do so with it, then it has a dignity, a superlative non-instrumental value that must be treated morally by us and specifically with respect. In contrast, if an entity cannot itself befriend others but we can befriend it, it matters morally but lacks a dignity. I have already suggested that it follows from this account that nearly all human beings have a dignity and that many animals have a partial moral status.

In the second place, though, I also mean that large, and not merely incremental, differences in degrees of ability to be either a subject or an object of a friendly relationship constitute differences in moral status. So, for example, if, by virtue of the nature of human beings, elephants, and molluscs, a moral agent were in principle *much* more able to identify with and exhibit solidarity towards elephants than molluscs, then elephants would have a greater moral status than molluscs. The qualification about 'much' is important. Of those who believe in degrees of moral status, most implicitly think of it in a way that can be captured well with an orbit metaphor. Supposing that elephants were only marginally more capable than, say, dolphins of being befriended by a moral agent, then dolphins would intuitively get 'pulled into' the same moral status orbit of elephants. Similarly, if a stereotypical Mother Teresa's capacity to identify with and exhibit solidarity towards others were greater than the reader's, their moral status would be the same; that is, they would both have a dignity, supposing her capacity was not qualitatively superior.

Interesting questions arise at this point about the moral status of God, Jesus, and angels. One puzzle concerns the fact that these are persons who, if they existed, would have a much greater ability to befriend than we do. Would they have a higher moral status than we do?

[2] Counterexamples abound once one interprets vitality in physical terms such as liveliness. For example, it seems to follow that severely depressed persons, persons debilitated by cancer, and those with severe physical disabilities count less from the moral point of view than persons who lack these impediments, while sloths seem to matter less than lemurs. Although I am open to the ideas that a person such as God could conceivably matter more than us and that some animals do matter more than other animals, I do not draw the lines in places where it appears the vitalist must.

One way to answer would be to 'bite the bullet' and answer in the affirmative. Perhaps because of their much greater capacity for other-regard, they would be greater than us and entitled to more respect, with many religious people inclined to accept that implication. Another way to answer would be to maintain that, upon reaching a certain threshold of the capacity to be a subject of communality, no being has any moral status greater than any other one—the approach of Immanuel Kant and typical neo-Kantians such as John Rawls (1999: sec. 77). I am unsure which answer to provide at this stage, and simply note the options to consider further.

A second puzzle about a spiritual being such as God concerns the fact that God is a person who might seem unable to be the object of communal relationship, at least with us. How could we improve God's quality of life? How could we sympathize with God when God would lack a biology that is presumably essential for feelings? If we could not, does that mean God would lack a dignity by my account?

Again, there are two natural options available, and I currently lack a definitive view about which to prefer. One is to revise the approach to moral status by maintaining that, although we could not commune with God as an object to an appreciable extent, it is sufficient for dignity to be able to be a subject of communality with us, as God of course would be to the utmost degree possible. The second option is to retain the current approach but to argue that it might in fact be possible for us to relate to God communally as an object. It does seem as though one could enjoy a sense of togetherness with God and work to advance God's purposes, for instance. Furthermore, if God would have emotions such as being glad or displeased, there would seem to be a way to improve God's quality of life and to do so for God's sake. These are fascinating issues, but, as they are not essential to the question of how to interact with beings in nature (at least given a secular background), I now set them aside.

8.3.2 Capacity versus Potential

Returning to physical beings, let us consider the issue of whether, instead of focusing on the capacity for friendly relationship as the relevant ground of moral status, I should rather focus on the potential for it. Both a tree and a human embryo lack the capacity for friendliness; they cannot by their nature share a life with others or care for others' quality of life, and nor can others do so with them. However, the human embryo has the potential for such ways of relating, whereas the tree does not. In time the embryo can become a different sort of being that can commune and be communed with, but the tree cannot. There are two sorts of modality from which to choose, and I need to motivate the choice of capacity over potentiality.

I deem capacity to be the crucial feature precisely because of, amongst other things, my prior stance on the abortion debate. My intuitions are that the 'morning after pill' and abortion are permissible in the very early stages of pregnancy, that infanticide is wrong, and that worse than both is murder of a person (which I try to defend below in 8.4 and 9.5). In addition, I find compelling the point that, despite a human being's skin cells having the potential to develop into her clones, the skin cells lack a moral status.

I realize that these intuitions are more contested than many others in this book, and so do not want to close off theoretical avenues at this stage. Those who believe that abortion of a human foetus in the first month of pregnancy is no less wrong than murder of an adult human person, or that human skin cells have a dignity, and who furthermore find a modal relational theory broadly attractive might appeal to the potential to be the subject and object of communality (cf. Molefe 2020).

8.3.3 The Nature of a Being

Above I noted that the relevant sense in which a being 'can' be party to communal relationships is not tied to contingencies (7.2.1). For example, the fact that an animal is hiding in the wild and so is unknown to us does not mean that we 'cannot' benefit it in the relevant sense, and the fact that we are asleep does not mean that we 'lack the ability' to cooperate with others. Often appealing to such intuitive examples of accidental conditions will be enough to apply the modal relational account. However, other times drawing a specific conclusion from it will require a contested account of when a being necessarily or essentially has the ability to relate communally in certain ways.

A key distinction here is between an intrinsic and extrinsic account of a being's nature, a metaphysical issue that parallels, but is logically distinct from, the individualist versus relational distinction in respect of moral standing (8.2). Take a late-stage foetus, for example. What is essential to it? By an intrinsic account of its nature, it is identical to certain biological features, perhaps with a certain history. In contrast, by an extrinsic account of its nature, it is identical to a being with certain biological features, perhaps with a certain history, that is furthermore in a mother's womb and lives in a certain society and environment. These metaphysical distinctions can make a moral difference when specifying how a being might 'by its nature' be able to commune in certain ways.

With most of the African tradition, I will at times appeal to an extrinsic metaphysics, maintaining, for instance, that there is indeed something essentially different about a foetus and a newborn infant, despite having identical intrinsic properties. Despite having striven to defend such a metaphysics elsewhere (Metz 2018), I lack the space to do so here. These claims are not as contested as those about the existence of ancestors and witches, for philosophers from a number of other non-African cultures, particularly those in East Asia, will find them convincing (see, e.g., Nisbett 2003). However, an extrinsic account of a being's nature remains controversial, particularly to a Western audience, and so the conclusions I draw from it are more tentative.

8.3.4 With Whom to Relate

A final outstanding question about the view that moral status varies according to the capacity for communal relationship is with what the being must be able to relate. I have been supposing that a being must be able to relate with us, i.e., characteristic human persons. I am inclined to hold, first, the view that a being can be a subject of communality if and only if it can (by its nature and ours) befriend us, and, second, the view that a being can be an object of communality if and only if we can (by our nature and its) befriend it. Each view admittedly faces prima facie challenges.

With regard to being an object of communality, why not adopt the alternative view that a being has a partial moral status insofar as some agent or other can identify with it and exhibit solidarity towards it? Suppose that we could not commune with a being but some other, alien kind of person could. Why should the focus be on its ability to relate with us? Is this not an unwelcome focus on humanity these days?

My answer at this stage is to urge the reader to think carefully about the concept of moral status and what it would really mean for us to be unable to commune with a being. For something to have a moral status is for a moral agent to owe it dutiful treatment for its own sake. In this book I am strictly interested in our moral duties, those of human persons as the relevant moral agents, with the duties of possible Martian or Vulcan persons being a large, distinct matter for another engagement.[3]

Now, if characteristic human persons are utterly unable by their nature to relate communally with another entity, it is in fact plausible to think that it lacks a moral status. If we cannot commune with a being because of its nature, that means that we, no matter what we do, cannot advance its ends or improve its quality of life. Why might that be? One straightforward thought is that it is an animal too distant for us to influence, thousands of light years away on another planet. Now, ought implies can, meaning that you can have a moral reason to act in a certain way towards a being only if it is possible for you to perform the action. If there is truly nothing you could do to further the ends of these alien animals or to improve their quality of life, then it is plausible to maintain that you have no duties in respect of

[3] Although I am not sympathetic to an earthly relativism, instead believing that there are some substantive moral norms that apply to all human persons (7.5.1), I am more open to an interplanetary relativism, given the plausibility of a causal theory of reference for moral terms (cf. Metz 2013a: 88–96).

them and hence that they lack a moral status. You could still describe them as 'valuable' beings or 'good for their own sake', but you could not plausibly ascribe the specific label of 'moral status', which carries normative, and not merely evaluative, connotations.

Consider, now, my suggestion that the capacity to be a subject of communality means not merely being able to identify with and exhibit solidarity towards some being or other, but us in particular. Again, one might not want to make a being's full moral status depend on its ability to relate as subjects to us, but rather on its general ability to commune, perhaps just with members of its own alien species.

My reply again appeals to the concept of moral status, as a normative notion and not merely an evaluative one, as well as to the details of the case. If these alien persons are unable to commune with us, why is that? If, like the alien animals case, they are simply too far away to cooperate with us or to help us, then we are too far away to cooperate with them or to help them, and so it is likewise plausible to deny that they have a full moral status. If we cannot influence them, we can have no duties towards them. The case suggests that we should differentiate the concept of dignity from that of full moral status, which I have admittedly treated as equivalent up to now; perhaps these aliens would have a dignity, understood as a certain kind of value, but not a full moral status.

However, what if, somehow, alien persons were here on Earth, and we faced a situation in which we could advance their ends and promote their good, but they could not do so with us despite being able to do so with one another? I find the case difficult to make concrete and to appraise. It might be enough reason to alter my approach, by according a full moral status to a being able to commune with some beings or other, even if not with us. However, here is some reason for resisting such a change. Suppose you had to choose between rescuing a member of an alien species that was capable of being friendly towards us and one that was incapable of that. Would you not have more reason to save the former than the latter? The thought experiment is hard to pin down, but insofar as you would favour rescuing the relatable species, a reasonable explanation of why that would be appropriate is that the ability to relate with us has some importance. A further point to make is that even if another person lacked a dignity for being unable to be the subject of communal relationship with us, below I explain how it could still have a partial moral status that is greater than what animals characteristically have (8.4), which might be enough to account for the standing of persons who could not commune with us but with whom we could commune.

As I currently interpret the modal relational account of moral status, humanity admittedly plays a central role in determining which beings have it and which do not. However, the relational approach decidedly does not warrant the 'anthropocentric' label, when that is understood to mean that only human beings or even persons matter from the moral point of view. My approach clearly entails that many animals have a moral status—that is, are owed duties because of facts about themselves—insofar as we are capable of enjoying a sense of togetherness with them, advancing their goals, making them better off, and doing so out of sympathy and for their sake. Roughly speaking (and not meaning to flout the findings of Chapter 2 regarding is and ought), since we can come closer to many animals, we have some moral reason to do so. I now point out that the property of being able to relate to characteristic human beings appears essential to entail and explain a variety of intuitions about differential degrees of standing between a variety of beings. These are strong advantages for the modal relational account of moral status.

8.4 Humans and Animals

Here I consider what the modal relational account of moral status from the previous section entails in a variety of contexts for earthly organisms, bringing out its strengths in relation to dominant Euro-American-Australasian approaches, which are individualist. I first apply the theory to 'normal' cases of human persons and animals (8.4.1) and afterwards to 'abnormal' or 'marginal' cases of human beings that are not persons and human persons who cannot be a subject of communal relationship (8.4.2). I conclude that communality provides a unitary ground for plausible views about moral status, and particularly about gradations of it, held by an array of entities.

8.4.1 'Normal' Cases of Humans and Animals

When it comes to human persons, it follows from the modal relational account that (nearly) all of them have a full moral status or a dignity that merits respectful treatment. According to it, full moral status inheres in beings that by nature can be both subjects and objects of communal relationships, and typical humans not only are capable of being identified with and being cared for by others, but also can identify with others and care for them. The account grounds a robust impartiality, where virtually all human beings have an equal standing from the moral point of view (7.3.3).

When it comes to *entailing* the full moral status of human beings, the theory does no worse than Kantianism, the view that moral status is constituted by a being's capacity for rationality, and utilitarianism, the view that moral status is constituted by a being's capacity to experience pleasure/pain or for preference satisfaction/frustration. Characteristic human persons indeed manifest these properties to no less a degree than they do the capacity to relate communally.

However, there are reasons to think that the relational account of human moral status is *explanatorily* more attractive than at least some of the Western individualisms. First off, utilitarians deny that dignity is a genuine moral category; while they readily think in terms of a being warranting moral consideration for its own sake, they do not believe that any being has, in virtue of its nature, a superlative non-instrumental value, respect for which grounds basic human rights. However, many of those who believe that we have a full moral status conceive of it in terms of being in a position to affect beings with dignity, with the relational approach being able to account for that intuition. It may be interpreted to say that humans have a dignity warranting respect in virtue of their natural ability to be both a subject and object of a friendly relationship. The moral reason to avoid killing human persons is that they have a superlative capacity to befriend and be befriended.

Adherents to Kant's and Kantian views, of course, also believe in the dignity of characteristic human beings. Although Kant himself maintains that the capacity to act for a moral reason is definitive of dignity (1797: Ak. 423, 434–5), morality is not strictly other-regarding for him; if there were just one agent alone in the world, the categorical imperative would still apply to her and she would have duties to herself. Such an account of morality would be somewhat heretical in the African tradition.[4] Similarly, contemporary Kantian accounts usually ground moral status on a being's more general capacity for reasoned deliberation, with no essential tie to morality or other-regard. Unlike Kant's and neo-Kantian approaches, the relational account entails that a rational being who can, say, neither think of himself as a 'we' nor act for the sake of others lacks a full moral status, which many readers—though, I accept, not all—will find intuitive. I discuss such cases more below (8.4.2).

For now I point out that, *contra* Kantianism, part of what gives us a full moral status by the relational account is our capacity to be an object of communality. According to it, when someone acts in an unfriendly way towards us, reducing our quality of life, he is thereby degrading us, treating our ability to be related to in a friendly way with disrespect. Rape, for instance, is degrading not merely because of the lack of consent, but also because of the physical and psychological pain involved as well as the harm done to the capacity to enjoy romantic relationships. Kantians will reply that the degradation consists of frustrating a person's highly ranked ends of living without pain and with intimacy, but that cannot be correct since frustrating a person's highly ranked end of making everything she can the colour pink would not be as degrading.

Turning to animals, along with most in the contemporary field of ethics, I believe that it is possible to wrong certain animals themselves, and that we owe direct duties to many kinds of them. Recall that if one has to run over either a plant or a mouse with one's vehicle, one morally ought to run over the plant, a good explanation of which is that the mouse matters for its own sake. There are two ways to be party to a communal relationship, to be either a subject or object of

[4] I admittedly have flirted with duties to oneself, e.g., in terms of treating oneself in a friendly way, which would align my view with Kant's in this respect (see 7.3.5).

it, and many animals clearly have the capacity to be objects, i.e., they are capable of being befriended by us. Characteristic humans are naturally able to think of themselves as bound up with certain animals, to adjust their actions to comport with the animals' teleological behaviour, to act in ways likely to improve their quality of life, and to do so for their sake and consequent to sympathy.

Animals with whom we can relate in these ways have a partial moral status, meaning that instructions to avoid anti-social behaviour towards the innocent as well as to commune with them (7.2–7.3) apply to them. We generally must not exhibit extreme unfriendliness or enmity towards animals we could befriend, and being indifferent towards their good, too, could be wrong, when going out of one's way to help them would not take away much from human persons (which have a greater moral status) and one could do a lot of good at little cost to oneself. In general, the urgent interests of a being with moral status should not be traded off for the trivial interests of another being, even one with a higher moral status. So, if the urgent interests of animals that can be objects of communal relationship with us are at stake, it would be wrong to sacrifice them to satisfy our trivial interests. Such an approach forbids a wide array of practices that are commonly done by human beings, such as hunting for sport, eating meat for the taste, and testing cosmetic products.

Not all animals are in fact equal, however; it follows from the relational account of moral status that there are gradations of it amongst them. There is evidence that some animals, such as chimpanzees and gorillas, are capable of being subjects of communality to some rudimentary extent, at least in that they can coordinate their behaviour, exhibit sympathy, and act consequent to it (e.g., de Waal 1996). Although I do not currently believe that these other-regarding capacities are sufficiently robust to ground a dignity, it is surely apt to deem these and other creatures with such abilities to be 'higher' members of the animal kingdom, as they are in fact commonly called. Below them are animals that are utterly incapable of being subjects of a communal relationship (either with us or any other being), but have a substantial ability to be objects of one with us. We are clearly able to identify with and exhibit solidarity towards giraffes, cows, pigs, goats, sheep, deer, buffaloes, dogs, cats, ferrets, and mice. Further down are animals that are perhaps capable of a better or worse life and so could be objects of a friendly relationship with us, but that are less able to be objects of one than other animals because of their comparative lack of goal-directed behaviour or sentience, for instance molluscs and worms. Finally, there are some animals that, by the relational approach, lack a moral status altogether since, for all we can tell, they utterly lack both intentionality and a (welfarist) good, presumably mosquitos and bacteria.[5] If moral considerations

[5] Some suggest that factors besides sentience or even well-being more generally can ground a being's moral status. For instance, Martha Nussbaum (2006) argues that the capacity to be a good member of

pertain to the treatment of these beings, they are indirect, obtaining because of what the treatment of them means for some other being.

Insofar as the reader would, like me, save a chimpanzee before a mouse, a mouse before a worm, and a worm before a bacterium, modal relationality should be found attractive for according them differential standings. Kantianism can draw none of these distinctions, as none of these animals is a person. Utilitarianism also cannot do so, for if a chimpanzee and a mouse both feel pain to a comparable degree, their status is the same. In contrast, the relational account naturally entails that various members of the animal kingdom have different degrees of moral status, since their capacity to be party to communal relationships with us varies to qualitatively different degrees. Where the urgent interests of two animals cannot both be satisfied, a moral agent ought to consider how great its (partial) standing is.

However, the same principle entails that the urgent interests of human persons must be satisfied before those of animals, in cases of unavoidable conflict. Recall the intuition that it would be wrong to shoot a person if essential to feed a pig but not wrong to shoot a pig if essential to feed a person. The modal relational account makes sense of that judgement by according the person a full moral status in the light of his ability to commune and to be communed with by us, but the pig a partial moral status given its mere ability to be communed with by us. The idea that human persons have a greater moral status than animals is a persistent intuition, even amongst many of those sympathetic to animal welfare and rights, and invoking degrees of capacity for communality provides a common foundation for ascribing differential degrees of moral status to both kinds of beings.

In my view, a glaring weakness amongst the prominent Western accounts of moral status is that they cannot entail all the following: (a) most human persons and many animals have a moral status; (b) human persons have a greater moral status than animals; (c) both human persons and animals have moral status for a unitary reason. On (a), I find it incontrovertible that at least some animals have a moral status, and even those who question the existence of animal *rights* and defend practices such as eating animals and experimenting on them often admit at some point that they do (e.g., Frey 1983). The best explanation of why it is wrong to put a live cat in a microwave merely for the thrill ultimately has to do with facts about the cat, not solely the agent or other persons; Kant's ethic and similarly indirect views are simply mistaken on that score.

its kind grounds moral status to no less a degree than the capacity to live a good life. However, even she maintains that in order for the former, perfectionist good to matter morally, it must inhere in a being with the latter, welfarist good. With Nussbaum, I suggest that exhibiting solidarity with a being can involve acting for its perfectionist good, particularly as an other-regarding being, but if and only if it also has a welfarist good. Such a qualification most easily enables one to exclude, say, knives and cancers from being objects of moral status.

Although utilitarianism accounts for (a), standard forms of it fail with respect to (b). It and related welfarist views (e.g., Horsthemke 2018) entail that many animals have the same moral status as human persons, for both kinds of beings are capable of pleasure/pain, preference satisfaction/frustration, or more generally of having better/worse lives. In reply, some utilitarians argue that people's 'global' desires, with regard to their lives as a whole, are more important than 'local' ones, giving them priority over the severely mentally incapacitated or animals in cases of conflict (Singer 1993: 121–34). But what if a person, such as Galen Strawson, lacked such desires, or were even incapable of them? Another utilitarian reply would be to invoke John Stuart Mill's distinction between higher and lower pleasures, ascribing a higher moral status to those beings capable of higher pleasures. But what if a person were born incapable of experiencing pleasure upon doing such things as undertaking scientific enquiry and reading poetry?

A similar objection applies to Tom Regan's (2004) subject of a life criterion, according to which a being has moral status roughly insofar as it has attitudes towards the past and the future, as well as Paul Taylor's (1986) biocentric view, which prescribes respect for all living organisms. These individualist accounts also entail the equal moral status of human persons and many animals, something that I, and I presume most readers, find counterintuitive, at least upon reflecting on what to do when the urgent interests of both kinds of beings are in unavoidable conflict.

Finally, there are accounts of moral status that entail (a) and (b) but that are pluralist and hence do not satisfy (c). For instance, Christopher Stone (1985) and Mary Anne Warren (2003) hold that several features ground moral status of differing degrees, ranging from rationality to sentience to actual relationships to landscapes to species. However, all things being equal, a view is more desirable the greater its simplicity and explanatory power, meaning that a plausible monist theory would be preferable.

Modal relationality accounts well for (a), (b), and (c): it appeals to a singular property to ground moral status that entails differing degrees of it between humans and many animals and also between various classes of animals. I take the ability to account for gradations of standing between human persons and animals as well as between different kinds of animals to be major points in favour of the communal account relative to dominant Western ones. Even adherents to the Kantian or utilitarian theories of moral status typically feel the pull of intuitions about differential standing, some evidence of which is the attempt to accommodate them by appeal to, say, indirect duties or differential kinds of well-being, respectively. The modal relational approach is a realistic contender in the light of its natural ability to ground judgements of different degrees of moral status both between us and animals and within the animal kingdom.

I have the most to say about moral status, but comparatively little about what it entails for right action, for many of its implications are familiar. For example, I have said that vegetarianism is morally required when it is possible to satisfy the urgent interests of a person in health without killing and harming an animal, and also said that hunting for sport and cosmetic testing are forbidden since these sacrifice an animal's urgent interests for our trivial ones. In addition, I note that the ascription of moral status to so many entities on the planet grounds many obligations in respect of environmental matters. Those in a position to make a real difference to global warming and ocean acidification, for just two examples, owe it not just to present and future generations of human persons, but also to many animals, to effect change. It is unlikely that the urgent interests of present human persons require the burning of fossil fuels in the way we currently do, where doing so is harming the urgent interests of others with full and partial moral status and hence is wrong.

However, there is one implication of relationality that is unusual, which is that our duties in respect of animals would have us come closer to them. More specifically, by the relational moral theory we appear to have duties of some weight to identify with and exhibit solidarity towards animals capable of being related to in that way, such as elephants and wolves (not so much insects and bacteria). That, in turn, appears to permit, if not require, domestication, amongst other ways of integrating our lives with animals, such as routinely entering what had been wild spaces. Many will baulk at that judgement.

In reply, I can say that often supporting an animal's intentionality would mean leaving it alone; a bird naturally seeks to fly and inhibiting its ability to do so would be subordinating. In addition, in those instances where it is possible to interact with animals in ways that comport with their aims and foster a sense of togetherness, many times doing so would risk reducing their quality of life, viz., either harming them or reducing their liveliness. Where identity would come at serious cost to solidarity, considerations of communal relationship would plausibly entail that we have most reason to leave them in the wild.

However, there are admittedly occasions when it would be possible not only to share a way of life with animals, but also to do so in ways that would not compromise our ability to care for their quality of life. And, here, I am inclined to bite the bullet and say that there is nothing inherently wrong with integrating our lives into theirs—in the name of love. When we can interact with animals on a trusting basis, meet their needs, and foster their liveliness, as it appears we often can with cats and dogs, then the communal ethic entails that it is permissible to do so. Pets can indeed be parts of a family, where familial relationships merit pursuit as ends, by the relational moral theory.

8.4.2 'Abnormal' Cases of Humans and Animals

There are further gradations of moral status that I intend to capture, which are between 'normal' cases of human beings and 'abnormal' or 'marginal' cases of them, on the one hand, and between abnormal cases of human beings and animals with a partial moral status, on the other. I advance the position that human beings that cannot be subjects of a friendly relationship have a lower moral status than those who can, but that they have a higher moral status than animals that likewise cannot be subjects of one.[6]

Recall that a contrasting case between the relational approach and at least contemporary Kantianism is a rational being capable only of self-regard. My suggestion is not that individuals who have acted wrongly have a lower moral status than us, but rather that individuals who are utterly incapable of other-regard do, whereas recent Kantian views have different implications. Although the relational approach probably cannot claim a definitive advantage relative to an individualist Kantianism with respect to this sort of case, I submit that the former is not much, if any, worse off than the latter. First off, note that an appeal to communality need not entail that autistic humans, or at least 'higher'-functioning ones such as the well-known Temple Grandin, lack a dignity or full moral status. While these individuals might be incapable of empathetic awareness and sympathetic emotion, the evidence indicates that they are typically capable of additional forms of other-regarding behaviour (Kennett 2002). They are able to coordinate their actions with others, to do what is likely to make others better off, to act for the sake of others, and so on. Given the orbital account of degrees of moral status I advanced above (8.3.1), the relational approach entails that many autistic individuals have a dignity in the way we do.

However, considerations of modal relationality do appear to entail that *extremely* autistic, psychopathic, and mentally incapacitated human beings lack a dignity comparable to ours, supposing they are indeed by nature utterly incapable of being subjects of a friendly relationship. The Kantian, of course, is also committed to the view that severely mentally incapacitated human beings lack a dignity. So, the nub of controversy between the Kantian approach and the relational one appears to concern extremely autistic or psychopathic persons.

It might be that an extreme psychopath can in fact be a subject of a friendly relationship to some degree, viz., by virtue of being able to coordinate with and to aid others, even if we imagine that he cannot do so consequent to other-regarding propositional attitudes such as 'we-ness' or sympathy. Suppose, however, that this is not enough to count as being a subject of communality to the requisite extent for a dignity, or consider an *extraordinarily* autistic individual who by his nature cannot even engage in these kinds of behaviours. The relational view entails that, although these individuals would lack a dignity equal to ours, their moral status would be higher than that of animals. These persons would have the capacity for being an object of a friendly relationship with us to a *much greater* degree than that had by other beings such as mice and elephants. Compared with animals,

[6] I save discussion of embryos, foetuses, and newborns for the next chapter (9.5).

characteristic human beings are more able to include 'deformed' humans, such as extremely autistic, psychopathic, and incapacitated individuals, in a 'we', cooperate with them, act in ways likely to improve their quality of life, exhibit sympathetic emotions with them, and act for their sake. We do much more for the autistic, psychopathic, and incapacitated than we do animals, which is *evidence* of a greater ability to make them an object of a friendly relationship and hence a higher moral status than what animals have.

The modal relational account of moral status is interesting and worthy of consideration for ascribing a 'middle' standing to the extremely autistic, psychopathic, and incapacitated. Neither Kant nor contemporary Kantians can consistently grant any moral status to the severely incapacitated; at least Kantians seem to have to ascribe full moral status—indeed, a dignity—to individuals who can reason but are utterly incapable of other-regard; and the utilitarian would naturally grant full moral status to all of them, as they are comparably capable of pleasure or preference satisfaction. The relational approach presents a plausible alternative of granting to these individuals a greater moral status than animals have, but a lesser one than the dignity of normal humans.

Notice that the relational account is to be credited with providing a reasonable explanation of why members of two different species that have the same internal properties, viz., animals and severely mentally incapacitated humans, might have a different moral status. It grounds a real reason to doubt the influential 'argument from marginal cases', the rationale that at least some animals are entitled to as much moral status as humans since the two are biologically similar (e.g., Singer 1993; Dombrowski 1997). My approach entails that even if there is no intrinsic difference between two beings, there could be a relational difference between them, *qua* capacity to have a life that is shared with, and cared for by, characteristic human beings, that grounds differential degrees of moral status.

My view is not that it is impermissible to eat a grandmother with dementia but permissible to eat an animal with the same intrinsic properties. In fact, I believe that, because of their moral status, it is usually wrong to kill animals if not necessary for us to remain alive and healthy, e.g., for the fairly trivial interest of taste. My point is rather that if all human beings have a greater moral status than animals, this would be well explained by the idea that we are able to commune with the former more readily than the latter. And such an approach well explains the intuition that in cases where one cannot save the lives of both a human being and an animal, one ought to favour the former, even supposing they have similar internal traits.

8.5 Plants, Species, and Ecosystems

In the final section of this chapter I address beings in the natural environment other than humans and animals, and, not coincidentally, respond to two major objections that are likely to be made to the modal relational account of moral status. To some readers, the glaring weaknesses of this view are that it is, first, anthropocentric and, second, unable to account properly for ecological concerns. However, I reply that the first objection is simply incorrect, while the second is questionable.

The relational approach might appear to be anthropocentric in that it analyses moral status in terms of certain human capacities. To be able to be an object of a friendly relationship, on this view, is construed as the capacity to relate to characteristic human beings in a certain way, i.e., for them to be able to befriend it. There is an irreducible appeal to humanity in its conception of moral status. However, this approach is not anthropocentric in the clearly objectionable forms. First, I reiterate that it does not entail that non-human beings have a merely instrumental value for us or lack moral status altogether. The relational account instead entails that many animals have a moral status, which means that they are the proper objects of ethical concern in their own right and have urgent interests that may not be frustrated for the sake of at least our trivial ones. If a being is something that, by its nature and ours, we can identify with and exhibit solidarity towards, then we have some moral reason to do so and for its sake. Lots of animals meet these criteria, usually making it wrong to trick them, cause them serious pain, or reduce their liveliness in order for us to look at them, enjoy a taste, or adorn ourselves.

It is true that, in cases where the urgent interests of human beings and animals cannot both be satisfied, the relational theory directs one to meet those of human beings (as well as any other being that can be a subject and object of communality). However, that is frankly a clear advantage of the view. Would you really shoot a person to feed the pig, or refuse to kill a pig if necessary to feed a person? Would you truly think it morally appropriate to flip a coin to decide whether to run over a person or a mouse with your car? I do not believe that saving human lives in these cases counts as 'anthropocentrism' in the way the word has most often been used.

Note, too, that the relational view is not speciesist in the usual sense, for it does not imply that human life *qua* human constitutes moral status. The theory is capacity-based, making it an empirical matter to determine not only which beings have the capacity to identify with and exhibit solidarity towards us (perhaps chimpanzees and gorillas fit the bill), but also which beings can be the objects of such a relationship with us. The relational view admittedly conceives of the relevant capacity as including reference to humanity, but, on balance, I submit that it is appropriate, given enquiry into a conception of moral status for human agents and the unique ability of the theory to account for an array of intuitive gradations of moral status between beings.

At this point, a number of friends of an ecological perspective will provide prima facie reason to find the relational approach to moral status unsatisfactory. For one, the theory entails that all plants—even Redwoods—lack a standing, so that any duties with regard to them will be indirect. Although there is a sense in which a tree can 'flourish', as Stone (1972) helped make clear to the field long ago, that is a matter of being able to be a good instance of its kind, and not being able to live a good life, which is necessary to be an object of solidarity (see note 5). For another, groups such as species and ecosystems are incapable of being subjects of friendship, and also cannot be objects of it, as they are not individuals with intentionality and lives that can be better or worse off. In this day and age, when concerns about damage to the non-human, natural world loom large, one might find the relational approach to be outmoded.

In reply, I suspect that these kinds of ecological concerns can be plausibly captured without ascribing moral status to plants and groups. To put it tersely, not all final value has a moral standing. As Robert Nozick points out (1989: 163–4, 170–1), scientific theories and the game of chess are organic unities and for that reason plausibly have a worth that is not merely instrumental, but it is implausible to think that they are ever the direct object of moral obligations. We do not owe them anything. Even if the modal relational approach to moral status denies it to plants and groups, there could be other respects in which these things are good for their own sake and so warrant admiration, protection, promotion, etc. Furthermore, if morality is not invariably overriding, there could even be situations in which one has the most practical reason on balance to attend to these final values at some cost to the interests of beings with a moral status.

Here is some reason to believe that a tree and an ecosystem do in fact lack moral standing, even though they might well be good for their own sake in virtue of, say, traits such as beauty or complexity. Consider how a person (or at least one not yet in the grip of a theory) would likely feel if she destroyed a tree or an ecosystem. I submit that, if she would feel guilt, she would most likely feel guilt with respect to the animals or humans affected by this behaviour, and she would probably not feel guilt with respect to the tree or the ecosystem as such. She would not feel as though she owes these things compensation but rather the communal beings affected by the destruction done to these things. And if others were to force her to engage in reparative work in respect of the tree or ecosystem, it would not be for their sake but rather for the sake of, say, future generations of people and other intentional creatures with needs.

I accept that a person could well feel shame with respect to the way she has damaged a tree such as a Redwood. However, guilt is a much more reliable marker of moral status than shame. People often feel shame about their unattractive appearance, or their impoverished condition, or their having been the victim of wrongdoing—conditions that are quite unrelated to their having violated moral norms, at least those concerning how to treat other beings.

I also accept that it might be useful for people to think that trees and ecosystems have a moral standing. The climate crisis is in full swing, and pretty much anything that will stop it is to be welcomed. However, even if there is pragmatic reason for people to believe that certain things have a moral status, in this book I am strictly interested in what there is evidential reason to believe about the topic.

In any event, I am most concerned to replace utilitarian and Kantian accounts of moral status, and so to account better than they do for the sorts of considerations to which they straightforwardly apply, which are roughly organisms. Perhaps it is incomplete to accord moral status to only humans and animals (in respect of what is on Earth), so that the relational approach needs supplementation. So long as I have shown that utilitarianism and Kantianism should be supplanted in respect of organisms, much will have been accomplished.

To bring this chapter to a close, I note that those deeply committed to a version of holism or individualism, or even a combination of them, may well not be convinced by its analysis. My aim has not really been to get anyone to change her mind, and not even to show conclusively that appeals to welfare and autonomy are inadequate. My goals have instead been the more limited ones of articulating a new, modal relational account of moral status and showing that it gives standard Western theories a run for their money when it comes to accounting for a variety of widely shared intuitions about what has moral status and to what degree. Many of these intuitions are captured neither by holism nor individualism and have lacked a firm philosophical foundation up to now. Of particular importance here is the relational theory's apparently unique ability to account for the ideas that humans and animals have a moral status grounded on the same property that differs in degree and that severely mentally incapacitated humans have a greater moral status than animals with the same internal properties.

9

Biomedical Ethics

9.1 Treating Bodies and Minds

Much of the field of biomedical ethics has traditionally been divided into three parts: issues about how doctors and nurses ought to interact with patients, how such medical professionals ought to make decisions in respect of life-and-death controversies, and how to allocate scarce medical resources justly. In this chapter I address the first two large clusters of topics, my aims being to draw out the relational moral theory's implications for interpersonal matters in a healthcare context and to show that they are plausible alternatives to those of familiar forms of utilitarianism and Kantianism.

Since my aim is to develop and defend a certain moral theory, and since it is apt to evaluate like with like, I contrast it with these dominant Western moral theories. It is true that a notable portion of the bioethics literature does not appeal directly to utilitarianism and Kantianism, but rather to the Four Principles, which are meant to cover common ground between them. However, I believe that such 'mid-level' norms ultimately need to be interpreted in the light of a theory that is fundamental and comprehensive. What exactly counts as 'harm', 'beneficence', or even 'autonomy' is best understood by appeal to a background moral theory. For example, acting beneficently for a utilitarian means promoting another's subjective well-being, for a Kantian doing so consists of realizing the other's particular ends or general ability to realize them, and for the relational moral theory doing so means meeting others' needs, fostering their liveliness, or enhancing their virtue *qua* communality. The overlap here is minimal, and a philosopher needs to decide what it really means to help others. Most often I argue that the relational moral theory easily entails an intuitively attractive conclusion about a bioethical issue that the Western moral theories have difficulty entailing, but sometimes I point out that it entails the same conclusion as they but for a different reason that is at least as plausible.

I start by considering the proper aims of medical treatment (9.2). Most would readily say that they are to prevent illness and injury, to improve people's health, or more generally to make people's lives go well. However, different moral theories can have divergent accounts of these conditions. I argue that the relationality of the communal ethic enables it to account for certain attractive ideas about the final ends of medical treatment to a degree that is no worse, and sometimes

A Relational Moral Theory: African Ethics in and beyond the Continent. Thaddeus Metz, Oxford University Press.
 DOI: 10.1093/oso/9780198748960.003.0009

better, than the principles of utility promotion and of respect for autonomy. One topical controversy regarding the proper aims of medicine to which I devote a separate section is about enhancements—technological interventions that could bestow positive traits on a human being far beyond what have usually been available to members of the species (9.3). My contribution on this matter amounts to showing that the relational moral theory raises a prima facie problem with enhancements that has not been salient in the literature, concerning their tendency to foster alienation and indifference amongst people. Having addressed issues of how to treat others, I move on to the question of precisely whom to treat (9.4). What do medical professionals owe their extant patients compared to new patients they could take on? What do they owe the society in which they grew up and were trained compared to a different society to which they could emigrate? After contending that communality grounds plausible answers to these kinds of questions, and delaying interpersonal issues of informed consent and confidentiality until the next chapter (10.2–10.3), I turn to debates about life and death. I first argue that the account of moral status from the previous chapter grounds a moderate approach to abortion that can rule out infanticide, which is difficult for utilitarianism and Kantianism to do (9.5). Finally, I contend that the relational moral theory also grounds a moderate and compelling approach to euthanasia and physician-assisted suicide, which is likewise difficult for the Western moral theories to justify (9.6).

9.2 The Point of Medical Treatment

A medical professional is someone who is in a better position than most to help people avoid or overcome sickness and related forms of debilitation and who hence should do what she can in those respects. Indeed, one might sympathize with the suggestion some have made that there is no controversy about what the proper goals of medicine are, and that the only controversies are about the proper means to achieve them and the constraints on doing so. Responding to previous work of mine on the present topic, two theorists say: 'It is not evident that the first issue—the point of medical treatment—poses an ethical problem or dilemma. The point of medical treatment is, plain and simple, to treat the sick and either cure or palliate the patient's condition' (Macpherson and Macklin 2010: 32).

Upon reflection, though, one finds genuine contestations about what a medical professional ought to be aiming to achieve. What truly counts as 'being sick' or a 'patient's condition'? Is abortion when unnecessary for the health of the mother a proper aim of medicine? Is circumcision, when done for religious reasons? Should medical professionals write out scripts for the 'treatment' of baldness? Should psychotherapists help a client navigate an uncomfortable and scary path of asking for a raise from a boss? Should insurance companies or public funds be used for any of these interventions? What makes one illness or injury more serious than another? Do the most serious cases invariably warrant priority in situations of scarcity, or might the aim of medical interventions be realized by instead treating a greater number of people with somewhat less serious conditions? I do not answer all these questions here, but they do deserve answers and the answers to give are not obvious.

For the utilitarian, if medical interventions are going to be morally sound, they must be expected to minimize woe and maximize well-being, taking the interests of everyone into account. Protecting health is an important way to help someone, according to this approach, because normally a reduction in health means a reduction in the chances of living well. Few utilitarians would say that being healthy *just is* to live well to some degree; instead, on the dominant, i.e., subjective conceptions of welfare as pleasant experiences or satisfied desires, health counts as a particularly effective route by which to obtain welfare. On this view, the diseases that are most urgent to treat are those threatening death, intense pain, or some other gross interference in the ability of a person to feel pleasure or to obtain what she wants. Specific conditions of the mind or body, whether cancer, diabetes, foreskin, baldness, anxiety, or whatever, merit intervention insofar as a medical professional would best promote the general welfare by preventing or treating them.

The Kantian answers the question about the point of medical treatment with the claim that, to be respectful of autonomy, it should help people realize their various higher-order ends as well as to protect, if not enhance, their capacity to revise ends and perform actions to achieve them. The less healthy one is, the less one is able to adopt and to pursue a wide variety of goals. Even pain, on this Kantian view, is something for a medical professional to help others avoid either because it inhibits their general ability to deliberate and choose (e.g., Rawls 1988), or because one of their particular ends is to avoid pain (and not because pain inherently makes their lives worse, as per the utilitarian). The more that a condition threatens people's ability to reflect on which ends to pursue and to pursue them, or the more that it undercuts a person's specific end that has priority for her relative to her other ends, the more urgent the condition is to prevent or correct.

Each of these theories is a plausible account of the proper ultimate purpose of medical treatment from a moral point of view, but there are counterexamples to both that might reasonably lead one to search for another approach. For instance, utilitarianism has prima facie difficulty entailing that psychopathy, mania, and opium addiction are serious mental illnesses. People with all three psychological conditions could be capable of happiness, whether construed as pleasant experiences or satisfied desires. A psychopath might happen not to encounter resistance to his manipulation; a 'maniac' might not 'come down' all that much and instead be lucky enough to experience recurrent highs; and an addict might have a never-ending supply of his drug. In reply, the utilitarian may suggest that a medical professional should treat people with these conditions because doing so would substantially improve the welfare of those who interact with them, particularly family members. However, this is not the best explanation, for the primary reason for a healthcare worker to treat these conditions is for the sake of the people who have them.

Turning to physical conditions, consider that it is commonly said that losing a limb is not all that harmful when it comes to people's subjective well-being. To be sure, amputees are not happy in the short term, but after about a year it appears that on average they return to their previous levels of contentment, such as they were. Suppose that empirical claim were true. Then, for the utilitarian, losing an arm or leg would be bad, but, resulting in just one life-year of poor quality, not all that urgent. However, I presume the reader shares the intuition that it would be urgent to prevent the loss of a limb, even if subjective well-being would remain intact without it.

The Kantian is better able to account for all these cases. Without a limb, Kant himself would say (1797: Ak. 445), one would be less able to pursue all manner of possible purposes; one could not *do* as much, even if one *felt* the same. Both mania and addiction patently interfere with one's ability to act in accordance with reasons, while psychopathy is an inability to act in accordance with moral ends.

However, consider the following counterexamples to Kantianism. Think, first, about someone who has difficulty feeling emotions, e.g., he tends neither to get angry at others nor to feel sympathy for them. Second, consider people who have sex with the dead, or whose primary intimate 'relationships' are with life-like dolls. In both kinds of cases, people need not be any less able to deliberate about the good and the right and to act in accordance with their deliberations, and yet it would be implausible to describe them as fully mentally healthy. The natural reply to make on behalf of the Kantian is that emotions provide reliable information about oneself and others, meaning that one would be less likely to act as one should if lacking emotional intelligence, something that is likely true of most necrophiliacs and doll-lovers. The point is fair. However, imagine someone who had a variety of epistemic aids to correct for his emotional deficiency. If a person were missing emotional intelligence but had enough other sorts to facilitate action in accordance with his reflective judgements of which ends merit pursuit, many would still deem the emotional disconnection to be something worth treating.

There are also physical conditions that seem to count as diseases or to be otherwise worth treating but that seem to have little connection with end-pursuit. Consider people who are at risk of losing not a limb, but, say, a pinky finger. Or think about women who are losing their hair, or men losing not just hair on their head but also their eyebrows. Or reflect on those who face reproductive sterility. Losing a pinky finger, hair, or the ability to procreate poses no serious risk to the capacity to judge ends and act on the basis of ends of chosen. What the Kantian can say in reply is that many people have highly ranked ends to keep their fingers, hair, and ability to procreate. Upon reflection, though, this is a poor explanation of why these conditions merit treatment. Recall the earlier counterexample of the individual whose highest or at least highly ranked end is to colour everything she can pink (8.4.1). She does not merit assistance from any professional, let alone public tax money, in support of her aim. However, medical professionals and public hospitals should indeed help people avoid losing fingers, hair, and the ability to procreate, meaning their importance is not merely a function of patients having set some end or other.

In any event, I invite the reader to consider an alternative understanding of the point of medicine. The reader should note that both the Kantian and utilitarian accounts of the proper function of medicine are 'individualist' in the sense that they prescribe treatment in order to support something intrinsic to a person. The utilitarian would have healthcare workers promote a patient's (or others') happiness, which, understood as pleasant experiences or satisfied desires, makes no essential reference to anyone besides the individual who has them. Similarly, the Kantian would have healthcare workers support a patient's theoretical and practical reasoning, which also does not essentially include anyone but the individual rational being.

In contrast, my relational account of the ultimate purpose of medical treatment from a moral standpoint prescribes it as a way to honour people insofar as they have a communal nature. Respect for people's capacity to be subjects and objects of communal ways of relating, which involve identity and solidarity, can avoid the above counterexamples to the Western principles while providing a reasonable account of the general point of healthcare.

First off, by the relational moral theory, a medical professional is obligated to act communally with regard to the patient, with the solidarity condition involving doing what is likely to promote her good and for her sake. Recall that, with much of the African tradition, I recognize two distinct sorts of final value (6.2.3). On the one hand, there is what is good for a person, what will make him better off, or what is in his self-interest, as distinct from what a good person is, what will make him better, or what will constitute his self-realization.

Both sorts of good are intuitively relevant to a moral relationship that includes solidarity, or at least I stipulate that the relational ethic prescribes promoting not merely others' well-being, but also their excellence. Regarding the latter good, consider that the normativity of friendliness suggests that being a good friend involves doing what is likely to make one's friend not merely happier, but also a better friend. Regarding the former good, recall that well-being is understood centrally in terms of meeting people's biological, psychological, and social needs.

What all this means is that a healthcare worker ought to be not only aiming to make the patient better off, but also working to overcome obstacles to developing her character, neither of which utilitarianism or Kantianism standardly prescribes. By the relational moral theory, medical interventions should serve the dual functions of meeting people's needs and enabling them to exercise their capacity to identify with and exhibit solidarity with others.

Applying this approach to common ailments such as physical illnesses and injuries, such as cancer, diabetes, and broken legs, the theory easily entails that they should be treated as a way of meeting people's biological needs and enabling them to commune with others. That is a plausible explanation that contrasts with doing so in order to make people subjectively happy or to foster their autonomy. Prioritizing disease or more generally distributing healthcare will, by the relational moral theory, be a function of the degree of neediness and extent to which a person's ability to act in friendly ways is threatened.

In the light of this sketch of the relational moral theory's implications for healthcare, consider how the counterexamples to utilitarianism and Kantianism do not apply to it. Recall that it is difficult for a focus on subjective well-being to explain why psychopaths, 'maniacs', addicts, the emotionally stunted, necrophiliacs, and doll-lovers merit psychological treatment. In contrast, the relational moral theory grounds a plausible, unitary explanation: these conditions interfere with people's ability to be subjects of communal relationships. All these people are isolated from others in various ways, specifically being unable to enjoy a sense of togetherness, to cooperate with others, to empathize and sympathize, to act for other people's sake, and so on. The relational moral theory entails that part of the point of medical treatment is to overcome such distance by improving people's ability to be friendly towards others. And then recall the divergence between the intuitive seriousness of the loss of a limb despite an insubstantial loss of subjective well-being; on this score, it is plausible to suggest that people have a need for bodily integrity, regardless of how that may or may not affect their moods or desires.

Turning to the problems facing Kantianism, remember that they involve conditions that do not necessarily impair end-pursuit but that seem to merit medical treatment all the same. These include having difficulty feeling emotions such as sympathy, avoiding sexual intimacy with people, and losing a finger, hair, or the ability to procreate. Feelings, sexuality, and the body are prima facie troublesome for a Kantian account, focused on our rationality. In contrast, they are not for the relational moral theory, which directs medical professionals to meet people's physical and psychological needs, including for bodily integrity, and to improve their ability to exhibit identity and solidarity with others, including emotionally and romantically.

I acknowledge that there are versions of the Western principles that might be more powerful than the ones I have addressed here. The point is not so much to show that the relational moral theory is preferable in respect of any particular moral controversy, but more to demonstrate that it has plausible implications for a wide array of controversies. The burden is on utilitarians and Kantians to provide an account that adequately captures not merely, for instance, the point of medicine, but also the myriad issues discussed in this part of the book.

9.3 Enhancements

The previous section addressed the question of what the purpose of medical treatment is, with the answer basically being to commune with patients by meeting their needs and enabling them to commune in turn with others. It is not clear from this statement whether medicine ought to be in the business of providing enhancements—say, tinkering with an embryo's genes in order to make it more beautiful, intelligent, strong, or the like.

On the one hand, doing so is unlikely to count as 'meeting needs'. It would be just for a public healthcare system to offer cosmetic surgery to the grotesque and deformed, although not, say, to the beautiful who would like to become downright gorgeous. A good, communal explanation of the difference is that such surgery is warranted particularly when necessary to facilitate a romantic relationship, but not warranted when unnecessary for that.

On the other hand, solidarity involves not just meeting other people's needs, but also improving their ability to relate communally as subjects, where enhancements could, at least in principle (if not yet in practice), foster friendliness. Imagine that people were engineered to become more sympathetic with strangers and less inclined to view members of out-groups as akin to pollution or subhuman. An ethic of honouring the capacity for communality, which, in turn, often prescribes improving that capacity, would seem to justify moral and related enhancements.

However, there are different ways of interpreting the relational ethic's prescription to exhibit solidarity. Does respect for people's capacity to commune mean helping others by improving their deformed capacity so that it approximates the norm, or might it mean helping them to become more like a stereotypical Mother Teresa, whom we presume to be beyond the norm? I lack a firm comprehensive view at present about what the relational moral theory entails for enhancements. I am not sure whether it would require moral ones, and I also cannot say whether it would permit non-moral ones. In the following, I offer some tentative, piecemeal considerations on these difficult topics.

First off, I do think that there is no question that enhancements would be justified for certain reasons. As Stephen Hawking has famously pointed out, the sun will not last forever, and in order to survive as a species we will probably need to modify our genes in order to be able to travel in space for long times in search of a new planetary home. If enhancements were required in order to keep the human race—or a transhuman species closely related to it—from going extinct, surely they would be justified.

The harder question is whether enhancements are justified for less urgent purposes. A principle of respect for autonomy seems readily to entail an affirmative answer, as neither a parent's nor a child's autonomy would necessarily be impaired, or otherwise degraded, by the former authorizing genetic modification of the embryo from which the latter grew. In addition, so long as enhancements were safe, in the sense of not threatening the child's well-being, utilitarianism would appear to permit them, if they would be put to good use.

I suspect, though, that the relational moral theory provides *pro tanto* reason to doubt the permissibility of enhancing, even when it involves our moral agency. Communality grounds a criticism of enhancement different from the usual suspects of contending that it would: degrade human nature *qua* biological configuration; consist of playing God; foster injustice in the form of greater inequalities between the rich and the poor; and evince base desires for perfection and total control. Instead, a principle requiring one to respect people's communal nature entails that enhancing would be morally objectionable insofar as it would be likely to put distance between people.

In particular, enhancements could threaten to make it harder for people to share a way of life. Recall the major parts of what that involves (6.2.2). For one, it includes enjoying a sense of togetherness, including things such as thinking of oneself as a 'we', cultivating a sense of 'who we are', feeling good about being with others, and taking pride in others' accomplishments. To be avoided are more divisive attitudes, of thinking of oneself as an 'I' as opposed to others, developing senses of identity that are defined in opposition to one another, disliking other people's presence, and being envious of others.

For another, sharing a way of life includes not merely cooperating, but also living together and undergoing some of the same experiences. As the most influential sub-Saharan political philosopher of the past twenty-five years remarks, African communitarianism 'advocates a life lived in harmony and cooperation with others, a life of mutual consideration and aid and of interdependence, a life in which one shares in the fate of the other' (Gyekye 1997: 76). Salient examples in the African philosophical tradition are living with a family, participating in the rituals of one's society, and collective harvesting and building (3.4.3). However, there are additional ways to ride in the same boat, as it were. For example, if there were a choice of distributing two units of a burden on ten people or ten units on one person, the communal principle would, *contra* utilitarianism, prescribe the former, despite the fact that there would be double the aggregate amount of harm. Similarly, the communal principle would likely entail that it would be more apt to distribute one unit of a benefit on ten people rather than twenty units on only one. In both cases, more egalitarian distributions would foster communality.

Now, enhancements would probably interfere with people's ability to share a way of life, at least if some were substantially enhanced and others were not. Large differences in abilities, even moral ones, could be expected to impede psychological identification in the way that great inequalities of wealth tend to do. It is well known that it is harder to form friendly and loving relationships across class divides. In addition, studies show that large gaps between rich and poor tend to foster indifference to others' suffering on the part of the former as well as feelings of envy on the part of the latter. The present point is not the common one to make—that by allowing enhancements the rich would become biologically superior and hence all the more wealthy and otherwise dominant. Instead, the point is that biological hierarchy, regardless of whether it is only the wealthy who are on top, would likely have negative influences on people's ability to share a sense of self with one another, like economic stratification does. Giving a handful of people qualitatively superior intelligence, for example, would be akin to distributing a large amount of wealth on a minority, instead of opting for a more egalitarian and inclusive allocation. Hence, those authorizing or voluntarily undergoing enhancements would probably be failing to honour people's capacity to identify with each other.

I do not mean to suggest that honouring people's ability to share a way of life requires 'levelling down' or demands that everyone live identical lives. Rather, the point is that enjoying a sense of togetherness and undergoing the same fate can be important instantiations of sharing a way of life, and that they would be much harder to realize if enhancements were distributed such that only some people received them and their abilities were noticeably greater.

Of course, there is nothing intrinsic to enhancements that would require that sort of distribution. Perhaps they could be allocated reasonably equally. Or perhaps if they were allocated unequally, they would not facilitate *great* divergence in abilities. Or maybe if there were only some who were genetically gifted, the value of communality could still be honoured on balance if they were to use their gifts to help others. Although there are these promising ways to avoid the concern about divisiveness, the point is that divisiveness is a relevant moral concern, and that it has not been salient in discussion about the ethics of enhancement. The relational moral theory highlights an under-theorized objection to enhancement—an objection that, if it does not forbid it altogether, would require that it be undertaken in certain ways rather than others.

9.4 Whom to Treat

The previous two sections considered which medical treatment to provide and why, whereas this one is instead about who should receive it. There are a variety of patients to whom healthcare workers could attend, and this section provides some guidance about which ones are appropriate. I first consider the obligations of a medical professional in respect of his own, actual patients relative to other patients (9.4.1), then obligations in respect of his colleagues' patients in contrast to other ones (9.4.2), and finally obligations pertaining to patients in his country versus those elsewhere in the world (9.4.3). In each case, I contend that the partiality of the relational moral theory grounds *pro tanto* special obligations that are plausible and difficult for Western moral theories to capture.

9.4.1 One's Actual Patients

Intuitively, a doctor should seek to ensure excellent treatment for his actual patients, those with whom he has already had a relationship, whether as a general practitioner or a specialist. That is most clearly true if the relationship with them has been long-standing, but even a few consultations might be enough to provide reason of some strength to continue to treat them relative to other, potential patients.

Consider that if a medical resource were scarce, it would be wrong for a doctor to flip a coin to determine whether his actual patient should receive it or whether another doctor's patient should, supposing both would be expected to benefit from it to the same degree. It would also be wrong for a given doctor to flip a coin to determine whether his actual patient should receive it or whether a new patient that he could take on should, again supposing the same health outcomes. Instead of randomizing amongst equally needy patients, once a doctor has had a patient for some time or with some intimacy, it becomes the former's *pro tanto* duty to act in a zealous and partisan fashion on the latter's behalf, relative to those who are comparably needy. If there is an agent who should consider the interests of patients impartially, it would instead be a hospital's management or a government's Department of Health, not the physicians who have treated them so far.

Utilitarianism has difficulty accounting for these intuitions, for this principle prescribes impartial consideration. Since a medical professional is obligated to do whatever would produce the best results, giving equal weight to the interests of all, there is no reason for him to direct a scarce medical resource to his actual patients relative to other patients, if the outcomes would be the same. One might reply that the expectations of actual patients would be disappointed, or that, having engaged with patients for a while, the doctor knows them best such that it would be most efficient to treat them. However, the doctor need not tell his patients that he elected not to give them the treatment and instead has given it to another doctor, where that other doctor indeed knows his patients best and could prescribe it effectively.

What goes for the issue of how to allocate a certain treatment, whether to one's own patient or the patient of another doctor, also goes for the issue of which patients a given doctor should have at all. If all new patients would have marginally more serious illnesses to treat than those of a physician's actual patients, then, according to utilitarianism, the right course of action for him would be to dump the latter and take on the former. It would take time for him to get to know the new patients, of course, and for his former patients to find a new doctor, but in the long run it could well be that doing so would produce the most social benefit. I presume the reader agrees that, while a large-scale patient swap could be justified if the illnesses and injuries of the new patients were *much* more serious than those of the old ones, it would not be justified if they were only marginally so, despite the prospect of maximizing the general welfare.

I submit that it is also difficult for a Kantian, one who places a principle of respect for autonomy at the centre of her moral thought, to make sense of a special obligation on the part of a doctor to act in the interests of current patients. Some doctors or their hospitals will have promised to prioritize the interests of actual patients, where it is degrading of another's capacity for self-governance to break promises. However, the deep issue is why such a promise should be made in the first place, something the Kantian cannot easily answer. Furthermore, even in the absence of a promise, there would intuitively be some moral reason for a doctor to act for the sake of present patients, and not to balance their interests against the similar ones of other, potential patients or another doctor's actual patients. However, the standard view of Kantianism when it comes to whom to aid beyond the voluntary assumption of an obligation to do so is that it is an imperfect duty and so up to the agent's discretion whom to aid.

The relational moral theory does better. Unlike utilitarianism, it can ground special obligations to aid, entailing that there is extra reason to help certain individuals even when doing so would not be optimific. Unlike Kantianism, the communal ethic can do so without the voluntary assumption of an obligation to help such as an agent having agreed to do so for certain individuals or having accepted benefits from a cooperative scheme with them. Recall that partiality is characteristic of the African tradition (alongside a dignity-based impartiality), where I reconstruct that in relational terms, such that the more one has communed with a person, the more reason there is to continue doing so compared to others with whom one has not communed (7.3.3). Recall that one would not intuitively be honouring people if one stopped relating to them any time one could be expected to maximize relationships with others. Instead, upon having identified with and exhibited solidarity towards certain people for some time and to some degree, one is liable to assist them, at least when one can do so at relatively little cost to oneself and to other moral considerations.

This corollary accounts well for the aptness of a division of labour between doctors, on the one hand, and hospital managers and government ministers, on the other. Doctors should be partial towards their patients with whom they have already related communally, where the longer and stronger the bond, the greater the obligation. In contrast, since managers or ministers have not communed with any patients themselves, and since they run institutions that should commune with the general public, it is appropriate for them to take more impartial decisions about how to allocate resources.

9.4.2 The Patients of Colleagues

Consider, now, a medical professional's obligations not to his own, actual patients, but instead to patients who are in the care of colleagues. Suppose you are a nurse or doctor in a certain hospital or clinic, and a fellow medical professional needs to attend to some personal matters for a shift. Would you not have an obligation of some weight to cover for him? Could you with moral justification consistently refuse such requests? The natural answer is that one indeed has moral reason to assist one's colleagues—greater reason than one has to assist medical professionals at other institutions.

The question now is why one owes more to colleagues, and hence should do more for their patients, than to others working in the same field. Considerations similar to those from the previous sub-section apply. The principle of utility entails that whoever would be inconvenienced the least, as well as would inconvenience others the least, by taking over should do so. Often that will align with covering for one's institutional colleague, but not always. Imagine that one's colleague works in a closely related area of medicine, whereas a physician at another institution whom one does not know works in precisely one's area. Then it would be most efficient to fill in for the stranger, but I presume the reader shares my intuition that one would still have some greater reason to help one's colleague.

The Kantian will be tempted to suggest that an agreement amongst colleagues to help each other is what accounts for the duty to do so. I submit, though, that there probably is not any such agreement and, furthermore, that such a duty would remain in the absence of one. If you are an academic reading this, consider, by analogy, whether you have *promised* to stand in for your departmental colleagues when they need someone to cover a lecture to students. When, exactly, did you do that? I doubt that you ever did, either explicitly or tacitly, but suggest that you have some moral reason to help your colleagues nonetheless.

Kantians and related moral theorists might at this point plausibly appeal to the principle of fair play, which is the view that one who has freely accepted benefits of a cooperative scheme (or perhaps involuntarily received substantial benefits) has some moral obligation to undertake his fair share of the burdens necessary to generate those benefits (Davis 1992; Klosko 1992; Rawls 1999: sec. 18). Just as it would be wrong for a doctor routinely to take chocolates lying out on the administration desk and never pitch in to replenish the supply, so it would be wrong for a doctor never to help out other doctors at her institution, since she benefits from their labour but not (or not nearly as much) from the labour of doctors at other hospitals and clinics.

This argument is powerful, and I accept that it accounts for some of the collegial obligation involved. However, I deny that it accounts for all of it. Consider that the principle of fair play requires only one's *fair* share of burden, which is presumably proportionate to the degree to which one has received net benefit from the cooperative scheme. Suppose, now, that a certain doctor has already undertaken her fair share of burdens with respect to the cooperative scheme; perhaps she was unfairly burdened before by the other doctors as a whole, so that she has benefits, and not burdens, coming to her from them as a group. In that case, the principle of fair play would entail that no obligation exists for her to cover for a colleague who needs some time off to deal with family matters. However, my intuition is that she could still have an obligation of some defeasible weight to aid the colleague under those conditions, if she could help him at little cost to herself.

The relational moral theory provides a more powerful account of why one can be obliged to go out of one's way for one's colleagues, more so than for others in the same profession. Even if one has not exacted a net benefit from colleagues' labour and other burdens, one can, by this theory, have a duty to help specific others with whom one has been in communal relationship. Upon identifying with and exhibiting solidarity towards colleagues, both as subject and object, a medical professional has established a morally significant relationship with them that demands respect as a way to show them respect as relational beings. If medical professionals have thought of themselves as a 'we', engaged in the joint project of running a ward or clinic, performed actions that have been good for one another, and done so for one another's sake, then they have acquired special obligations to support and help each other, obligations that can go beyond those assumed in the course of promising or accepting benefits from a cooperative scheme.

Furthermore, the relational moral theory provides a powerful account of *how* a medical professional is obligated to aid colleagues. A plausible corollary is that the form that solidarity should take with respect to those with whom one has communed is substantially influenced by considerations of identity. The way that a person should care for others' quality of life is determined in large part by the way in which they have shared a way of life together.

For example, consider that it would be wrong for a doctor to ask one of her medical colleagues to mow her lawn, clean her garage, or babysit her children, even if she really did need these things done. The intuitive problem is one of disrespect, but it is not disrespect for a colleague's *autonomy*—his capacity to make decisions for himself. In making such a request, she need not be employing any coercion, deception, exploitation, or other manipulation, but could simply be making a fully informed request that the other is completely free to turn down. Instead, the object of disrespect appears to be the *relationship* or the person's relational nature. The explanation of the disrespect includes the idea that the kind of aid that one may reasonably expect from another person, or that he may be required to provide, depends on the way they have identified with each other in the past. As medical colleagues think of themselves as a 'we' in the context of the collective ends of understanding, preventing, and treating injury and illness, unassumed duties to aid each other would normally (barring extreme emergencies) be a function of helping one another with regard to these ends, not ones pertaining to home life.

9.4.3 Patients in One's Country

Suppose a medical professional has a choice of helping people in the country in which she has grown up or those in another country with comparable needs.

Concretely, imagine that she could either practise medicine in her own country or emigrate to another one where she would be similarly employed. Does she have any obligation not to emigrate, at least for a while, accepting that it could be overridden by other considerations? If the reasoning in the previous two subsections has been sound, then it follows from the communal ethic that it is *pro tanto* wrong for at least a newly trained medical professional to emigrate, supposing she has not given much to her country yet.

According to the communal ethic, positive duties to help specific others arise upon having been party to (at least) intense or long-standing relationships of identity and solidarity. When people have thought of themselves as a 'we', participated with each other on even-handed terms, engaged in mutual aid, and done so for one another's sake, then there is a tie that encumbers to some degree. And since a recently graduated medical professional has, by hypothesis, been in such communal relationship with her state and broader society, she has some moral reason to go out of her way for others, according to her ability to do so. Should a skilled citizen who could substantially cooperate and aid her compatriots fail to do so by emigrating, she would be failing to honour people's communal nature.

This judgement that there can be something wrong with emigrating is more controversial than those elsewhere in this section. I believe the judgement is considerable in the case where a person has grown up in a certain country, has just acquired her qualifications in it, and has yet to put them to use in that country, but, even so, I accept that it is not as strong as other intuitions discussed above and so I do not invoke it as evidence in favour of the relational moral theory. It appears, though, that the best explanation of those less contested intuitions entails the judgement that there can be moral reason of some weight not to emigrate.[1] Perhaps because the ties with one's state and society are not as strong as those with patients and colleagues, the obligations to them are not as weighty, explaining why there is disagreement about whether there is any obligation at all.

9.5 Abortion and Infanticide

In the rest of this chapter I turn to debates about whether—and, if so, when—it can be permissible for medical professionals to kill human beings. In the next section I consider whether it can be right for medical professionals to kill those who are suffering from terminal illnesses, but here address whether they may terminate a human pregnancy. While it is difficult for utilitarianism and Kantian

[1] For discussion of the inability of Kantianism to ground a duty not to emigrate, see Metz (2017b).

to answer in a moderate way, avoiding counterintuitive implications about infanticide, it is easy for a certain interpretation of the relational moral theory to do so.

Utilitarianism easily justifies an early-stage abortion insofar as the embryo or young foetus cannot feel pain (or lacks preferences), the eventual child would live a relatively poor life, and either the foetus or the eventual child would make those around him miserable (or dissatisfied). The trouble with this rationale for abortion is that it counterintuitively entails that even late-stage foetuses and new-born infants may be killed whenever doing so would satisfy enough trivial interests of others (cf. Singer 1993: 150–1, 169–74).

Kantianism can also justify abortion straightforwardly, since neither an embryo nor a foetus has the capacity to reason. Lacking a dignity, there is no disrespect of the human life that is ended, with consent from the relevant persons, viz., clearly the mother (there is controversy about the father), being necessary and sufficient to make abortion permissible. However, this rationale for abortion also counterintuitively entails that even late-stage foetuses and new-born infants may be killed since they, too, lack the capacity to reason (cf. Warren 1973). Any reason not to kill a new-born infant must be indirect, which, I submit, is implausible; we have a duty not to kill babies because of facts about the babies themselves, not merely persons who might have set ends in relation to them.

In contrast, the relational moral theory permits an early-stage abortion, while normally forbidding a late-stage one and, especially, infanticide. It can uniquely do so because of its gradualist approach to moral status. Recall the principle that a being has a moral status (roughly) to the extent that it is in principle capable of communal relationships (8.3). While a full moral status goes to beings with the capacity to be subjects and objects of communal relationships, a partial moral status goes to those with the capacity to be only objects of them with us, where there are degrees to which that is possible.

Applying this account, gametes, zygotes, embryos, and very early foetuses lack a moral status altogether. They obviously cannot exhibit identity and solidarity with us, but, in addition, they are capable neither of any intentional action that we could support or feel a part of nor of a quality of life that we could sympathize with or foster.[2] Since they are not yet organisms that can have aims and or be better or worse off, if they ever warrant protection, it is only on indirect grounds. Of course, an embryo and foetus are alive, and so there may be a perfectionist sense in which it would be 'better' if they were to stay alive, but not in the relevant sense of being 'better off', i.e., having an improved quality of life, where our ability to enhance it is requisite for moral status (even though not exhaustive of that—on which see Chapter 8, note 5).

[2] It might be that characteristic human persons, particularly pregnant women, can enjoy a sense of togetherness, a sense of 'we', with young foetuses, but this is not sufficient for a moral status or at least for a moral status robust enough to rule out abortion.

Although the relational approach entails that beings with human DNA younger than two months old lack a moral status, it also entails that they acquire a partial moral status upon becoming a mid- to late-stage foetus. Such later foetuses can be objects of a communal relationship with us, even if not yet subjects of one. Certainly by the sixth month (and perhaps a bit earlier), foetuses can feel pain and more generally have interests that enable us to have other-regarding reactions towards them such as improving their well-being, doing so for their sake, and feeling sympathy. In addition, while it is true that some people, particularly pregnant women, are inclined to think of themselves as a 'we' with beings with human DNA that are not yet organisms, the ability for us to identify with them increases substantially as they develop. Characteristic humans much more readily think of themselves as a 'we' with mid- to late-stage foetuses than they do with a clump of rudimentary cells, upon a clear awareness of their nature. Since we can be friendly in relation to the former, but they cannot in relation to us, they have a partial moral status.

Finally, it is plausible to suggest that new-born infants have an even greater (albeit partial) moral status than late-stage foetuses since there is a qualitative difference in the degree to which characteristic human beings can commune with them.[3] New-borns and foetuses, while potentially identical in biological terms, are not identical in respect of essential functions, and partly for this reason might not be identical in respect of capacity to be the object of identity and solidarity with characteristic human beings.[4] Babies cry, look people in the eyes, ingest food through their mouths, are out in the world, and, at least at a certain point, engage in goal-directed behaviour, which more readily enables us to enjoy a sense of togetherness with them, realize their aims, foster their good, and sympathize with them. The point is not that new-borns are more similar to us than are foetuses, but rather that the latter are, by their nature, *cloistered* in such a way as to make communal relationship with them markedly more difficult than with the former. If that metaphysical claim were indeed true, then it would follow from the relational approach that new-borns have a greater moral status than foetuses, an interesting, under-considered view that merits consideration.

Before returning to the question of when abortion might be permissible, notice that the relational approach to moral status can probably claim credit for accounting for a long-standing and widely shared intuition that has not been firmly captured up to now, which is that moral status increases along with the development of a being from embryo to mid-stage foetus to new-born. Utilitarianism cannot entail or explain that intuition, for once a foetus is capable of pain or

[3] This line of reasoning is inspired by some remarks from Slote (2007: 17–19).

[4] I presume here that a being's nature is determined not merely by its intrinsic properties, but also by its relational ones (see 8.3.3). That is, I rely on a contested metaphysical claim, making the conclusions here more tentative than others that do not rely on it.

preferences, there is no difference in moral status between it and a new-born. Kantians also have difficulty accommodating the differential moral status of embryos, foetuses, and infants, as they all lack moral status for being non-rational (or, alternatively, they all have moral status for exhibiting the potential for rationality). Only a *relational* theory of the present sort has a real chance of differentiating between degrees of standing amongst these beings. And nothing else plausibly could, given the *intrinsic* similarities.

Moral standing is one thing, and right action is another. Let us move from considerations of how morally important an embryo, foetus, or new-born is to those of how we are obligated to treat them. The relational moral theory instructs an agent to honour a being insofar as it is capable of being party to relationships of sharing and caring. As the mother has a full moral status, her urgent interests come before the urgent interests of any being with a merely partial moral status, when a trade-off has to be made between them (8.4). Hence, if there were an unavoidable choice to be made between the mother's life and that of her foetus, even a late-stage one, it would be permissible for her and medical professionals to make the tragic decision to abort.

Furthermore, it follows that abortion is permissible for less than urgent interests on the part of the woman, when there is merely an embryo at stake or when the foetus is very young and undeveloped. As a robust communal relation is not possible with these beings, they lack a moral status altogether (or at most have one that is very low), meaning that abortion would not degrade them. Although abortion would 'stop a beating heart', it would not count as very unfriendly or discordant in the way that has been conceived here: there would be no subordination of a being capable of intentional action and no harm done to a being capable of living well.

However, once the foetus has developed such capacities, abortion for the sake of realizing the less than urgent interests of the mother is at least *pro tanto* wrong. Recall the corollary that it is wrong to trade off the urgent interests of a being with a partial moral status for the trivial interests of a being with a full moral status (8.4), which entails that many non-persons should often be protected from serious harm and extreme subordination such as killing. One would need a weighty reason—of a person's life, limb, or mind—to cause intense pain to, let alone kill, a being that we can, by virtue of its nature and ours, treat in a friendly way, particularly a human, with which we can commune more intensely than we can typical animals. In addition, since a new-born plausibly has an even greater standing than a late-stage foetus, for being all the more capable of being communed with, it would be even more wrong to kill it for a minor or even moderate interest of some other being, even if not as great a wrong as it would be to kill a normal person, viz., someone capable of being a subject of communal relationship.

I submit that this account of the morality of abortion will fit the secular judgement of many enquirers particularly well. Many moral philosophers, professional ethicists, and related thinkers believe that abortion is permissible early on, at least before the foetus is two months old, that at some point it becomes justifiable only to protect the health of the mother or something comparably important, and that killing a new-born would be even more unjustifiable. Ascribing differential degrees of moral status to these beings in the light of their divergent capacities to be objects of communal relationship with us naturally makes sense of these views. I take that to be an advantage relative to utilitarianism and Kantianism, which, as above, on the face of it can permit abortion only at the cost of permitting infanticide.

Despite what I find to be appealing about the implications of the relational moral theory for abortion, I note that many in the African philosophical tradition and in the Judeo-Christian-Islamic one will not. What they have in common is the valuation of life, whether a force in the former or a substance in the latter. If a living human being is sacred and demands honouring, then abortion for the sake of just about any purpose is immoral.

However, such an approach has the well-known implication that it cannot easily provide any justification for favouring the life of the mother, where the life of the foetus threatens it and the choice must be made between them. Both the foetus and the mother are living human beings, making it difficult to articulate any moral reason to differentiate between them by a principle of respect for human life. Such a principle entails that a medical professional should randomize when it comes to whom to save, supposing only one could be saved. However, I, perhaps even with many drawn towards a life ethic, believe that the mother's life should invariably be preferred (at least supposing she wishes to be saved), if there were an unavoidable forced choice to be made. If so, then it is likely that dignity inheres in something other than life and that there is differential standing between the mother and her foetus.

9.6 Euthanasia and Physician-Assisted Suicide

Like the previous section, this one addresses when it might be permissible for medical professionals to cause the death of human beings knowingly. Instead of considering the very young, though, I now consider the very old, or at least those adults who are expected to die soon and are suffering. As with abortion, I maintain that the relational moral theory grounds a moderate approach to euthanasia and physician-assisted suicide, one that will appeal more strongly to many readers than the implications of the principles of respect for autonomy and of utility, and that, in any event, is not to be easily dismissed.

In the way that utilitarianism justifies abortion but 'proves too much' by also justifying infanticide, so too it justifies euthanasia and related practices in 'too many' cases. If someone were not destined to live long, would live the rest of her life in agony, and would not benefit others by remaining alive (perhaps because she has no relatives), utilitarianism would permit a physician to help her to take her own life. That is not an unreasonable implication. However, utilitarianism would, furthermore, permit (indeed require) a physician to kill such a patient, even if she were mentally competent and did not consent to being killed. Consent in itself has no moral relevance for the utilitarian, and so if considerations of well-being tell in favour of death, it would allow forced killings, which I presume the reader agrees would be wrong.

Consent does matter to the Kantian, of course, but a principle of respect for autonomy also justifies euthanasia in 'too many' cases. If a patient makes a free and informed decision to end her life because it is painful and it will end soon anyway, then, by this principle, there would be no disrespect in helping her to do so. However, the principle would also permit active euthanasia and physician-assisted suicide when a patient is perfectly healthy, so long as he made a free and informed authorization to be killed. For an example, consider the members of Heaven's Gate. The reader might not have heard about this cult, since its members killed themselves some time ago. At the time when Comet Hale–Bopp was approaching Earth, members of Heaven's Gate believed that it would take them to a much better place and that the only way to ride the comet was to kill off their bodies, freeing up their spirits. According to the logic of the principle of respect for autonomy, there would be no disrespect in a medical professional helping them to die or even intentionally killing them, supposing they were not mentally ill to a degree that undermined their capacity for consent. However, I again presume the reader believes, with me, that it would be inappropriate for doctors to kill individuals merely upon autonomous request.

In contrast, the relational moral theory can justify euthanasia and related practices without 'proving too much'. Whereas the utilitarian allows killing without the other's consent when it would be best for his welfare, and whereas the Kantian allows killing with the other's consent when it would not be best for his welfare, the communal ethic is naturally understood to allow neither course of action. Instead, it explains why euthanasia and physician-assisted suicide are justified when and only when there is both consent from the other and a need for him to prevent a fate worse (or perhaps no better) than death.

According to the relational moral theory, we have a dignity in virtue of our capacity to be party to relationships of cooperative participation (part of identity) and aid (part of solidarity). We have a full moral status because we can advance others' ends and improve their quality of life and also because others can do so in respect of us. Respect for such a capacity normally means avoiding very unfriendly ways of treating other innocent parties (7.2.2–7.3.1), where unfriendliness consists of subordination and harm. Now, killing someone who has only a fate worse than death to look forward to might not amount to causing her harm, but, if it were done without her consent, it would constitute extreme subordination and hence a degrading treatment of her capacity to be related to cooperatively (and to cooperate with others). And then killing someone who has given his consent to be killed might not amount to subordinating him, but, if it were not necessary to avoid him facing a fate worse than (or equal to) death, it would constitute a serious harm to him and hence a degrading treatment of his capacity to be helped (and to help others). Rightness as friendliness requires a moral agent such as a physician interacting with patients to attend to both their choice and their good, and hence is uniquely able to ground a moderate approach to euthanasia and physician-assisted suicide. Choice without good is lacking content; good without choice is misdirected.

Finally, just as many in the African philosophical tradition[5] and in the Judeo-Christian-Islamic one reject abortion by appeal to the value of life, so they reject euthanasia on the same ground. Sometimes a way of expressing respect for the lives of human beings might be to protect or improve their quality of life, but a standard interpretation of the principle of respect for human life is that it cannot entail that one may ever end a person's life for the sake of avoiding a poor quality of life, for that would be to treat life itself as worth less than its quality—a serious kind of degradation. However, I submit that one is not treating the dignity of another person with respect if one refuses to help her die when she would die in the next few weeks anyway, be in a state of intolerable suffering until death, and elect to die as the only way to end such suffering. A good explanation of the lack of respect is that the physician would be ignoring her special capacity to be cooperated with and aided.

Drawing this chapter to a close, I again acknowledge that I have worked with straightforward or familiar versions of the Western moral theories, and that there might be other ones able to avoid the objections made in this chapter. The point is not to provide knock-down arguments in favour of the relational moral theory in respect of a given applied topic, but rather to demonstrate its promise as a new, comprehensive alternative to familiar Western principles in the light of many intuitions that I expect will be shared by their adherents or at least by many global enquirers. Although I believe that it would be difficult for utilitarians and Kantians to entail and powerfully explain the intuitions advanced in this chapter, it would be reasonable for them to try to advance versions of their views that do. I submit, though, that it would also be reasonable, should this kind of argumentation continue in the remaining chapters, to accept the relational moral theory as a replacement and develop it instead.

[5] For a rare and recent exception, see Molefe (2020).

10
Research Ethics

10.1 Learning about Bodies and Minds

While the previous chapter applied the relational moral theory to matters concerning which patients a medical professional should treat and how, this chapter applies it to those about how a medical researcher should interact with participants in a study. The usual example is a clinical trial being undertaken to ascertain health-related outcomes, with key questions being when informed consent is required, which sort of confidentiality is appropriate, and whether ever to compensate for harm the study did not cause. Many of the answers given to these questions in the context of medical research will equally apply to other settings, such as medical treatment and non-medical research.

Most of the time in this applied part of the book I try to show that the relational moral theory entails intuitively attractive approaches to practical controversies that differ from those of rival theories. For two of the three major topics in this chapter, however, I try to show that my favoured ethic can entail plausible conclusions shared by rivals, but for a new, powerful reason.

That is particularly true in the case of informed consent (10.2), which I accept is normally required before conducting medical research on a person. In contrast to intrinsic properties such as a participant's subjective well-being or autonomy, the communal ethic explains why informed consent is apt by appeal to a relational property of sharing a way of life. When it comes to confidentiality, the communal ethic provides reason to doubt the default view that it may not be infringed except when essential to save lives (10.3), which might mean that its implications differ from standard interpretations of utilitarianism and Kantianism. Finally, regarding standards of care, both utilitarians and at least one prominent Kantian support the claim that a researcher can be obligated to compensate study participants for harm that the study did not cause, and I work to show that the relational ethic entails the same conclusion, but for a more compelling rationale (10.4).

10.2 Free and Informed Consent

Most moral philosophers, professional ethicists, and the like these days around the world hold that one may normally conduct medical research on participants (or

A Relational Moral Theory: African Ethics in and beyond the Continent. Thaddeus Metz, Oxford University Press.
 DOI: 10.1093/oso/9780198748960.003.0010

treat patients) only once they have given a certain kind of consent to be studied (or treated). Roughly, participants must be mentally competent adults who not only understand the basics of the researcher's plan, but also have, consequent to this understanding, agreed without coercive, deceptive, or exploitive manipulation to let the plan proceed. Rejecting a corporatist interpretation of African morality that would invariably subordinate individuals to the interests of their group (7.5.2), I accept that there is normally a requirement to obtain free and informed consent before conducting medical research on a person.

It can sometimes be difficult to obtain informed consent. Perhaps the prospective participant is being pressured to participate by an authority figure in her community or does not understand what scientific research involves. Even so, a researcher usually must do what he can to ensure that her consent is both free and informed or find another participant.

In addition, there might be times when a participant's right not to be studied without informed consent may permissibly be infringed. Perhaps having a prior understanding of the study would contaminate the ability to obtain extremely useful data from it, or there could be situations in which research on vulnerable populations, such as refugees or prisoners, would likely do them so much good that conducting the research in the face of a relative lack of freedom is permissible. Even so, there would be a moral cost to be acknowledged in these situations.

The utilitarian defends a default requirement of free and informed consent on the ground of its consequences for subjective well-being. Obtaining such agreement is expected in the long run to avoid disappointment and similar negative emotions and to foster participation by subjects in a study (or adherence to a treatment regimen by patients).

The Kantian, in contrast, appeals to non-consequentialist reasons and specifically to a moral right that follows from the principle of respect for autonomy. It would be degrading of a person's capacity to make decisions for herself if a medical researcher were to study her (or physician were to treat her) without having first obtained her voluntary and knowledgeable authorization to do so. Doing so would treat her ability to choose in the light of reasoned reflection merely as a means to the ends of the researcher.

Both of these Western rationales for a requirement of free and informed consent are admittedly plausible. However, the relational moral theory presents another reasonable explanation of why such consent is normally required prior to experimenting (or treating). Its basic claim is that it would be unfriendly or discordant to study (or treat) a person without her free and informed consent, and so almost always wrong since the person is innocent.

Think about what is involved in genuinely identifying with others (6.2). One cannot *share* a life with other people when: they are unclear about the basic terms of one's interaction with them; one uses force or takes advantage of weaknesses to pressure them into doing one's bidding; or one interacts with them in ways that undermine trust. Failing to obtain free and informed consent amounts to flouting the other person's capacity to be identified with and also to identify with the researcher and others. In particular, failing to do so undermines the capacity of the innocent participant both to be cooperated with and to cooperate (see 7.2.2), and so would be wrong by the relational moral theory.

Since the participant is innocent, she warrants instead friendly/harmonious treatment and hence engagement in joint projects. That involves transparency between actors about their goals, willingness on the part of each to achieve them, and interaction on the basis of trust. Such a relational rationale for the moral importance of free and informed consent is, I submit, a plausible rival to the more Western explanations.

Some might object that a concern for harmonious relationships would routinely permit a medical researcher (or physician) not to obtain free and informed consent. Consider a case in which, if a researcher manipulated a person into 'agreeing' to participate in a study that he otherwise would not have, the participant would obtain a new treatment, one that enables him and many others in society to enjoy more and better harmonious relationships in their lives.

In reply, the objection supposes that right action is a matter of promoting a final good of harmony, in the way that happiness is something to maximize according to a utilitarian model. However, I have been at pains to emphasize in this book that the relational moral theory is instead a deontological theory, where right action consists of *respecting* an individual's *capacity* to be party to harmonious relationships. My claim is that it is normally degrading of an innocent individual to treat her in an unfriendly way, even if done for the sake of promoting friendliness in the long run (7.2.2–7.3.2). Conducting research on a person's body or mind, say, without her knowing that it is happening or consequent to a threat degrades her ability to be the subject and object of a shared way of life between them.

Even if the relational moral theory can sensibly entail deontological restrictions on the promotion of good outcomes, one might have another reason for thinking that it fails to support a sufficiently robust right to free and informed consent. Imagine that a patient were aware of the communal ethic's injunction, which has been widely adopted in her society, to share a way of life with others, including by participating with them in their projects. She might then feel pressured to agree to procedures that she does not understand or would prefer to avoid, so as to avoid being nonconformist.

In reply, if this is a problem for the relational ethic, it is equally a problem for utilitarianism, which is all the more demanding of a moral agent, and also for Kantianism, at least insofar as it requires that another's ends 'must as far as possible be also *my* ends' (Kant 1785: Ak. 430). Were these ethical principles socially accepted, similar results would presumably ensue. Since the concern applies to any ethic imposing substantive positive duties on people, it does not constitute grounds to reject rightness as friendliness relative to its key competitors.

However, I deny that the present objection in fact poses a real problem. It is one thing for a theory actually to prescribe certain behaviour, and it is another for people to engage in certain behaviour based on their misinterpretations of a theory. I am interested in a moral theory that is epistemically justified to a global audience of philosophers, and hence am interested solely in evaluating the theory's real implications, not what people might do upon misconstruing them. Now, it is true that the communal ethic instructs people to commune with (innocent) others, meaning that a given person would have moral reason of *some* weight to help researchers achieve their aims. However, it does not follow that she would owe researchers anything in particular, supposing there had been no prior interaction between them. In addition, her duties to her family, co-workers, and neighbours would likely be stronger, given that she had been party to communal relationships with them in the past. Furthermore, by one interpretation of the relational ethic, there are duties to oneself for her to take into consideration (7.3.5). For all these reasons, it would be inappropriate for her to judge herself to be obligated to prioritize participation in a study or for society to suggest otherwise. Where a researcher has reasonable grounds to suspect a participant has been pressured or has such a skewed judgement, he should emphasize that she has a right not to participate and that morality permits her to take advantage of this right. He could also simply find another participant.

10.3 Confidentiality

I have argued that the ethic requiring respect for people's capacity for communal relationship *qua* sharing a way of life and caring for another's quality of life entails a right to free and informed consent. If a researcher is going to share a way of life with his participant (or a physician with his patient), then he must be transparent about their interaction and seek out her willing engagement. However, when it comes to confidentiality, I suspect the relational moral theory might put less weight on considerations of privacy than is the default in the West and for what are, upon reflection, plausible reasons.

First off, note the difference between the two distinct privacy-oriented issues in medical ethics of a right to free and informed consent, on the one hand, and a right to confidentiality, on the other. The consent issue concerns whether a research participant (or a patient) has voluntarily made a decision about which, if any, medical procedures she will undergo consequent to an accurate understanding of what they will involve. Whether a participant is sufficiently knowledgeable of the study's procedures and has agreed to them without inducement is distinct from whether those overseeing the study tell others about her medical condition.

The existence of free and informed consent to participate in a study is, both in principle and in practice, consistent with a lack of confidentiality. Just because others have been informed of one's medical condition without one's permission does not necessarily mean that one failed to give free and informed consent to be part of a research project. Conversely, the maintenance of confidentiality is consistent with a lack of free and informed consent. Even if one is part of a study but did not give such consent, it could be that the medical researcher nonetheless has not divulged to anyone else what he has discovered about one in the course of the study.

Not only are consent and confidentiality logically distinct matters, I suspect they are also morally distinct; having a right to one might be coherent with not having a right to the other. In the West, the standard view is that a research participant (or medical patient) has a right to have medical information about her kept confidential. More carefully, a medical researcher or other professional may not disclose information about a person obtained in the course of the study (or treatment), unless doing so is essential to prevent imminent and serious harm to third parties, often construed in terms of life and death.

Such an approach is sometimes grounded on the idea that it would be degrading of her autonomy to reveal information about her without her permission, as per Kantianism. Other times the notion is that such revelation would lead to withdrawal from the study or the reticence of others to participate in future studies, or would subject a participant to stigma on the part of an employer or her neighbours, which are natural utilitarian concerns.

However, rightness as friendliness suggests there are two reasons of relationship for thinking that medical researchers (and other professionals) are not obligated to maintain patient confidentiality in the way that is currently expected in the West. First, one's relationship with family might mean that they are entitled to know about one's health, a point that a number of other African ethicists have maintained. Because individuals are, by a characteristically African moral perspective, normally understood to have weighty duties to aid specific others, particularly family members, it is not merely up to the individual what she does with her body and mind. Since others have a stake in the individual being healthy, some have held that they ought to be aware of her illness and play a role in discussing how she ought to treat it (Gbadegesin 1998: 194; Kasenene 2000: 349–53, 356; Dube 2009: 192–9; Murove 2009b: 170–1).

Now, I reject the suggestions from some sub-Saharan moralists that it 'is the group which is the owner of life' (Kasenene 2000: 349) and that '[c]onfidentiality is based primarily on atomic individualism and the incorrigibility of the individual who is assumed to be endowed with intrinsic properties' (Murove 2009b: 171). However, I accept the ideas that one has substantial obligations to support those with whom one has intimately communed for a long while and that those whom one owes substantial labour, money, and other resources have a legitimate interest in knowing about conditions that risk precluding one's ability to provide them. It probably follows that a person has a duty to tell his dependents of foreseeable risks to his being able to continue to help them, and that, if he refuses to do so, a medical professional would do no wrong to him if she revealed such to his dependents. Ideally a medical professional would indicate such a policy up front with patients, so that they could know what to expect.

It does not follow that a medical professional who has obtained information about one's health in the course of a study or treatment has no duty of confidentiality whatsoever and may reveal anything to anybody. Instead, a medical professional should maintain confidentiality (unless there is serious risk to, say, the general public) when it comes either to a person's medical conditions that do not risk impairing his ability to live up to his special obligations or to third parties who are not the ones owed such special obligations. If sharing a way of life means interacting with others on a voluntary basis, then one may not divulge intimate information about them without their consent, supposing they are upholding their obligations to others.

The first exception to a confidentiality requirement was based on a duty of a person to provide material aid to family members or those similarly related to him, whereas the second is based on a duty of a person to provide information to others. Imagine that a genetic test conducted on a woman in the course of a study (or as part of treatment) reveals that her male partner incorrectly believes that he is the biological father of a child they are rearing together. May the tester tell him that he is mistaken?

The communal ethic entails that familial relationships matter morally, and, indeed, are to be pursued as an end, meaning that a broken family would be a serious ethical cost to avoid if at all possible. That would provide some reason for the tester not to tell the man, supposing there would be some likelihood that he would abandon the woman and the child.

However, the communal ethic also entails that there is a moral cost to interaction based on ignorance of important truths such as paternity. If the mother has known that the man is not the biological father and has led him to believe otherwise, she has treated him in an unfriendly way. The same is true, albeit to a lesser degree, if, while not having lied to him, she has taken advantage of his false belief. The mother has had a duty, of some weight, to the one who thinks that he is the biological father to inform him that he is not.

Now, it does not immediately follow that the genetic tester may indeed tell the male partner if the mother continues not to tell him herself. However, one point highlighted by the relational moral theory is that the tester would at least not be wronging *the mother* if he were to disclose to the partner, with the more salient moral concern being the likelihood of the prospective child not having enough support and aid. So long as the tester had not promised to keep the information confidential, disclosing to her partner would not be disrespecting her capacity to commune; her interests carry less weight since she is not adequately respecting her partner's ability to share a way of life as a subject and object.

10.4 Ancillary Standards of Care

Setting aside matters such as consent and confidentiality, what does a medical researcher (or, more carefully, his team, which includes sponsors and fieldworkers) morally owe participants in his study when it comes to resources? There is no debate that if a study ends up harming participants, the researcher must compensate them for their losses. That applies not merely to the time taken and inconvenience caused, but also for any unforeseen physical or psychological injury produced by the study. In contrast, there is some debate about whether there is any additional respect in which a medical researcher has a moral obligation to provide resources to participants in his study. This debate concerns what is sometimes called 'ancillary care obligations' or 'ancillary standards of care', with the 'ancillary' indicating what in addition to harm caused by the study might warrant the provision of aid to participants.

There are two familiar illustrations of ancillary standards of care (found in Slack et al. 2005; Stobie and Slack 2010; Richardson 2012). First, someone conducting a two-week study on malaria might encounter evidence of long-standing schistosomiasis in a participant. Must the researcher tell the participant that she has this disease and provide treatment, which typically involves medication for a few days? Second, consider a scholar conducting a two-year clinical trial on an HIV vaccine who discovers that some participants have acquired HIV during the course of the study. Suppose that he had done everything he could have in order to help them avoid becoming HIV+, such as providing information about how to avoid it, offering free condoms, and the like. Even though his study did not cause the harm of acquired HIV, should the researcher provide antiretrovirals or other relevant treatments, if he could do so at little cost to his other obligations?

Affirmative answers to these questions are controversial, with ancillary care obligations typically unrecognized in day-to-day practice around the world. While I now point out how the two prominent Western moral theories might seem to entail that these obligations indeed exist and should be acknowledged, I note some weaknesses in their rationales, after which I indicate how the relational moral theory more naturally supports the existence of robust ancillary care obligations.

For utilitarianism, the above researchers should often bear the costs of schistosomiasis and HIV, respectively, despite not having been responsible for study participants having acquired them. That is because often enough a researcher (or, again, his team) is in a better position to repair harm than would be an individual participant who is undergoing it. For the utilitarian, it does not in principle matter who has caused or otherwise been responsible for the presence of harm, and instead all that counts is who now could improve the situation, doing the most good with the least bad.

Although utilitarian reasoning does often entail that a researcher should pay for harm suffered by a study participant, there are limits to its scope that will be found counterintuitive to those sympathetic to the category of ancillary care obligations. Notice that there would no utilitarian reason for a researcher to help his study participant as compared to someone marginally more needy who is completely unrelated to the study or even to the researcher. Where the options include both helping a study participant keep her HIV load low and giving the money to a charity that would produce a bit more subjective well-being in the long run, utilitarianism would direct the researcher to do the latter as the uniquely right act. Another way to put the point is that utilitarianism does not recognize special obligations, where ancillary care obligations are plausibly understood to be an instance of them. There is something about having participated in the researcher's study that gives the researcher extra reason to aid participants relative to non-participants who are similarly needy.

At first blush, Kantianism seems to entail that a researcher is never obligated to compensate for harm that he did not cause, since this ethic bases duties substantially on the way a person has exercised his capacity to make reasoned decisions. If the researcher did no wrong to the participant, the researcher is not liable to help her, by a straightforward understanding of respect for autonomy. Of course, Kantians believe in positive obligations to aid others in need, but very much like utilitarianism, there is nothing in the logic of such 'imperfect' obligations to direct a researcher to help those in his study as opposed to others who are not. For typical Kantianism, a duty to aid a particular person must arise from having made a promise to do so or having accepted benefits from her in a cooperative scheme, but these are inapplicable to a typical clinical trial.

However, there is one Kantian, Henry Richardson (2012; see also Richardson and Belsky 2004), who has provided an elaborate theoretical justification for thinking there are ancillary care obligations, which he calls the 'partial-entrustment model'. It is roughly the view that, upon waiving privacy rights and providing information to the researcher, he becomes obligated to support participants' health in the light of the information acquired from them, even if the researcher's study did not cause their need for medical assistance: 'The central claim of the partial-entrustment model is that, simply by providing researchers with these special permissions (to conduct research on them), participants effectively entrust the researchers with special responsibilities to look after needs they discover by acting on those permissions' (Richardson 2012: 35). The entrustment is only partial, as participants naturally retain significant responsibility for looking after their own needs. However, upon receiving private information from participants, which places them in a vulnerable position, the researcher is thought to become obligated to help participants, even if their need for help was not caused by his study.

The view is Kantian in that respect for self-governance is the value at the bottom of Richardson's explanation of ancillary care obligations. Basically, since the researcher has compromised the participants' autonomy, he has a duty to protect them in other ways: 'The basis of the special ancillary-care obligation, then, lies in the special responsibility for protecting participants' autonomy that falls to researchers when they accept the participants' waivers of their privacy rights' (Richardson 2012: 96). Upon giving informed consent to participate in a study, participants waive their right to retain certain kinds of information about themselves—e.g., about their body and intimate behaviours as they pertain to the object of study—and thereby put themselves in a compromised position, which, for Richardson, means that the researcher incurs a special obligation to protect them in particular from harm discovered by means of that information.

The account is powerful, but, rather than point out its advantages, which Richardson (2012) has done quite ably, I focus on what I think are some important weaknesses, so as to motivate the relational alternative. One of these problems is that there are places in Richardson's complete theoretical account where autonomy does not do the sole—or even the main—justificatory work, as it is supposed to do according to the official line of argument adumbrated above; autonomy is supplemented by an ad hoc appeal to an altogether different, relational value.

For example, according to Richardson, a researcher has a duty to offer treatment or funds to participants after, and because, she has notified them of harm that she discovered in the course of the study about them. Once she tells them of a sensitive matter, *the relationship becomes more intimate*, which is what obligates the researcher to offer aid as well:

> The warning or, more generally, the broaching of the sensitive issue deepens the relationship between these two parties.... Insofar as the demandingness of beneficence obligations varies directly with the depth of relationships, this deepening of the relationship is itself a basis for firmer obligations of beneficence (than merely warning). (Richardson 2012: 92; see also 93–6)

My point is this: it is *not* so much the fact of reduced privacy or compromised autonomy that, by Richardson's full account, generates the duty to aid beyond providing a warning of a discovered illness, but, rather, the intensity of the relationship between the parties. Richardson's appeal to intensity of relationship in order to ground obligation fits naturally in a communal ethic, but not in an autonomy-based one.

Continuing the dialectical move against Richardson, notice that he also appeals to the depth or intensity of the relationship—e.g., how close the parties are and how long the relationship has lasted—in order to determine how much a researcher is obligated to aid participants (while also including a 'little cost' rider) (2012: 42, 48–9, 188). However, this factor again has nothing inherently to do with the participant's autonomy, and instead fits best within a fundamentally relational ethical framework.

In reply, Richardson could seek to give up the appeal to intimacy as a factor determining the ground and content of obligations. He might instead maintain that it is indeed a reduction of autonomy, or threat of such, that creates the obligation for a researcher to aid a participant. Sometimes, for example, Richardson contends that when a researcher warns a participant of a disease revealed in the course of the study, 'the gaze of another threatens to inhibit how one deals with particularly sensitive matters' (2012: 93), or that the participant 'will likely feel temporarily at a loss when suddenly confronted with the issue' (2012: 94). Imposing these autonomy-related risks on participants, the researcher incurs a duty to make up for them, by offering treatment for the disease.

This reasoning would be more coherent for Richardson, but, I maintain, less plausible. If there is indeed an obligation to offer treatment to participants, then it probably existed *before* such threats to autonomy obtained. My intuition is that, supposing the researcher has a duty to warn participants of a disease they are revealed to have in the course of the study, he also has a duty to offer more than that *at the same time, prior to having actually warned them* and thereby having negatively affected their autonomy. And if the duty to offer treatment existed prior to the participants being warned, then it of course was not the warning that created the duty. It must have been something else that created it.

For another major objection, I suggest that a principle of respect for autonomy is a prima facie poor explanation of how one can acquire a partial duty to aid without having wronged a specific person, promised to aid her, or benefited from her contributions to a cooperative scheme. If a person makes a fully free and informed choice to give information to a party, then, *in the light of autonomy*, she is responsible for any foreseeable vulnerability that doing so may normally entail, and the one who now has the information is not liable to aid the donor *on that basis*. So long as the research participant was not exploited—i.e., she had the robust ability to avoid becoming a participant—and so long as the participant was neither deceived nor otherwise ignorant of key facts, autonomy-based factors mean that it is her responsibility to bear the cost of having disclosed the information about herself. When thinking from the perspective of autonomy, there is no apparent difference between deciding to put personal information about oneself on the internet and giving the same information to a researcher. Of course, the researcher probably has asked for the information, but we can imagine that people on the internet have made similar requests. In both cases, the logic of autonomy suggests that others do not become obligated to help one by virtue of becoming aware of information that one elected to share with them, even if one thereby has made oneself vulnerable.

To sum up, I suggested that where the partial-entrustment model appears strong in accounting for ancillary care obligations, it is so by illegitimately invoking relational values that are distinct from autonomy, and that where it seems weak, it is so because of its appeal to autonomy as the ground of ancillary care obligations. In any event, I now point out how the relational moral theory provides a different and strong rationale for ancillary care obligations, ones that, *contra* utilitarianism and a general principle of beneficence, are specially owed to research participants.

Recall how the communal ethic entails partial duties, viz., that upon having communed with someone, one incurs extra moral reason to commune with that person relative to those with whom one has not communed (7.3.3, 9.4). Roughly, to the extent that one has been friendly with someone, one has a *pro tanto* duty to continue to do so. Now, upon relating communally or being friendly with participants in a study, particularly by sharing a way of life with them, a researcher has formed a morally significant tie that demands respect and hence a response in the form of caring for their quality of life. Concretely, once a researcher and participants have begun to think of themselves as a 'we' engaged in the context of a study, once they have cooperated with each other to advance the end of acquiring knowledge, and once participants have presumably helped the researcher, then they have related in a way that imposes special obligations to aid each other (with the one in a greater position to aid having much more of a duty to do so). Just as extant patients are normally entitled to treatment from a doctor with some priority relative to strangers (9.4.1), extant participants in a study have a claim to receive aid from a researcher, such that it would be *pro tanto* wrong for her to allocate it to strangers with whom she has not related communally.

In addition to providing an explanation of whom it is that a researcher has special moral reason to aid, an appeal to communality can account for how she should aid them. Basically, the form that caring should take is determined by considerations of the way of life that has been shared. When a communal way of relating is responsible for a partial obligation to help another person, the proper way to help him is in large part a function of the nature of the relationship of which they have both been a part. Since a medical researcher and participants have been involved in a joint project of discovering information about health, health-related care is the appropriate sort of aid to provide. Recall the point that when a doctor owes a colleague aid, it is for help with such matters as taking over his shift when he has family obligations, and not, say, assistance with cleaning his garage (9.4.2). By the same token, if a researcher owes participants aid by virtue of having related communally in the context of a study about disease, the aid should in the first instance be a matter of informing them about diseases and treating them.

When it comes to how much aid to provide, remember that Richardson is drawn to the view that the more intimate or deep the relationship between a researcher and her participants, the greater the obligation to them. While I find it hard for autonomy-based considerations to make sense of that attractive point, rightness as friendliness does so with ease. Note that the moral reason one is required to give one's family the lion's share of one's resources is plausibly that one is closest to them, not that one has promised to do so or that one could do the most good by helping them rather than others (7.3.3). Even if one had not promised to do so, and even if one would not maximize good outcomes by doing so, one would still have some weighty duty to help one's family before non-family. Communal relationships encumber.

By extension, the longer and stronger the ties between a researcher and participants, the more that the former, presumably with more resources, is obligated to help the latter. So, a researcher would owe more to those in a longitudinal study than to, say, those subjected to a few drawings of blood. Of course, often it is not literally the researcher who develops ties with participants, but rather those acting under his direction, such as fieldworkers and nurses. However, insofar as the latter's agency is a function of those who are directing the study, the ties they form with participants are also plausibly considered to be those of the principal investigator and his sponsors.

For those who are inclined to accept ancillary care obligations, I submit that an appeal to communality provides an attractive explanation of them, one that promises to improve on what utilitarianism and Kantianism can provide. Rightness as friendliness explains why a researcher can be obligated to aid participants apart from any agreement to do so, but not to aid, say, those who work at a shop till. It accounts for the judgement that a researcher can be obligated to aid participants with regard to their health, but not for everything they might need in life. And it also makes good sense of how much aid a researcher owes different participants. For those who went into this section not already convinced that there are any ancillary care obligations, the relational moral theory might have provided enough reason for them to change their mind. Specifically, I submit that the analogies between duties of doctors to aid their patients and colleagues (9.4.1–9.4.2), on the one hand, and duties of researchers to aid their study participants, on the other, are strong.

11
Education Ethics

11.1 Teaching Students

The previous chapter addressed the ethics of acquiring new information from participants in a study, while this one is mainly about transmitting information that has already been acquired to students in a school.[1] Specifically, here I take up some moral controversies about teaching students in higher education institutions such as public universities. I am principally interested in what the proper final ends of such institutions are when it comes to imparting knowledge, i.e., what they should strive to teach students.[2]

Nearly everyone agrees that students at a university must be taught the knowledge and skills that would make them competitive on the job market; few doubt that public higher education ought to facilitate equal opportunity, which involves enabling those from lower economic classes to acquire the qualifications to make them eligible for jobs and the wealth attached to them. However, it is also the case that virtually no one believes that this is all that students may or even must be taught, with much controversy existing about what else students should have learned by the time they earn their degrees.

Surely it is morally appropriate to teach university students about culture, but which one(s)? Utilitarianism and Kantianism appear to support a cosmopolitan approach, whereby students would learn about an array of cultures from around the world, with it left up to them to determine which one(s) to pick. In contrast, I argue that the relational moral theory would prioritize the instruction and development of a local culture, albeit without being utterly parochial (11.2). Next, I argue that the communal ethic entails that it would be appropriate for a university to impart moral knowledge that constitutes or enhances virtue (11.3). In this, it accords with the dominant approach amongst African educationists and contrasts with standard applications of utilitarianism and Kantianism, which instead focus, in liberal fashion, on student preference or choice. Finally, I address a puzzle about whether students should be taught any knowledge for its own sake, information that is of no practical use or at least much less than other

[1] For discussions of related topics in media ethics, see Metz (2015a).

[2] I do not devote space here to other educational controversies, such as which students should be taught, where affirmative action would be relevant, or how to teach students, which would include proper pedagogical techniques or assessment methods.

A Relational Moral Theory: African Ethics in and beyond the Continent. Thaddeus Metz, Oxford University Press.
 DOI: 10.1093/oso/9780198748960.003.0011

sorts of knowledge (11.4). After showing that it is difficult to provide an affirmative answer in the light of the dominant Western moral principles, which direct us to what would facilitate preference satisfaction or end realization, I consider whether the relational moral theory entails otherwise. Although I note that a plain reading of it suggests not, I also offer another way to interpret rightness as friendliness according to which knowledge about fundamental aspects of human nature and our environment is a gift that is in itself worth bestowing on students.

11.2 Culture as an End

What should be the aim when teaching matters of culture to students in public schools, ranging from secondary to tertiary education? For many indigenous African societies, and according to some philosophers inspired by them, the point of education in regard to culture should be to enable young adults to help sustain a local way of life. In contrast to this parochial approach, an influential, and perhaps even dominant, educational philosophy in the West is the cosmopolitan view that such students should be informed about a wide variety of cultures, with it left up to them which one(s) they will choose.

These two views are at the opposite ends of a spectrum. From a parochial perspective, only one culture matters for its own sake in the classroom, while, from a cosmopolitan one, all cultures merit equal consideration there (at least insofar as they are not unjust).

In contrast to both perspectives, I articulate and advocate a third approach, according to which it would be right for schools to give priority to understanding and enriching local culture, while also informing students of many other cultures. I show the relational moral theory entails making the local first and the global second.[3] Respecting people as capable of communal relationship means teaching students so as to support a local way of life,[4] while taking care to ensure that they are not ignorant of the rest of the world, a plausible alternative both to the cosmopolitanism that follows from the impartial Western moral theories and to parochialism.

By the word 'culture' I include things such as languages, values, belief systems, social relationships, aesthetics, and knowledge. For example, what counts as Chinese culture would include (but hardly be exhausted by) the written language of Mandarin, the value of harmony, Confucianism and other non-theist worldviews,

[3] My approach to cultural instruction is broadly similar to what Appiah (2006) advances, but my defence of it differs from his.

[4] For ease of discussion, I assume that a given society has a single culture, although I of course acknowledge the reality of multicultural societies. My aim is to show that the local should receive priority relative to the global, which nonetheless also merits a place in cultural instruction, leaving for another occasion the distinct issue of how to balance the instruction of different local cultures.

the norm of saving face, the practice of calligraphy, and the tendency to be pragmatic and holist when seeking to understand the world. In contrast, European culture includes (amongst other things) written Romance and Germanic languages, the value of autonomy, monotheism and especially Christianity, the commonness of a nuclear family, the prizing of abstract visual arts, and a theoretical and analytic orientation towards the pursuit of knowledge. So construed, culture excludes large facets of medicine, technology, engineering, economics, domestic politics, international relations, chemistry, and physics. There can of course be cultural dimensions to these fields, but there would be something substantial to them that would remain if one abstracted from those. In any event, in order to make the discussion tractable, I mainly address what should be taught in university departments such as music, visual art, architecture, literature, languages, religion, and philosophy.

In indigenous sub-Saharan societies, and in philosophical work inspired by them, when it has come to teaching young adults about culture, the dominant theme has been the need to enable them to sustain and participate in the local way of life. In an article that surveys the major aims of education in pre-colonial Africa, a leading scholar of it, Augustus Adeyinka, and a colleague remark:

> Children developed a sense of obligation towards the community and grew to appreciate its history, language, customs and values. This is perhaps one of the greatest attributes of indigenous education as opposed to Western education which has been rightly accused of alienating young Africans from their cultural heritage.... Most traditional communities in Africa perceived education as a vehicle for maintaining or preserving the cultural heritage and *status quo*. This partly accounts for why traditional teachers discouraged their pupils from probing into the unknown and imposed heavy sanctions on those who tried to do so.
> (Adeyinka and Ndwapi 2002: 18–9)

Notice how the descriptive and prescriptive are interwoven in the quotation. On the one hand, the authors are recounting how traditional African societies have typically educated so as to sustain their respective cultures, while, on the other, the authors express support for such an approach.[5]

What would make sense of this narrow sort of approach to cultural instruction, one that does not consider it essential, or that even considers it inappropriate, to teach young adults about cultures from other parts of the world? An armchair anthropology suggests that many indigenous sub-Saharan peoples formed small-scale societies that did not routinely come into contact with cultures radically different from their own (e.g., Busia 1962: 80; cf. Appiah 2006: xii–xiii). If there were little prospect of interacting with those from alien cultures, let alone ever

[5] For similar views, see Adeyemi and Adeyinka (2003: 228–9) and a number of the contributions to Seepe (1998).

leaving your society for one, then there would be little incentive to learn about them. However, as is well known, in the twenty-first-century globalization is in full swing. Rural villagers often access the internet and see their livelihoods depend on decisions made in other societies.

It could also be that some underlying moral values have been taken to prescribe parochialism when it comes to culture. Recall that there have been relativist, corporatist, and traditionalist interpretations of African communitarianism (7.5.1–7.5.3) suggesting that the folkways of only one's people matter. According to some, the community is in some sense 'prior to' the individual, which, in turn, means that one's foremost aim should be to accept 'the rituals of incorporation and the overarching necessity of learning the social rules by which the community lives' (Menkiti 1984: 173). However, beyond having cast doubt on these interpretations of African ethics, there is the point that, even if one must learn the local rules, it does not follow that the rest of the world's peoples and their ways of life should be considered irrelevant for a young adult.

Not all African philosophers favour a parochial approach to education, with Kwasi Wiredu objecting to the sort of education he finds prominent in 'traditional' Africa, namely, one that accords 'a low priority, if any at all, to the discussion of alternatives or even to the rational justification of the one given alternative' (1980: 3). Wiredu prefers an approach in which students would be enabled 'to perceive, in relation to any given issue, as many as possible of the relevant alternatives' (1980: 3). That approach is at the heart of cosmopolitan cultural instruction that has been a salient, if not dominant, theme in contemporary Western philosophy of education.

A cosmopolitan orientation towards education in respect of culture includes an 'intellectual and aesthetic stance of openness to divergent cultural experiences' as well as 'respect and enjoyment of cultural differences with a sense of global belonging' (McCarty 2011: 7). A cosmopolitan education teaches students a wide array of languages, values, belief systems, social norms, and aesthetics, imparting 'the ability to think as a citizen of the whole world, not just some local region or group' (Nussbaum 2002: 289). In addition, the attitude towards the world's cultures would be a substantially neutral one, in the sense of avoiding favouritism towards the culture of the students' own society. Indeed, by a cosmopolitan approach, students 'would be encouraged to question their narrow attachments' (Waks 2009: 589), as opposed to being expected and prompted to uphold them.

Cosmopolitanism is the natural companion of the egalitarianism and individualist ethical systems that grew out of the European Enlightenment (Appiah 2006; Kleingeld and Brown 2013: sec. 1.2). If what confers a moral standing on us is our ability to govern ourselves with our rational faculties, as per Kantianism, or to satisfy our informed preferences, à la utilitarianism, then it is immoral for educators to restrict students to any one conception of the good life. What matters instead is either the individual student's choice, made in the light of an awareness of as many options as possible, or her satisfaction, potentially achieved from any source.

However, just as a purely partial morality is incomplete, so is a purely impartial one. You really should save the life of your mother before that of a stranger, if you had to choose between them, such that you should feel more guilt for not having rescued her than for not having rescued him. It is difficult for Kantianism and utilitarianism to entail and plausibly explain why, when you have never promised to rescue your mother in such a situation or when rescuing her would promote marginally less subjective well-being down the road, respectively. In contrast, the relational ethic easily does so in terms of the idea that long and strong bonds provide extra reason to aid those party to them relative to those who are not (7.3.3, 9.4, 10.4). My suggestion is that, although the tie to one's society is of course weaker than that with one's mother, there is enough of one for a student to have reason to prioritize his culture relative to a foreign one.

I now consider what such priority would mean, after which I show how relationality justifies it. With this approach to cultural instruction, the focus would be on the local while not ignoring the global; to speak of 'prioritizing' one's own culture means that other cultures are not entirely neglected and do receive some attention. To use an analogy, it would be neither a monarchy, where one person has all the power, nor a consensual democracy, where power is equally shared; instead, all would have some power, but some would have a greater share than others. I maintain that a school's emphasis should be on understanding, enriching, and participating in the prominent culture(s) in which the school is set, while also ensuring students learn about ones elsewhere in the world that might be quite different from their own.

From this perspective, *contra* cosmopolitanism, it would be inappropriate merely to construct 'world citizens', with no particular ability to support their culture or interest in doing so. Instead, the aim should be to produce citizens who identify with their culture and are in a position to contribute to it, more than with other cultures. However, *contra* parochialism, the aim should also be to produce citizens who understand and are open to learning from cultures other than their own, so that it would be wrong for teachers to discourage pupils from probing into the unknown and considering changes to the status quo.

Consider a concrete example of what a priority approach entails for the curriculum. When it comes to literature, a school in an African country should focus on novels that were written by those from it and that are about it, supplemented by works written by those from other African cultures. In addition, given that a large majority of African societies have featured oral 'texts' for several centuries, students should listen to stories, proverbs, and poems recounted by elders, either in person or in digital form. Although a majority of the literature curriculum in an African school should be African, it should not neglect texts from, say, the Indian, Latin American, and Euro-American-Australasian traditions. And where styles, techniques, or insights from non-African sources would be revealing when adapted to an African context, students-*cum*-writers should borrow them. Such an approach would differ from the parochial one of excluding the foreign, on the one hand, and from the cosmopolitan one of according equal weight amongst global sources, on the other.

When it comes to the attitude of the teacher, she would not impose sanctions on students for being interested in non-African texts, and instead should readily facilitate access to them. However, she might especially enable and encourage students to engage with the local culture. For example, she might point out that it would be revealing to develop it in a certain way, suggesting that pupils should continue their studies with an eye to making a contribution someday. Or she might organize a written or oral competition whereby students would demonstrate their knowledge of texts composed by their people. Or she might arrange field trips so that students listen to readings by local authors and poets and ask questions of them.

Now, cosmopolitans will object, to use Wiredu's terms, that there is no 'rational justification of the one given alternative', i.e., that the emphasis on the local is not defended and perhaps is not defensible in the face of a global array of options. To respond to this concern, as well as provide more general support to the priority approach, I invoke the relational moral theory. According to it, we should treat individuals with respect insofar as they are capable of relating communally or harmoniously. Recall that simply having the capacity to relate communally confers moral importance on people, entitling them all to some protection and concern, but that treating people with respect in virtue of their capacity to commune will mean taking into account the ways they and others have actualized this capacity (7.3.3–7.3.4). Where an agent has communed with other parties in the past, that provides some moral reason to continue to do so with them, relative to others. Family members and co-workers are the sorts of persons who straightforwardly merit extra cooperation and help from a given agent, because of the relationship that agent has shared with them. I submit that the same is true of one's compatriots.

Consider, now, what the communal ethic entails for the way a school ought to instruct a young adult regarding culture. Against the cosmopolitan approach, the communal ethic entails that such students have weightier obligations to identify with and exhibit solidarity towards the society in which they have been embedded. At least insofar as young adults have enjoyed a sense of togetherness with a certain society and participated in it, and this society has helped them by having socialized them and supported their studies, they have an obligation to commune with it that is to some extent stronger than they have in respect of some other society. It follows that when it comes to cultural instruction, students have extra reason to think of the local culture as theirs and to take pride in it, to participate in it as opposed to remaining aloof from it, to help enrich it, and to do these things 'because this is who we are' and not merely for self-interested reasons.

As noted above, cosmopolitans are likely to object that there is nothing special about one's own culture—that its interpretations, styles, and the like demand justification in the face of so many competing alternatives on the globe. That might be relevant for a Kantian ethic that would prize 'training intended to enable people to make deliberate rational choices' (Wiredu 1980: 3). However, it is not so relevant to a communal ethic, roughly according to which 'immorality is the word or deed which undermines fellowship' (Kasenene 1998: 21). The plausible reason to give greater attention to local culture than to other cultures throughout the world is not that the former is better or somehow more justified, but rather that it is one's own. Putting it on an even footing with other cultures would undermine one's fellowship with the members of one's society.

11.3 Virtue as an End

Although a society's conception of virtue plausibly counts as part of its 'culture', I did not discuss moral education in the previous section. Partly that is because the literature by and large treats cultural instruction and moral education separately. However, mainly it is because I am interested in whether university students should learn the true or most justified conception of virtue, not whichever one is prominent in their respective societies. Morality admits of norms and values that are universally applicable, unlike, say, those for making music or participating in rituals, or so I have been contending (7.5.1).

In this section I argue that a public university ought to strive to make students more virtuous, where that centrally includes doing the right thing. Notice that this aim is not reducible to merely teaching university students about ethical views—say, by conveying propositional knowledge of utilitarianism, Kantianism, or even the present communal ethic. The aim would instead be to enable students to improve their moral decision-making in day-to-day life. It would mean instruction oriented towards not merely imparting an abstract apprehension of moral claims and controversies, but also prompting some sound moral practice. In other words, the aim would be not so much *moral education*, an orthodox focus on belief formation, but more *education for morality*, an orthopraxy.

Whereas there is real debate amongst Western philosophers about whether universities should strive to make students morally better (for just a sample, see Kiss and Euben 2010), there is little amongst African philosophers. Those working in the sub-Saharan tradition normally accept that one final end of education is the realization of personhood, where 'personhood' connotes good character (for some examples, see Letseka 2000; Wiredu 2004; Nkondo 2007; Balogun 2008). It is common to hold that the point of education is to develop wisdom, where wisdom is understood to be a mainly moral-practical trait—roughly an ability to navigate social relationships with good judgement.

Rightness as friendliness supports the default position amongst African philosophers of education. Lecturers at a public university should act in friendly ways with their students, where doing so includes, but is not exhausted by, meeting their needs and so enabling them to acquire wealth, particularly if they come from lower economic classes. However, an intuitive part of being a good friend to others is enabling them to be a good friend in turn. That is, being friendly means not just making people better off, but also better people. Insofar as the solidarity element of the relational moral theory involves enhancing people's communal dispositions (and probably their liveliness, too, for it is a plausible candidate for excellence) (5.4, 6.2), lecturers ought to aim for that in the classroom.

Although the communal ethic in principle does entail that public higher education ought to strive to enhance people's virtue, in practice its reach would probably be limited. In the light of some reasonable empirical claims, a university would typically fail to impart virtue understood in a 'thick' way, for example, as a person being motivated by the right reasons or feeling emotions such as being glad when others flourish. There are likely not the time and other resources available for a university to make students better people in these attitudinal ways, at least if it is going to teach them intricate knowledge and refined skills in fields such as chemistry, engineering, medicine, economics, sociology, and metaphysics. In theory, a government could tack an additional six or twelve months onto the bachelor's degree, but most students and also governments already find higher education expensive and something to streamline on the road to economic productivity.

Although there is reason to doubt that a university can foster much virtue understood in terms of certain attitudes, it is probably in a good position to advance it when it comes to performing actions. Here are several respects in which instructors could prompt their students to act in friendly ways towards each other and those in the broader society and to do so in ways likely to prompt more friendliness down the road to boot.

For one, some instruction could be done using what are often called 'communities of practice' (Wenger 1998), where students would learn by collaborating with others to realize shared goals. Relationships of sharing a way of life and caring for others' quality of life are more likely to be realized in the context of joint, public activities than isolated assignments done at home in which students are competing against each other for marks. In the context of communal learning projects, instructors might highlight how to become more aware of implicit biases, how to identify and deal with conflicts of interest, and how to become more attuned to other people's points of view and feelings.

Beyond coordinating with and helping one another, students could be taught to do so with those beyond the university. Enabling students to excel at the right sort of job, meaning one that would meet people's needs (as opposed to satisfy market demand for trivialities), would plausibly count as a way that a university could impart moral behaviour. If the state must treat people as having a dignity because of (in part) their capacities to be cared for and to care for others, then it must care for each of them by enabling them to work at jobs in accordance with their particular abilities and inclinations to care for others. Part of such training could involve internships or related forms of work-based education.

In addition, a university could teach students how to be cooperative within the institution and also facilitate cooperation beyond its confines. There are certain policies that, when routinely enforced by the state or otherwise adhered to, would enable people to avoid interfering with one another and would foster joint projects. Key examples are certain constitutional laws, good governance policies, principles for resolving conflict, and rules to regulate debate, all of which a university could readily impart to students. Note that universities could teach students about cooperative participation not merely theoretically, but also practically. For example, they might do more than they often do to include students in decision-making bodies. From this standpoint, a university Senate should consist not merely of full professors and senior managers; it should also include a number of student representatives, at least to watch as observers to learn how to share opinions, to disagree constructively, and to forge consensus. Perhaps students should in fact have their own governing body.

In sum, part of honouring people's ability to relate communally is relating to (innocent) people in that way, which, in turn, includes enabling them to relate communally to still others. Part of what a state university ought to be intrinsically striving for is helping others to improve their character at least to the extent that it is feasible during the time of a degree. That is a plausible, even if contested, view of one point of higher education, which, I now argue, is more naturally entailed by the communal ethic than it is by the dominant Western moral theories.

For utilitarians, who value only subjective well-being as good for its own sake, behaviour of the sorts just described is at best valuable merely as a means, if it is valuable at all. For example, training for a job that would give a great number of people small satisfactions could be right on utilitarian grounds, instead of training for a job that would meet a smaller number of people's needs. For another example, there could be situations in which a decision-making hierarchy would be marginally more efficient in the long run than democratic or otherwise cooperative interaction, and so would be justified by utilitarianism.

When it comes to Kantianism, there are ways of interpreting it so that it would prescribe instruction likely to improve students' character. However, the dominant applications of it in the context of philosophy of education for several decades have been otherwise. Instead, the overwhelming emphasis has been on developing the ability of students to decide autonomously, think critically, and evaluate rationally (for a range of proponents over the years, see Peters 1966; Hirst 1974; Mearsheimer 1998; Siegel 1998; Adler 2003; White 2010). One way of putting the point is that the focus has been on intellectual, and not moral, virtue, with many inclined to believe that, since there is reasonable disagreement about moral virtue, it would be objectionably illiberal for a public university to advance any particular conception of it. Instead, students should have the freedom to explore any conception of the good life they choose, except when it comes to political norms such as supporting constitutional democracy, advancing economic justice, or becoming a good citizen (e.g., Macedo 1990; Gutmann 1995; Enslin and Horsthemke 2004; Anderson 2007; cf. Nussbaum 2012).

This familiar approach differs from what a communal ethic entails, which would (also) prescribe making students better moral agents on a day-to-day, interpersonal level—say, by cultivating their sympathy or ability to resolve conflict. It is reasonable to think that much of a university's final end in respect of moral education would address more than just the political. Whereas good citizenship is a matter of the governmental roles of voter and advocate for justice, communality can also be manifested in the non-political contexts of being a romantic partner, friend, parent, neighbour, worker, colleague, mentor, therapist, manager, consumer, and member of a board. Voting takes place only once every several years; one's vote has virtually zero effect, while writing letters to the editor or lobbying a political party are only marginally more effectual; and one's odds of becoming someone with any real political power or influence are extremely low. In contrast, since communal relationships can be exhibited in a variety of everyday roles, and since a university can foster them, it ought to help students and the broader society by doing so.

11.4 Knowledge for Its Own Sake?

So far in this chapter I have argued that the relational moral theory prescribes prioritizing the instruction of local culture to support relationships of sharing a way of life and improving students' character as a way to support relationships of caring for others' quality of life. Transmitting these two kinds of knowledge has some kind of practical value to it; doing so facilitates certain ways of interacting between people. Should a public university also strive to impart knowledge that would do no or comparatively little practical good?

Debate about how to answer this question is often framed in terms of knowledge 'for its own sake' or sometimes 'blue-sky' scholarship. By such phrases I mean information or reflection that will not, or at least is very unlikely to, be of much concrete or tangible use for society with respect to goods such as health, wealth, liberty, or even improved interpersonal relationships. Examples of such enquiry are readily obtained from the humanities and liberal arts, and include seeking answers to questions such as: What is it to be a cause? Can you be certain that you are not dreaming right now? Do numbers have a real existence independent of our minds? What is the meaning of this poem? What were the earliest artworks done by human beings? However, the natural sciences also offer several examples of pursuit of knowledge for its own sake: Will the universe expand forever? Is there a multiverse? What is at the dead centre of a black hole? How did fish evolve into land-based creatures? What killed the dinosaurs?

Should a state university aim to teach students the answers to such questions? My own intuition is that it should. Suppose a cosmologist enlisted some students to help her ascertain with conclusive evidence what the fate of the universe will be, and then passed that knowledge on to other generations of students. I submit that she should be praised, instead of criticized, for the way she has used public resources. However, this intuition is not as widely shared as some others in this book, and so I do not maintain that it is a powerful strike against utilitarianism and Kantianism if, as I argue below, they cannot account for it. That said, the intuition is plausible, and I also sketch a way of understanding what is good for people that would enable the relational moral theory to account for it. For those who accept the intuition, the ability of a version of rightness as friendliness to entail and explain it provides some reason to accept it relative to the Western principles that, I now contend, cannot.

According to utilitarianism, any higher education institution should spend public resources solely in ways that are expected, relative to other available options, to result in the highest net improvement to people's subjective well-being in the long run. It appears true that such a cost-benefit approach would have to rule out seeking knowledge for its own sake, since the latter is *defined* as that which is unlikely to foster concrete social goods, including pleasant experiences and satisfied desires. Indeed, some theorists have made that kind of point, invoking a prescription to improve well-being in defence of strictly 'relevant' or 'responsive' instruction and against the pursuit of any knowledge for its own sake (e.g., Dowling and Seepe 2003: 45–8; and many contributions to Kraemer-Mbula et al. 2020). Concretely, teaching students about whether there is a multiverse would produce much less expected social welfare than other types of knowledge that a university could produce, e.g., how to produce affordable solar power.

However, there have been some who have tried to argue that a cost-benefit approach to public higher education in fact permits the promotion of knowledge for its own sake. First, there are some who have pointed out that we can never really know for sure what the long-term effects of knowledge will be, and from this have concluded that academics ought at least to be free to teach whatever knowledge they want. One scholar appeals to

> the truism that the future cannot be predicted, perhaps most obviously regarding the directions that the development of knowledge and technology will take. Thus even within the natural sciences, physical and biological, in technology studies and in business administration, there could be no sound rationale for steering teaching in line with too tight a specification of relevance.
>
> (Jonathan 2006: 21; see also Higgins 2000: 116; Flexner 2017)

Even if an instance of knowledge appears to be merely free-floating, chances are that its enquirer is on *terra firma*, so the argument goes.

The trouble with this rationale is that the alleged truism is patently false. Although we of course cannot predict outcomes with certainty, we can do so on the basis of probability. In a situation in which there are scarce resources, the rational thing to do, from the perspective of a cost-benefit approach, is nothing other than to weigh up the expected values and disvalues and to choose the option that will maximize the net amount of expected value minus expected disvalue. And we routinely are in a position to estimate which knowledge is more likely to benefit society compared with other sorts. After all, a physicist wanting to explore with students whether our universe is merely one amongst innumerable others in the light of extraordinarily difficult concepts in mathematics and physics is much less likely to foster subjective well-being than is one teaching them about solar power. It would be irrational and immoral merely to flip a coin about which knowledge to impart, supposing one were a utilitarian agent having to choose how to act so as to maximize satisfaction in the long run.

Here is a second strategy some have used to attempt to show that utilitarianism can permit the pursuit of knowledge for its own sake. It is that even if *knowledge* for its own sake would not be likely to do much good for society, the blue-sky *knower* would be. Citing the views of the British thinker Conrad Russell, one scholar suggests that 'the real value of the university lies in part with the teaching it does and the graduates it produces, graduates who "must be capable of wanting to pursue knowledge for its own sake" if they are to be socially useful' (Higgins 2000: 116). Why? Because those who pursue knowledge for its own sake come to prize the truth and to speak it more often than those who pursue other kinds of knowledge, where the more truth-appreciators a society has, the better off it is likely to be in the long term.

This is a clever manoeuvre by which to try to demonstrate that pursuing knowledge for its own sake can be of long-term social benefit. However, I think it also clearly fails in its aims. If the core premise of the argument, that blue-sky enquirers are more faithful to the truth and willing to speak it to power than more practical scholars, were correct, then philosophers and cosmological physicists would be, on average, better in these respects than, say, sociologists and medical researchers. However, I am, and I presume the reader is, unaware of any evidence suggesting that is the case. So far as truth-appreciation goes, these scholars are all on a par with one another.

In addition, a plausible reason for doubting that blue-sky enquiry makes one a better truth-appreciator is that the aspects of blue-sky enquiry that foster an appreciation of truth are equally (or at least comparably) available when conducting more practically relevant enquiry. For example, take an engineer teaching students what we know so far about solar power and collaborating with them to improve our understanding of how to make it affordable. They could appreciate the non-utilitarian facets of the research, e.g., the symmetry of the dynamics underlying the work, or the elegance of the theorems used, and thereby become useful truth-appreciators, while at the same time transmitting and developing knowledge that is likely to make a real difference to the general welfare. The present rationale, therefore, entails not that researchers should engage in blue-sky enquiry, but rather that they should engage in practical enquiry but along the way appreciate its non-practical facets, so as additionally to become truth-appreciators. Such research and researchers are what would be the most utilitarian.

Turning to Kantianism, any rationale in support of teaching knowledge for its own sake would have to be that doing so would be required as a way to honour autonomy in some way. Now, some cosmologists and their students have indeed set themselves the end of reflecting on whether there is a multiverse, and so if a state university were to support that, it would be helping them realize their ends and so respecting their individual autonomy.

However, this is not a plausible justification for how to spend public resources. For if the content of the ends adopted is left open (apart from, say, not interfering with other people's ends), then a small coterie's pursuit of knowledge about anything at all could be justified, including trivialities such as the number of people with red hair in a given society (Hurka 1993: 100) or non-causal correlations (cf. 9.2). The mere fact that some teachers and students have set themselves a goal does not mean the goal merits support, at least not from taxpayers or the rest of a university.

One might reply by invoking the value of collective autonomy, and not so much individual autonomy. That is, perhaps it is respect for democratic will that prescribes blue-sky enquiry. If public institutions ought to deploy their resources in ways that comport with what a majority has approved of via fair procedures (or what it would approve of were it to be consulted), and if the majority approves of the pursuit of knowledge for its own sake, then it would be right for those in universities to do it.

I wonder whether the above objection to spending public resources so as to realize the contingent ends of certain individuals applies to the ends of a majority, too. However, even if it does not, the present rationale for blue-sky enquiry backfires, in that an appeal to majority rule often entails that it is unjustified. Democratic principles instead frequently have the implication that the knowledge students acquire should serve a developmental agenda insofar as majorities have authorized that:

> A democratic society is expected to justify its investment in education. Thus, the question arises: what return does the country derive from its investment in higher education?.... [T]here is a growing public expectation that universities should contribute to the economic, social and cultural development of society.... [T]he traditional notion of the academic, with its emphasis on personal growth,

> implied that s/he worked in isolation from, or at least failed adequately to participate in, the wider life of society. Yet.... as academics are paid from the public purse, society is correct to expect some return from this investment.
>
> (Dowling and Seepe 2003: 45)

Of course, there are majorities in *some* societies who want publicly funded academics to pursue some knowledge for its own sake. I notice that often the most widely read news articles on the BBC's website are those relating to cosmology, which suggests that a poll of British people might go in favour of blue-sky enquiry. However, that is unlikely to be true of all societies, and, yet, in the more pragmatically oriented ones, a cosmologist who worked with students to discover the fate of the universe and shared the findings would arguably still merit praise.

Still more, even if an appeal to majoritarian will could entail that academics at public universities should teach some blue-sky knowledge, it would not adequately explain why they should. If a cosmologist and her students were to make a major discovery about the fate of the universe and then taught it to others, it would not be suitable to praise her merely, or even primarily, for having fulfilled one of the majority's aspirations. Instead, there is something about the object of the knowledge that explains why she should have sought it out and shared it and moreover should be praised for having done so. A similar criticism applies to the utilitarian rationale above; it would be inappropriate to praise this cosmologist simply for having done something that is likely to foster subjective well-being. Again, the appropriateness of the knowledge is a function of what it is about, not merely what it causes in the long run.

Now, on the face of it, it seems that the relational moral theory fares no better than utilitarianism and Kantianism when it comes to justifying the pursuit of any knowledge for its own sake. I have noted that respect for individuals' capacity to relate communally in the first instance means relating that way with them and enabling them to so relate with others. Communal relationships consist of the combination of identifying with others and exhibiting solidarity with them, where it does not look as though knowledge of the fate of the universe would do much to facilitate cooperation amongst people or to improve their quality of life.[6]

However, there is a way of understanding the objective human good that might enable the communal ethic to prescribe the instruction of some knowledge for its own sake. Up to now in this book, I have supposed that improving people's quality of life is best understood in terms of meeting their needs, enhancing their liveliness, or developing their virtue (6.2). What I propose now is that meaning in life is also a value that is not merely subjective and can make sense of why it is apt to teach blue-sky topics. Meaningfulness in a life roughly amounts to those

[6] So I myself once argued in Metz (2009).

facets of it that warrant emotional reactions such as great esteem or admiration or that involve a person realizing purposes that are higher than her own pleasurable feelings or satisfied desires. Such conditions are typified by loving or more generally beneficent relationships with others ('the good'), wisdom or more abstract kinds of knowledge ('the true'), and artworks and other sorts of creativity ('the beautiful'). Looking back on your life from your deathbed, which ends did you achieve that merit substantial pride on your part, or what did you do that was worth more than the mental well-being you enjoyed? Answering such questions involves making judgements of meaning in life.

If meaningfulness is part of the objective human good and if solidarity with others means promoting what is objectively good for them, then solidarity can include promoting meaning in other people's lives. What remains to be shown is that having kinds of knowledge can in itself make a life more meaningful, apart from any of its consequences. If knowledge for its own sake can make a life important, then solidarity on the part of a university provides some reason to prescribe its instruction to students.

To begin, consider how false beliefs about the nature of the world in which one lives can reduce a life's meaning. There is something sad about members of Heaven's Gate, a cult in the United States whose members killed themselves in the belief that only suicide would take them to a spacecraft trailing Comet Hale–Bopp that would, in turn, carry them to paradise. Or consider schizophrenics who incorrectly think that the devil is controlling their lives. The reaction of pity that I presume the reader has is well explained substantially by the idea that false beliefs about the fundamental nature of our environment reduce the meaningfulness of a life.

One might suggest that actual or expected harm is what accounts for the loss of meaningfulness in the Hale–Bopp and schizophrenia cases, but I do not think that is the entire explanation of them. Part of what is relevant is what the false belief is about, apart from the belief's causal influence on other parts of a life. To see that, consider a case of false belief that would neither have nor be likely to have bad consequences. Suppose one had radically mistaken views about the origin of the human species—say, one believed that we were put here by the Flying Spaghetti Monster 10,000 years ago. I submit that one's life would be somewhat less meaningful because of that, even if we suppose that no harm came from this belief and that only good feelings sprang from it.

Turn, now, to the intuitive meaningfulness of certain true beliefs. Charles Darwin's defence of the theory of natural selection conferred great meaning on his life, most plausibly in virtue of what the theory is about, and not so much whether it has made (or had been likely to make) people more healthy, creative, or the like. Indeed, it is reasonable to suspect that Darwin's 'dangerous idea' about the origin of our species made people feel insecure and anxious to a degree much greater than it provided comfort and reassurance. Even so, it was important knowledge to have established and to have shared with others. Similarly, if a cosmologist were to make a conclusive finding about the fate of the physical universe, e.g., whether it will forever expand, someday contract into a singularity, or rip apart, the discovery would confer substantial meaning on her life and it would be important for others to know.

It would be nice to have a theory of which beliefs reduce meaning in a person's life and which produce it. My hunch is that a person's life is less meaningful to some degree the more he fails to understand, and especially the more he is misguided about, the basics of the world and his place in it, and that his life is more meaningful the more he knows fundamental facts about himself, human beings, and their environment (on which see Metz 2013a: 222–30). Fundamentality, by which I roughly mean facts that explain many other facts about human existence, captures much about what academics do and intuitively should be teaching (and also researching).

Regardless of whether fundamentality comprehensively captures which beliefs merit pursuit (or conversely, avoidance) for their own sake, so long as some do and in ways that make people's lives more meaningful, it would be natural for the communal ethic to be understood to prescribe their instruction. Respecting others in virtue of the ability to be objects of care, in particular, means doing what is objectively good for them, where that plausibly includes making their lives more meaningful and hence sharing certain kinds of impractical knowledge with them. In contrast, the utilitarian values only subjective well-being, whereas the Kantian prizes the ability to choose some conception of the good or other, or at least has lots of explaining to do in order to account for why a university should teach some knowledge for its own sake.

12
Business Ethics

12.1 Producing Goods and Services

Other chapters in this part of the book have addressed how people should relate to the environment, doctors should treat patients, researchers should interact with participants, and teachers should instruct students. In this last applied ethical chapter, I consider how business owners, and related agents such as managers or state bank directors, should engage with others, particularly workers and consumers. As with the other chapters, the aims here are to present relational accounts of these obligations and to suggest that they are preferable to, or at least plausible alternatives to, the implications of familiar kinds of utilitarianism and Kantianism.

Those familiar with the African business ethics literature will know that it recurrently prescribes sharing both profits and power. That is, one commonly finds thinkers drawing on communal values to recommend that workers be given not only a real financial stake in the growth of a company (Bhengu 2006: 179–80, 192; Lutz 2009; Ncube 2010: 79), but also a real voice in its direction. Regarding the latter, managers are expected not merely to consult with workers before making major decisions, but also to enable workers to participate democratically in its formulation (e.g., Nussbaum 2003; Khoza 2006; Boon 2007; Msila 2015). In addition, one frequently finds the suggestion that business managers and related executives should adopt a servant leadership style (Khoza 2006: 58–9; Mbigi 2007: 298–301; Msila 2014; Ndlovu 2016). I realize that many readers of this chapter are not *au fait* with this literature, and might benefit from seeing why rightness as friendliness also supports these practices. However, broadly relational defences of servant leadership, profit-sharing, and power-sharing have already been made, and the Western moral theories would probably also support at least the first two of those three practices. I therefore turn my attention to topics that both have received somewhat less attention and admit of starker contrasts with utilitarianism and Kantianism.

I first consider what the final end of a firm ought to be, beyond making money for its owners (12.2). Most business ethicists in the West favour stakeholder theory—the idea that a company has a duty to go out of its way for not just its stockholders—but I maintain what the communal ethic entails in respect of what a company morally ought to achieve differs, and in a prima facie attractive way,

A Relational Moral Theory: African Ethics in and beyond the Continent. Thaddeus Metz, Oxford University Press.
 DOI: 10.1093/oso/9780198748960.003.0012

from utilitarian and Kantian models. Next, I address the question of who exactly counts as a stakeholder, showing that the partial element of rightness as friendliness has new and plausible implications (12.3). I then take up the question of how the production process ought to be structured, arguing that while the Western moral theories could well allow an unconstrained managerialism, the communal ethic probably does not (12.4). Finally, I consider how this ethic bears on a fresh topic in the field, concerning the role of oaths (12.5). Some business and related leaders are now taking oaths to live up to their fiduciary duties, and I try to show that a communal ethic makes better sense of why it would be wrong to violate these oaths than does utilitarianism or Kantianism.

12.2 The Point of a Firm

In a competitive environment, it is a given that one point of a firm should be to stay in business by making money for its owners. However, for most ethicists, that is not all that a firm should be striving to achieve. According to normative stakeholder theorists, a business has duties to go out of its way not merely for stockholders, but also for a variety of others. Saving discussion of precisely who (or what) counts as a stakeholder for the next section, here I advance an encompassing view of what a firm's proper role in society is.

According to the relational moral theory, a moral agent typically ought to relate communally (with innocent parties) and in ways that enable them to relate communally with others in turn. That is what a firm, or at least those in charge of it, ought to be doing. Honouring people's ability to be subjects and objects of harmony in the first instance means harmonizing with them, where that includes helping them to do so with others.

When it comes to customers, harmony or communality would normally mean selling goods and services that are expected to help them live objectively well. Recall that solidarity is largely a matter of meeting others' biological, psychological, and social needs, fostering their liveliness, enhancing their moral virtue (6.2), and, if the suggestion in the previous chapter was correct (11.4), producing more meaningfulness. Conversely, a firm has strong moral reason to avoid selling what would cause harm, occasion weakness, foster moral vice, or perhaps reduce meaning. Hence, for example, a firm would probably avoid selling cigarettes as these are well known to inflict serious bodily harm, cause addiction, and, as a consequence, disrupt the ability of someone to look after his family and friends.

In addition to customers, a firm has a duty to harmonize with future generations of people as well as many animals in the environment. As mentioned above (8.4), burning fossil fuels at the rate we currently are is immoral, and a company should strive hard to avoid doing so and support a transition to a green economy. It also follows from the communal ethic that it is wrong to run and support factory farms, insofar as they cause substantial mental distress and physical pain to animals that is unnecessary for human nutrition.

Still more, a company could and should relate communally with its workers. As a number of African business ethicists put it, doing so would involve forging community in the workplace (e.g., Dandala 2009; Lutz 2009), which by the present ethic means creating, sustaining, and enriching bonds of identity and solidarity amongst workers and ideally between them and managers/owners, too. Business owners with substantial resources would, for instance, go out of their way to pay workers well. Conversely, it would be wrong for a firm making substantial profits to cut healthcare benefits to its employees.

One interesting implication of building communal relationships in the workplace concerns the role of emotions. By the relational moral theory, cultivating certain feelings and attitudes merits doing so as an end, not merely as a means in order, say, to motivate employees to perform. A communal or harmonious relationship is not merely a matter of coordination and aid, but also includes emotional aspects (6.2). For one, part of identifying with others involves a sense of togetherness such as feeling pride in what others accomplish and liking being with them, and for another, exhibiting solidarity with others includes feeling sympathy and compassion. Insofar as one major task of a business leader is to foster communality in a firm, she must be committed to prompting such feelings and attitudes.[1]

Note that, by this general approach, harmony or communality is a way of relating that a firm is to pursue as an end, not merely as a means to other values such as, say, productivity or innovation. The relational moral theory should not be read as entailing the banalities that social capital or effective teamwork is useful to succeed in a competitive environment. Instead, the ethic supports the bolder claim that a certain way of relating is to be sought out for non-instrumental reasons, specifically as a way of expressing respect for the relational nature of people (and many animals).

In contrast, familiar Western models of stakeholder theory treat relationality as, at best, a mere means to some other value. Consider the utilitarian view that a firm ought to maximize the satisfaction of people's preferences and the Kantian view that it should live up to contracts and realize people's ends. Both Western forms of stakeholder theory can probably support stringent environmental practices for the sake of present and future generations of human persons as well as robust financial support for workers. However, a focus on satisfying people's preferences or fulfilling their ends does not as straightforwardly entail that factory farms are

[1] Such a theoretical rationale explains why some African leadership proponents have been right to recommend that an organization include activities such as observing rituals, singing, and dancing (e.g., Mbigi and Maree 2005: 50–2, 102, 108; Bhengu 2006: 186–7; Boon 2007: 68, 83).

wrong.[2] In addition, both of these approaches tend to support the view that a firm is right to satisfy whatever contingent and variable demand there is on a market, without much concern for the nature of the goods/services being sold. So long as smoking cigarettes is what people prefer over their health or what they rank more highly as an end than it, both approaches would naturally entail that selling cigarettes is justified. However, it is much harder to arrive at that conclusion with the communal ethic, where a firm must give consideration to what is objectively good for people. Consumers might freely choose to smoke tobacco, but that is not a sufficient reason to sell it to them, for an agent who is obligated to exhibit solidarity with others (cf. 9.6).

As with any stakeholder model, a firm needs to balance the interests of consumers against those of workers, stockholders, and the like, and so it does not necessarily follow that a firm would have all-things-considered reason not to sell cigarettes. However, rightness as friendliness does entail that selling cigarettes fails to treat the capacity of consumers to be objects of solidarity with respect to some degree, such that there is some moral reason to avoid doing so. That judgement is reasonable, and is one that is not as easily made by preference utilitarianism or Kantianism. One might invoke hedonic utilitarianism to address the case of selling cigarettes, which is fair. However, a focus on promoting subjective well-being, however that is construed, could prescribe selling, say, titillating gadgets or pornographic images that keep people isolated from each other in lieu of games that would bring families closer together or sexual/couples counselling that would facilitate romance.

12.3 Stakeholders

A firm cannot meet the needs of literally all in a society; it must rather attend to those of its stakeholders. But who counts as a stakeholder—that is, someone for whom a firm has moral reason to go out of its way—and how should it balance the interests of stakeholders? In the previous section I mentioned workers, consumers, animals, and future generations of persons as potential sites of communal relationship. Are there any stakeholders besides these? How should a firm prioritize amongst them when it cannot satisfy the interests of all?

In the Western ethical tradition, there are two main moral reasons to support someone's ends or improve his quality of life, setting aside non-ideal factors such

[2] Hedonic utilitarianism of course might rule out factory farms, but much would depend on how much pleasure humans get from the taste of meat as well as how many humans and animals are involved. Intense pain to a relatively small number of animals could be outweighed by the minor pleasures of many more humans. In contrast, a principle that the urgent interests of a being with moral status may not be traded off for the trivial interests of another such being has more stringent implications for meat eating when done for the purpose of mere taste.

as the fact that one has wrongfully subordinated or harmed him. On the one hand, he might be amongst the worst off (Kantianism) or has much to gain (utilitarianism) and so is owed aid because of a general duty of beneficence. On the other hand, he might be someone whom we have assumed a special obligation to aid—say, by having promised to help him or by having chosen to accept the benefits from a cooperative scheme of which he is a member (both are Kantian rationales, of course). By the former reasoning, a firm in principle has some reason to aid a person wherever he might be in the world or however unrelated to the firm he might be. Simply being in dire need qualifies one for consideration. By the latter reasoning, the firm usually had to have made voluntary choices that it knew would bind it to perform certain actions for particular people in the future.

In addition to these two moral reasons to aid others, the relational moral theory grounds a third: one has already related communally with others, at least to some substantial extent or intensity. For a few examples, recall that I have argued that having lived with and met the needs of children for many years is what gives parents a duty to continue to support them relative to other people's children (7.3.3), that having had a patient for a long while provides extra moral reason for a doctor to treat her instead of a new patient (9.4), and that having done a longitudinal study with a participant gives a medical researcher a *pro tanto* obligation to help her with substantial health-related needs that were not brought on by the study (10.4). Similarly, I maintain that where a firm has been party to a communal relationship with others intensely or for a long time, and especially both, then it has a duty of some weight to commune with these intimates as opposed to strangers, even if the strangers are somewhat worse off and one did not promise to do so.

Of course, the bonds with family are longer and stronger than those between a firm and, say, its workers or consumers. That means that the obligation of a firm or those in charge of it is weaker in one sense, specifically in that the kinds of moral considerations needed to outweigh an obligation to aid workers and consumers are not as strong as those needed to outweigh an obligation to aid family members.

However, there is another sense in which the obligation of a firm to help others is stronger than those on family members, for with power comes responsibility. Very roughly, can implies ought; the greater one's ability to support others' ends and improve their quality of life without imposing real burdens on oneself or on those even more intimately connected to one, the more one should do for others. So, a firm that is making more than 1 billion US dollars in profit in a given year owes its stakeholders millions, something family members are not typically obligated to provide.

In short, how demanding is the obligation to aid others is one matter, while how important that obligation is relative to other obligations is another. The obligation of an agent such as a business owner to aid those who are not family but have been party to communal relationship could be quite demanding, even if that obligation could be overridden more easily than could an obligation to aid family.

Suppose, then, that relationships of identity and solidarity ground obligations for a party to them who is well resourced to go out of its way for other parties to them whose ends and good it could advance. Applied to a business context, a firm could well have partial duties to cooperate with and aid suppliers, workers, and consumers. For instance, if a firm has a long-standing communal relationship with a particular supplier, the firm's leaders would have some moral reason to continue to contract with the latter, even if a new supplier would be marginally less expensive. The reason is merely *pro tanto* and not invariably conclusive, i.e., a firm's managers or owners need not continue to contract with a supplier regardless of how expensive its goods or how shoddy its services become. The point is that there would usually be *some* moral cost to dumping a supplier with whom there has been cooperation and mutual aid for many years. Furthermore, in those cases in which there would intuitively be little or no moral cost to breaking ties with such a stakeholder, a likely explanation would be that this supplier has itself failed to live up to its respective obligation to commune and has instead become exploitive or neglectful.

Running with this dimension of partiality in African ethics, two scholars have recently suggested that, when it is applied to the context of business ethics, the word 'stakeholders' should be replaced with 'relationholders' (Woermann and Engelbrecht 2019). For them, stakeholder-talk is 'contaminated' by the idea that 'different parties' interests are dependent on the power and influence that these parties can exert on the organisation due to the strength of the contractual underpinnings of their claims or stakes' (Woermann and Engelbrecht 2019). In contrast, the word 'relationholder' highlights the perspective that sometimes a firm can have some moral reason to aid particular individuals beyond contractual terms with them or any voluntary assumption of an obligation to aid them. Prior relationship of identity and solidarity can be sufficient to provide reason of some weight to continue interacting in that way.

Such a rationale entails that, in addition to suppliers, workers, and consumers, a firm can owe support and aid to its society—again, even if this society is not amongst those in the world who would benefit the most from resources, the firm did not promise to provide resources to it, and so on. For many, it is intuitive that a corporate social responsibility (CSR) programme should focus on those who reside where the firm operates (e.g., Mofuoa 2014: 233–4), such that, for instance, wealthy tech companies in Silicon Valley ought to be assisting those who cannot easily afford housing there. Utilitarianism cannot explain why, if helping these people who need assistance with rent would produce less subjective well-being than, say, helping those who have become downright homeless elsewhere in the world. Kantianism has difficulty explaining why, if the firm did not promise to aid these people and, say, is currently owed by those who are members of a society-wide cooperative scheme of which it is also a member. In contrast, the communal grounding of special obligations explains why the positive duty obtains: a firm has normally cooperated with and helped the society in which it is based, as has the society in respect of the firm, and, supposing its profits are substantial, it therefore has some moral reason to go out of its way for that society.

There is now a long list of those in respect of whom a firm has some moral reason to support and aid. When it comes to a general duty of beneficence, there are needy human beings anywhere in the world, future generations of them, and animals. When it comes to special obligations, a firm has presumably contracted with a variety of individuals and so has strong reason to abide by those agreements. And, then, with regard to those with whom it has been in communal relationship, there are at least long-standing suppliers, workers, consumers, and members of the society in which it operates. Which come first?

Of course, much depends on the details, but the relational moral theory can provide some broad guidelines, which I presume readers will find prima facie attractive. First, recall that the urgent interests of beings with a full moral status come before those with a merely partial moral status (8.4). A CSR programme should therefore help, say, hungry human persons before hungry animals.

Second, it is clear that special obligations often take precedence over general ones, for my duties to my sons surely come before my duties to other people's sons, even if the latter are somewhat worse off than the former (7.3.3). In a business context, then, normally contracts that have been made should not be violated, and long and strong ties that have been established should not be cut.

Finally, consider the principle that the longer and stronger the communal tie, the more there is a duty to provide to parties to it and the harder it is to outweigh this duty. It follows from this that a firm normally ought to give first consideration to meeting the urgent and moderate needs of its workers (cf. Woermann and Engelbrecht 2019), at least after those who created and still own the firm.

12.4 Managerialism

It is the presence of a strong duty to go out of its way for workers, whom a firm has cooperated with and aided for a long while and to an intense degree, that explains why I believe that managerialism in the workplace must be tempered. After indicating specifically what I mean by 'managerialism', I argue that the relational moral theory provides more reason to curb it than do the prominent Western principles of right action.

Managerialism, also known as 'rationalization' or 'Taylorism', involves seeking a certain kind of efficiency in the production process. In the contemporary era in both the East and the West, firms typically seek to maximize outputs such as profits and to minimize inputs such as labour costs, and they do so by steering workers with money or power to produce standardized outputs admitting of measurable criteria. Upon having accepted to provide labour-power in exchange for a wage, workers are directed by managers to perform the most discrete, repetitive tasks they can during the workday, thereby producing more goods or services that can be sold than they otherwise would. The assembly line is the quintessential example, but not dissimilar are cashiers in grocery stores, miners digging for gold, and lawyers totting up billable hours.

Although this model of production originated with businesses competing in a market, it is well known for having spread to many other spheres, including government bureaucracies. Here, high-ranking officials issue directives to subordinates to engage with clients according to inflexible form-filling and box-ticking. Although bureaucrats are not evaluated according to how much profit they bring in, they are according to how many clients they have dealt with, how many claims they have processed, or how much data they have entered into the system. And, as many readers will know, managerialism is now ensconced in academia, where in the main lecturers are evaluated according to how many students have passed their courses and researchers are judged by how many articles they have published in certain journals.

It is unlikely that, in a mass society, it is possible to avoid managerialism altogether, and it might even constitute a kind of social progress, as Jürgen Habermas (1987) has argued. Habermas does criticize managerialism for 'colonizing' too many spheres of life, but that is not my concern. Instead of how much of life managerialism takes up, I object to how intense it can be in a given sphere of life, namely the workplace. I believe that while the principles of utility and of respect for autonomy would permit more extreme regimented and standardized production processes, the communal ethic would not and is more plausible in that respect.

From the perspective of utilitarianism, managerialism is typically unpleasant for workers. It is boring. It does not allow for the pride that comes from creativity or otherwise having control over one's activity. It is isolating and inhibits conviviality. These are utilitarian reasons not to deploy such a production process. However, it is morally justified, and even required, so long as in the long term it produces a greater net amount of subjective well-being compared to any other available means. If the number of workers burdened by a mind-numbing and lonely managerialist process were few compared to the large number of consumers and stockholders only marginally benefiting from the outputs, a firm would be wrong not to subject the workers to it. My intuition, though, is that it would be wrong to do so.

Kantians agree that there are positive duties to aid others, and so the fact that a certain production process might enable many consumers to realize their ends is a moral advantage for them. However, Kantians of course deny that one may use any means whatsoever to achieve desirable outcomes, and in particular a firm may not treat workers' autonomy merely as a tool to satisfy the interests of consumers, let alone stockholders. Now, normally Kantians maintain that, upon having made a free and informed agreement to exchange labour-power for a wage, workers are not treated merely as a means when instructed how to act during the workday. For many in the Kantian tradition, a labour contract is sufficient to treat workers with respect, meaning that an extremely managerialist production process need not be wrong.

Some will suggest that workers do not make a genuinely free agreement to labour under such conditions. Borrowing from Marxian sources, it is open to the Kantian to maintain that employers take advantage of the weaknesses of prospective employees who have no real choice but to accept a contract. The problem with this reasoning, however, is that, if it is correct, it provides reason to criticize wage-labour in general but does not provide reason to criticize managerialism in particular. While I am open to the idea that all wage-labour is suspect, I submit that the nature of the labour workers are expected to undertake in exchange for a wage admits of independent criticism. My intuition is that even if a person did make a truly free and informed decision to submit to an extreme form of managerialism, it would be wrong for a firm to employ him in that way, at least if some other, less alienating production process would have comparable results.

I believe the relational moral theory does better in entailing and explaining why extreme forms of managerialism would be wrong, even supposing they maximized the general welfare or had been freely consented to by workers. In the previous section I noted that, of stakeholders with relations with a firm, workers tend to be amongst those whose ties with it are longest and strongest, meaning that their interests normally have some priority relative to, say, consumers (12.3). In addition, I earlier indicated that one major way of understanding the interests of workers is in terms of building communality in the workplace, construed as the combination of relationships of identity and solidarity (12.2). Putting these two claims together, one arrives at the conclusion that there is strong moral reason for a firm to avoid extreme forms of managerialism. In reducing labour to a series of discrete, repetitive tasks undertaken in isolation, managerialism hardly fosters a sense of togetherness between workers, let alone between workers and managers. Its use of steering mechanisms, such as financial incentives and punitive threats, is prima facie incompatible with cooperative participation on the part of workers. Although workers might gain financially from doing well by managerialist criteria, their own good in the production process is of little interest beyond avoiding health and safety violations; in particular, objective values such as liveliness, communality, and meaningfulness tend to be disregarded. Finally, managerialism is unlikely to foster sympathy, and probably encourages managers to view workers as human resources, not so much as people whose interests matter for their own sake.

In short, managerialism involves discordant or anti-social ways of relating as opposed to harmonious or communal ones. The relational moral theory does not, however, entail a blanket rejection of managerialism. For one, there could be situations in which it is essential for a firm to survive in a competitive environment that is, for all we can tell, here to stay. That is, the interests of stockholders are not irrelevant, while going out of business would normally not be in the interests of workers either. For another, consumers matter, too, and a production process that efficiently met many of their needs would be a plus.

It appears, therefore, that communality pulls in different directions when it comes to how to organize a workplace. The natural resolution of the tension is compromise. Here are a couple of examples of how those in charge of a firm might proceed in ways that arguably give adequate consideration to the relational dignity of all stakeholders. First, a manager might retain the use of numerical targets that workers must meet, but not set them down unilaterally. Instead, she could at least consult with workers about targets, or, still more, seek out their unanimous agreement to them, upon open and uninhibited discussion with them of what would be best for all those affected by the firm. Second, a manager might retain the use of a year-end bonus to express appreciation and to motivate, but not allocate it strictly in proportion to the quantified output of individual employees. Instead, she could award the same bonus to all those who have done well enough, if not also share profits in a more robust sense with them.

12.5 Breaking Contracts, Violating Oaths

Any plausible ethic for business has to account for the intuition that having entered into a contract provides *pro tanto*, and often quite strong, reason to fulfil its terms. Utilitarians do so on the ground that breaking a contract creates disappointment, erodes trust, and hence impairs the subjective well-being that would come from further trade. Kantians, in contrast, maintain that violating an agreement is primarily wrong 'in itself', as doing so interferes with the other party's self-governance. These rationales are sensible enough, but in this section I maintain that there is a third rationale that should be given consideration, and, furthermore, that it does better than the Western moral theories at making sense of a particular kind of agreement: an oath.

When it comes to a promise in general, the communal ethic entails that breaking one normally involves flouting a relational value. Like Kantianism, the deontological appeal to communality I advance has the implication that there is usually something wrong with failing to live up to a contract apart from the undesirable consequences of doing so. Unlike Kantianism, though, the explanation appeals not to autonomy but instead to identity. More carefully, for the Kantian, breaking a promise normally degrades the other person's ability to make decisions for herself; for when you make the unilateral choice not to live up to the agreement, you are deciding for her. In contrast, by my approach, doing so degrades the other person's ability to enjoy a sense of togetherness with you and to interact with you on a cooperative basis; when you make the unilateral choice not to live up to the agreement, you are typically putting psychological distance between her as well as subordinating instead of coordinating with her.

On the face of it, there is not much difference between these accounts. One way to see how they differ, however, is in the context of making an oath. An oath in general is, roughly, a promise of a heavy moral weight to abide by certain principles, made orally and publicly along with certain symbolic gestures, whereby the oath-taker puts his integrity on the line and expresses a willingness to undergo a penalty if he breaks his word.[3] Here I explore oaths made by business and more generally financial professionals, where a person working in these contexts has specialized knowledge or skills relating to economic matters that could greatly affect the course of people's lives and hence has a relatively unique ability to do substantial good or bad for them. Although many of my examples are in the private realm, the points should apply just as well to, say, a chairperson of a publicly owned bank. In addition, I have in mind mainly oaths made to the public as a whole or to an otherwise large segment of innocent and vulnerable persons such as stockholders, which tend to include the likes of union members and pensioners. I also note that oaths are typically made not merely *to*, but also *in front of*, the group whose interests could be substantially set back by failure to do what is being sworn.

A key example is an accountant swearing to her clients and the public at large to report accurately and not to engage in insider trading. Another example is a board member of a bank swearing to firms and the broader populace not to embezzle funds as well as to loan money in ways that are expected to balance the short-term profits of stockholders with the long-term concern to maintain a stable and equitable economic system.

I now consider what, precisely, is wrong with breaking these oaths and those like them. Of course, part of the explanation of why it is wrong is that one has not merely performed an immoral action such as insider trading or embezzling, but also broken a promise not to do so. However, there is a need to explain why breaking *this kind* of promise is *particularly* serious. There is an intuitive 'extra' wrongness of breaking an *oath* not to perform a wrong act that communality explains better than utility or autonomy, or so I now argue.

Why would breaking an oath not to engage in insider trading be an 'extra' wrong when compared to engaging in insider trading without having sworn not to? It appears impossible for utilitarianism to ground an answer to this question, for it does not recognize degrees of wrongdoing between different types of acts. By this ethic, there is nothing wrong 'in itself' with actions; their wrongness is entirely

[3] As Sulmasy points out (1999: 330), there is almost no literature analysing the concept of an oath, i.e., what it essentially is and how it differs from related concepts such as a promise. Above is a stab.

a function of whether they would produce comparatively bad results in a given circumstance. To know whether an act is wrong, one compares it only with all the *present* alternatives available, in the light of their (expected) results in regard to pleasant experiences, satisfied desires, or the like. So, in the case where one has already made an oath, one compares oath-keeping with oath-breaking in the here and now; one does not compare oath-breaking with another possible world in which one performed similar actions but without having made an oath in the first place. There is no such thing as degrees of wrongness, by utilitarianism. An act is right if and only if it would maximize good and minimize bad at a given time, and there are no degrees of that condition. Hence, the traditional version of utilitarianism cannot provide an explanation of why breaking an oath not to embezzle would be morally worse than embezzling without oath-breaking.[4]

Turning to Kantianism, it is able to account for degrees of wrongdoing; it does so in terms of degrees of degradation. The Kantian might suggest that, in the case of an economic oath, the promise has often been made not merely to one person, but to a large number of them. Hence, violating an oath treats many other people's rational agency as worth less than one's own ends and is for that reason more degrading that ordinary promise-breaking or ordinary immoral acts such as embezzling that one did not promise to avoid. Such an explanation, however, obviously would not explain why violating an oath made to an individual—say, by an investment advisor to a client—would be worse.

Another suggestion, then, is to note that an oath is a promise that has extra backing, i.e., for which the oath-taker has given another assurance beyond a normal promise that he will do what he has sworn to do. *Strongly* encouraging another to rely on one and then backing out is a particularly serious form of promise-breaking.

That is admittedly a forceful rationale. However, I doubt it is a complete one. There is a notable dimension of the wrongdoing that it is difficult for the Kantian theory to capture, namely the sense of *betrayal* people feel when oaths made to them have been violated. People tend to resent not merely having been used or treated as less important by the oath-breaker; they are also typically indignant at the *disloyalty* he has shown. As one thoughtful commentator on oaths remarks:

> An oath is a commitment to be a certain kind of person for other persons. Fidelity is a virtue that arises as a consequence of an oath, but does not arise as a consequence of a promise. One 'keeps' one's promises, but one is 'faithful' to one's oaths. One who swears an oath not only puts his or her own personhood on the line, he or she does so for the sake of a connection to the personhood of those who are the subject of an oath. (Sulmasy 1999: 333–4)

[4] As with the rest of this book, I focus on act-utilitarianism here. For critical discussion of rule-utilitarianism and oaths, see Metz (2013b).

I believe the communal ethic does better than the Kantian principle at capturing the infidelity facet of why oath-breaking is wrong—wrong in a way that goes beyond performing the wrongful act one swore not to do and beyond the mere breaking of a promise.

My basic suggestion is that breaking an oath is not merely failing to treat other people's capacity for *choice* as special, but also, or instead more fundamentally, failing to respect a *relationship* of a certain kind (and hence other people's capacity for it). Breaking an oath is particularly unfriendly, a serious failure to prize a way of relating in which one shares a way of life with others. Consider two respects in which this appears true.

First, recall that richly sharing a way of life is not merely coordinating to achieve ends compatibly, but also doing so consequent to trust. It is possible to jointly achieve ends on the basis of apprehension (even in the absence of threats), but a more robust sense of sharing a way of life includes cooperating on the basis of having (justified) confidence in others in the light of their motives. When one violates an oath, the problem is not merely the Kantian one of subordinating others' ends to one's own, but also, I suggest, that one is failing to prize a relationship of trust:

> Oaths essentially involve a deep level of interpersonal trust that is not part of a promise. I make a promise 'to' you, but I swear an oath 'for' you. The public may be angry that a President has failed to keep his or her campaign promises, but the public will justifiably feel personally aggrieved and deeply betrayed that a President has failed to remain faithful to his or her Constitutional oath.
>
> (Sulmasy 1999: 334)

'We trusted you!' is a common expression of outrage made to an oath-breaker, and I maintain that it is not merely an implicit reference to some other moral complaint regarding well-being or autonomy. A trusting relationship has some moral worth in itself that is forsaken when one violates an oath, something that the communal ethic best captures.

A second respect in which an oath-breaker is disloyal, and hence degrades people's communal nature, is by distancing himself from others and, more than that, by doing so consequent to initially having come close to them. I noted above that it is characteristic for people to make an oath before the group to whom the solemn promise is being made. Rather than taking an oath to the public (or other group)—say, behind closed doors to a representative or merely in writing—it is typically done verbally in front of it. That is, there is a face-to-face encounter between the oath-taker and the public, which I submit has some moral significance, as it makes the oath-breaking *personal* in a way it would not have been otherwise. Consider the indignation one feels when another lies to one's face, as opposed to in an email, or when a family member, as opposed to a stranger, steals from one. Deceiving and cheating are often deemed morally worse when done by those related to oneself, and I suggest something analogous is true of an oath-breaker, in virtue of the presence he has had before the public. He does not have an impersonal relationship with those to whom he has sworn the oath, meaning that when he thinks of himself as an 'I' in opposition to a 'them' and engages in behaviour unlikely to foster a sense of 'we-ness', he is tearing down the right sort of relationship, not merely failing to build it up.

It is difficult for Kantians to make sense of this point. There appears to be nothing in their theory that enables them to say that a lie to one's face is worse than a lie in an email or on the phone; the treatment of one's capacity to *make decisions* looks equally degraded—whereas my point is that the capacity to *relate* in certain ways is differentially so. The Kantian might reply that the reason a lie to one's face is worse than a lie in writing is that the liar in the former case is providing extra assurance that he is telling the truth and hence is manipulating to a greater degree. However, I suspect that the point backfires: for *why* is it the case that meeting in person provides extra assurance of truth-telling? Is not the best explanation that both parties recognize that it would be morally appalling to tell a lie in that situation?

The above respects, at least together, add up to a promising explanation of the sense of betrayal members of the public often feel when a businessperson or financial professional violates an oath. He has subordinated their projects to his; he has violated trust; and he has created distance between them, where there was an initial sense of togetherness fostered partly by a personal encounter. While the principle of respect for autonomy can plausibly account for the wrongness of subordination, the other facets, well captured by the notion of disloyalty, are better underwritten by the relational moral theory. Only it can capture intuitions that sometimes relationships are what is degraded, not merely end-setting (9.4.2, 10.4).

13
Conclusion

Ex Africa semper aliquid novi.

13.1 Some Strengths of a Relational Moral Theory

The above saying is usually translated as: 'There is always something new coming out of Africa', and has been common in the West since the time of ancient Greece. It was initially made in reference to the kinds of animals discovered on the African continent, which seemed strange, and for that reason by and large unwelcome, to the Greeks.[1] The biological and negative connotations of the statement have dropped away, so that now it normally indicates beliefs and practices, particularly from below the Sahara desert, that are different and potentially admirable. It is in this sense that I use the statement to begin this concluding chapter.

In the rest of this section I highlight some of the respects in which relationality, which has been so prominent in African ethics, is revealing about moral matters and in ways that rival dominant Western principles of right action. After that, I indicate three projects that it would be natural to undertake, supposing that the central ideas advanced in this book have been convincing or at least are worth taking seriously. First, while I have been strictly concerned to present and defend a normative theory—that is, a certain prescription of how to act—one might wonder what relational implications there are for how to describe moral behaviour in the ways moral educationists, psychologists, and sociologists do (13.2). Second, while my normative theory has been about right action, i.e., which choices are permissible as opposed to impermissible, others will be interested in good character and want to know how relationality might inform our understanding of moral virtue (13.3). Third, while I have focused on right action in mainly interpersonal or dyadic contexts, where one person is affecting another individual, some will be keen to consider institutional matters—those concerning criminal, economic, and other forms of justice (13.4). For all three matters, I sketch some respects in which relational perspectives merit further application.

At the start of the book I suggested that the great divide between utilitarians and Kantians for more than 200 years in Western philosophy shares a common premise, one of ascribing a moral status to an individual on the basis of her

[1] For discussion of the history of the maxim, see Feinberg and Solodow (2002).

A Relational Moral Theory: African Ethics in and beyond the Continent. Thaddeus Metz, Oxford University Press.
 DOI: 10.1093/oso/9780198748960.003.0013

intrinsic properties—features that make no essential reference to anyone but the individual, or at least not a positive way of relating to others. For utilitarians, what matters is an individual's capacity for pain/pleasure (or preference dis/satisfaction), while, for Kantians, it is one's capacity for rationality (or autonomy). Similarly individualist views in the history of modern ethics include the ascription of moral status to being the one acting, having a soul, being a living organism, and being a subject of a life. There have of course been exceptions, but individualism has been salient in works by Western moral theorists for centuries.

My proposal has been that, to make headway in moral theory, we should cast doubt on the individualist assumption shared by many Western rivals, and consider what moral theory might look like upon ascribing moral status on the basis of relational features. That alternative approach has not meant claiming that relationships matter morally and individuals do not; instead, my suggestion is that individuals matter morally because of their relational properties, features that do make essential reference to something beyond the individual. I have sought to defend this broad approach to morality with normative argumentation, i.e., by appealing to moral claims that are less contested than those being evaluated, instead of by invoking metaphysical claims, particularly ones that are highly contested at a global level (Chapters 2–3).

Although my specific account of relational moral status and its companion principle of right action are advanced as new, I have been inspired by large swathes of long-standing African ethical thought that have been nearly altogether ignored in global philosophical debates. Although relationality has been prominent in the African tradition, it has often been unclear what role it plays in the works of philosophers or should play in our moral thinking. Some thinkers are aptly read as treating it instrumentally, i.e., as an essential or particularly reliable means to another end such as the common good (Chapter 4) or vital force (Chapter 5). I argued that, in contrast, deeming relationality to be an end is the most promising theoretical interpretation of the African tradition (Chapters 6–7); doing so accounts best on balance for intuitions about right and wrong salient in it and for those shared with philosophers working in many other traditions.

I then sought to show that taking relationality, and specifically a certain understanding of our capacity for communality, as of basic moral value should be given consideration not just by African philosophers since it sheds light on a variety of moral controversies (Chapters 8–12). A number of African thinkers over the years have suggested that the focus on relationship would be one of the continent's 'gifts' to the world, and, running with that idea, I have aimed to interpret it in a way that would be of interest to a global audience of moral philosophers and related enquirers. Specifically, I articulated and defended the principle that right acts are those respecting individuals' capacity to be party to communal or harmonious ways of relating, those of identity and solidarity. Roughly this means treating others in friendly ways, when they have not been unfriendly themselves, and above all avoiding enmity towards innocents. One major intended readership has been those adhering to contemporary Western moral theories, with me trying to show that rightness as friendliness can resolve problems facing standard versions of their principles, or at least offer fresh perspectives that even they would find prima facie plausible.

Returning to issues highlighted in the introduction (1.1), recall, first, that a powerful view of moral status, i.e., beings to whom we owe direct duties, is that animals matter for their own sake but not as much as human beings, particularly human persons. It is difficult for Kantianism to ascribe any moral status to animals as they lack rationality (including the potential for it), while utilitarianism tends to ascribe a full moral status to animals as they are sentient and have desires. In contrast, relational considerations ground a novel account of why humans and animals might have a differential moral status, albeit in virtue of the same basic property (8.4). Roughly, I proposed that the (markedly) more a being is capable of relating communally, the greater its moral status. One implication is that human persons are more capable of relating communally than animals, in that the former can do so as subjects and the latter (at least setting aside apes and the like) cannot and can do so merely as objects. Another implication is that even when it comes to human beings who are not persons and have the same intrinsic features as animals, the former are more capable of being related to communally as objects than the latter and so have a greater (partial) moral status.

Recall that I extended this reasoning to debates about abortion and infanticide, defending a novel, relational approach to them (9.5). I pointed out that utilitarianism and Kantianism have difficulty capturing a certain gradational account of moral status that is intuitive. Kantianism either accords no moral status to embryos, foetuses, and babies for lacking rationality, or it accords them the same moral status for all having the potential for it. Utilitarianism accords no moral status to embryos, but the same moral status to foetuses and babies. Both tend towards entailing the permissibility of infanticide under conditions in which it appears unjustified. I suggested a unique approach: that marked differences in the ability to be an object of communal relationship with us support the plausible view that a mid- to late-stage foetus matters more than an embryo, and that a baby matters more than a mid- and even late-stage foetus.

Another difficulty facing Western moral theories has been to find a way to make intuitions about the moral relevance of both dignity and welfare cohere. On the one hand, the natural thing for many of us to say is that the reason to avoid striking a person with a vehicle relative to a mouse or a plant is that the person is 'worth more' than they are; the person is plausibly ascribed a dignity because of her nature that the other beings lack. On the other hand, the pain caused to a mouse does matter morally, as does the pain caused to a person; furthermore, pain and other dimensions of a being's quality of life have essential and not contingent moral significance. Utilitarianism denies that persons are by virtue of their nature worth more than mice, while Kantianism treats pain as morally relevant only insofar as people have set particular ends against it or it would interfere with their general ability to set ends. In contrast, by my approach, moral status inheres in any being capable of relating communally, understood as the combination of identity and solidarity, where those that can be subjects of such a way of relating have a dignity, and where those that can be objects of it are owed moral treatment in part because we could relieve their pain and otherwise enhance their good (including their liveliness and virtue).

One attractive application of this approach was in the contexts of euthanasia and physician-assisted suicide (9.6, but see also 9.2, 11.3, 12.2, and 12.4). On the face of it, utilitarianism entails it can be right to kill someone without her consent if it would prevent her from suffering a fate equal to or worse than death, while Kantianism entails that it can be right to kill someone with her consent even if it would not prevent such suffering. The relational moral theory, however, requires a moral agent to attend to both identity and solidarity and so avoids these counterintuitive implications; it would normally be unfriendly either to kill without consent or to kill when it would not be good for the one killed.

For another respect in which the rightness as friendliness brings considerations of welfare and dignity into harmony (so to speak) in a promising way, consider its account of human rights (6.3, 7.3.1–7.3.2, 8.4.1). Utilitarianism does not recognize human rights at the level of principle, permitting extreme kinds of interference with innocent parties when it is for the greater good. Kantianism does recognize human rights, but grounds them on considerations of autonomy and so cannot easily account for the judgement that part of what makes torture, rape, and the like so degrading and horrible is the reduction of a person's quality of life, including her ability to relate to others in certain ways, not just of her freedom, say, to achieve whatever her highly ranked ends might happen to be, such as making everything as pink as she can. For the relational moral theory, a human rights violation normally consists of enmity towards an innocent party, where she is subordinated and harmed to an extreme degree and some of the harm characteristically includes impairing her ability to trust and be intimate.

For another weakness of salient moral theorization in the West, I believe it has had difficulty accounting in a unified way for these two intuitions: everyone (at least each human person) matters from a moral point of view regardless of how they might be related to a moral agent, but a moral agent is obligated to do more for those who are related to her in certain ways. Utilitarianism recognizes no principled special obligations at all, at best entailing that an agent sometimes has contingent reasons to support and aid those close to her, while Kantianism normally grounds special obligations on voluntary assumptions of obligation, such as promise-making or accepting benefits from a cooperative scheme. In contrast, the relational moral theory maintains that if one must honour people in virtue of their capacity for communality, then one must give everyone with that capacity some impartial consideration, while prioritizing communal relationships of which one is already a part. By this approach, the fact that one has identified with and exhibited solidarity towards others to an intense degree or for a long while provides extra moral reason to cooperate with and aid them, relative to others (7.3.3). I argued that this corollary makes good sense of why parents are more obligated to look after their children than other people's children, doctors have extra moral reason to treat their existing patients as opposed to new patients with marginally greater needs, firms have a *pro tanto* duty to act in the interests of their workers and the societies in which they operate, and several other partial duties that plausibly exist (9.4, 10.4, 11.2, 12.3).

Throughout the part of the book in which I targeted salient Western moral theories, I addressed familiar or standard versions of utilitarianism and Kantianism. I did not address literally all principles of right action, and did not systematically consider ways in which utilitarianism and Kantianism might be creatively interpreted to do a better job of capturing the intuitions I advanced. Even if these theories could be read in ways to avoid certain objections, I submit it would be difficult to present a reading that could evade and also explain all of them neatly, in the way rightness as friendliness appears to do. While it would be reasonable for moral theorists to consider whether there is a way of understanding a Western principle that can do as well as rightness as friendliness has in Part III of this book, another reasonable option at this stage would be to work with the latter, relational moral theory.

13.2 From Prescriptive to Descriptive: A Relational Theory of Moral Behaviour

By 'moral theory' in this book I have meant a general normative principle, i.e., one comprehensively distinguishing some actions as permissible from others as impermissible, which I have sought to evaluate mainly by appealing to particular moral judgements ('intuitions') that are less controversial than it. I have most often contrasted this prescriptive project, about which actions are right and wrong, from a descriptive one of recounting, perhaps in a similarly general way, what African peoples have tended to believe about right and wrong. However, there is an additional descriptive project pertaining to morality, one for which my prescriptive principle might have some implications.

I have in mind the work of moral educationists, psychologists, and sociologists: those who in one way or another seek to explain what moral behaviour is and how it arises. Key social scientific questions include what is involved in knowing something to be moral, what it means to be motivated or to deliberate morally, what it is for action to count as moral, and how one comes to learn how to be moral. In the way that it was sensible for Lawrence Kohlberg to have been influenced by philosophers such as John Rawls in the 1960s, 1970s, and 1980s, so it would be for twenty-first-century social scientists to consider the most up-to-date philosophical reflection on the nature of right and wrong action. In the following, for just one illustration, I briefly indicate how the relational moral theory might bear on thought about moral development, invoking the influential work of Kohlberg (1984, 1986) as a foil. My aim is merely suggestive—new normative thinking might have some empirical implications that merit exploration.[2]

When it comes to moral development, some psychologists have considered whether there is any kind of growth that occurs universally, i.e., in all human societies. According to Kohlberg, human beings, as they mature from children to adults under normal circumstances, tend to develop their thinking about interpersonal moral considerations in a series of invariant stages, with later stages being improvements over earlier ones. Kohlberg's hypothesis is that human cognition normally progresses in six stages, and while he did not empirically confirm the existence of a sixth stage (1984: 270), he thinks of it as the highest form of moral awareness about justice that human beings could be expected to obtain, and it has been very influential amongst social scientists. At stage six, people think about conflicts of interest in terms of the equal consideration of all persons. More specifically, resolving conflicts amongst people in the most defensible moral manner requires teasing out the implications of a procedural principle that even-handedly represents everyone as having a say about, or a stake in, the outcome. Rawls's (1999) original position is a classic example of stage-six reasoning.

Now, although the relational moral theory does accord all human persons a full moral status, and hence includes an impartial dimension (unlike some prominent versions of the ethic of care), it is not purely impartial. Of particular relevance, recall that rightness as friendliness accords, at a fundamental level, a greater moral obligation to support and aid persons who have been related in friendly ways to the agent (7.3.3). Honouring people's communal nature means prioritizing one's own communal relationships, as opposed to promoting communality as much as one can wherever one can in the world; it requires communing and then sustaining and enriching those ties. Hence, the communal ethic entails that it would be inappropriate *invariably* to tackle interpersonal moral dilemmas in a *purely* impartial way. Instead, the fact that certain people have been related to the agent in a communal way can provide some reason to resolve conflicts of interest in one way rather than another.

For example, in the famous Heinz case, Kohlberg clearly deems it merely stage-three moral reflection for Heinz to appeal to the fact that he loves his wife as a moral reason to steal a drug that is necessary and sufficient for her to stay alive and

[2] For a fuller case than is made here, including the suggestion that moral behaviour is not adequately captured by (even a combination of) justice and care, see Metz and Gaie (2010).

that he could not otherwise acquire (Kohlberg 1986: 493, 501, 528). Stage-six reasoning would explicitly exclude the fact of an intimate relationship as a reason to steal the drug, and would instead appeal, e.g., to the fact that the druggist could not reasonably reject, on grounds of an interest in taking advantage of superior bargaining power, a claim on behalf of another person to stay alive. While the relational moral theory might well include such impartial reasoning, it entails that it does not exhaust the relevant moral considerations. In fact, relying solely on impartial reasoning might be wrong, in that it could fail to recognize the greater obligation to one's wife when it comes to moral decision-making. One would plausibly do wrong to flip a coin when choosing between saving the life of one's wife and that of a stranger; one has most moral reason to save one's wife, and guilt would be appropriately greater if one did not. Likewise, the fact of a loving relationship is plausibly relevant to resolving the Heinz dilemma.

If there are special obligations of the sort the relational moral theory has been interpreted to entail, then there is strong reason to doubt Kohlberg's account of the final stage of moral maturation. In Kohlberg's heyday, analytic ethicists were drawn to conceiving what was often called the 'moral point of view' in strictly impartial terms (e.g., Frankena 1963; Baier 1965), and he is well known for having drawn on their analyses to ground his conception of morality. However, while it is sensible to think that the moral point of view includes an impartial dimension, it is plausible to think that it also includes a partial one. Or so some twenty-first-century philosophical reflection suggests.

13.3 From Right Action to Good Character: A Relational Theory of Virtue

Considerations of moral virtue, good character, or what African philosophers tend to call 'personhood' (Menkiti 1984, 2004; Wiredu 2009; Molefe 2019, 2020) have not been prominent in this book, the aim of which has been to advance a principle of right action. Now, rightness was conceived partially in terms of goodness, so to speak; part of the human good that a moral agent must consider in order to exhibit solidarity is other people's virtue (e.g., 6.2, 11.3). However, the question of which acts are right (permissible) differs at bottom from the question of which persons are good (virtuous). Furthermore, much of rightness as friendliness is not a function of that particular aspect of goodness; for its solidarity element includes consideration of well-being, and there is also the identity element, which is not a function of goodness at all. In any event, I have not said much in this book about what moral virtue consists of, but a natural extension of the ethic developed here would flesh that out. What follows is one strategy to consider.

One of the most prominent sayings in sub-Saharan Africa (particularly in the southern region) meant to capture morality is 'A person is a person through other persons', an overly literal translation of indigenous phrasings.[3] The first part of the phrase is saying that one ought to become a real person, or, in the influential talk of '*ubuntu*' from southern Africa, one should become a genuine human being or display humanness. The thought is that personhood or humanness comes in degrees and that one should develop it in oneself. The second part of the maxim indicates how to become a real person or exhibit human excellence, where 'through other persons' is shorthand for 'by relating to others positively'. Those who fail to do so are commonly labelled 'non-persons', 'zero-persons', or even 'animals', which are indications of vice (Nkulu-N'Sengha 2009: 144; Murove 2016: 185).

Accepting this widely held, broad view of human excellence, one way to proceed would be to interpret positive relations with others in terms of prizing identity and solidarity or, more carefully, the capacity of individuals to relate in those ways. A promising virtue-theoretic interpretation of the African moral maxim, which would align with my favoured principle of right action, is that one ought to develop one's personhood by respecting other persons because of their capacity to relate harmoniously. In this book 'respect' has invariably been used to signify which decisions are morally right, but it could be given a richer meaning, one that pertains to the agent's beliefs, emotions, desires, and motivations, beyond merely her choices. When it comes to virtue, one is not merely to treat others in permissible ways, but also should have and display attitudes that the other person has a superlative, non-instrumental value, a dignity, because of her ability to relate harmoniously. For instance, virtue includes actually believing another is good for her own sake to the highest degree on Earth and expressing that belief in one's behaviour, not merely acting in a way that is consistent with such an attitude.

It is worth considering the extent to which this account of moral virtue captures intuitions about it. Insofar as harmony or communality includes caring for others' quality of life, respecting people for being able to be objects of harmonious treatment easily makes sense of generosity, hospitality, care, compassion, sacrifice, kindness, benevolence, and similar virtues. By the same token, insofar as a failure to be harmonious means being indifferent or exhibiting ill-will, the ethic easily makes sense of the vices of insensitivity, hard-heartedness, selfishness, cruelty, and the like. Can communal virtue also account for the virtues of tolerance, peacefulness, honesty, fairness, humility, gratitude, and being polite as well as the corresponding vices of intolerance, aggression, dishonesty, bias, arrogance, ingratitude, and being impolite?

It would also be revealing to address prima facie objections to thinking of virtue in terms of communality. On the face of it, virtue can come not merely through

[3] For the maxim in two South African languages, see Mkhize (2008: 40), and for discussion in the context of a variety of sub-Saharan peoples, see Nkulu-N'Sengha (2009).

other *persons*, but also, for instance, by relating to certain animals; similar remarks go for vice, as when one takes pleasure in being cruel to an animal. It seems that one should broaden the account of virtue to say that a person should become a real person by prizing communal relationships with others, not merely other persons. And, then, there is also the objection that virtue does not necessarily come through *other* persons, but can be self-regarding. Consider practical virtues such as courage, determination, temperance, self-control, and self-respect, or corresponding vices such as cowardice, indecision, overindulgence, addiction, and self-denigration. I considered the possibility of interpreting the relational moral theory to include duties to oneself (7.3.5). The ideas there, particularly about 'relating' to oneself in one's action, would be of use when thinking about how to accommodate self-regarding attitudes.[4]

13.4 From Interpersonal to Institutional: A Relational Theory of Justice

Above I suggested that it might be worth extending the relational moral theory to address descriptive matters regarding the nature of morality beyond prescriptive ones as well as, when it comes to prescriptive matters, considerations of virtue beyond rightness. However, the most straightforward way to extend the relational moral theory would be to apply it to institutional controversies. In this book I have focused on providing answers to interpersonal controversies, mainly about how one person should treat another individual, and that has been true even when addressing settings such as medicine, education, and business in Part III. However, one could use the communal ethic to evaluate more large-scale choices, such as how to structure an organization, which laws to enforce, and what policy to adopt.

What does rightness as friendliness entail for how to effect just redress for crimes such as apartheid, colonialism, and slavery? Does it require compensating in ways that are likely to make their victims better off, or is what matters merely that stolen goods are returned to them, regardless of what good is expected to come in their wake?

What would the communal ethic mean for the final end of a criminal trial, and, in particular, would reconciliation, so prominent in 'traditional' African thought about criminal justice, be a plausible conception of it in a 'modern' society? Would the ethic justify punishment of the guilty, and, if so, for what reasons and in what ways?

[4] For some discussion of the pros and cons of a communal virtue ethic, see Metz (2021b).

Just war theory, too, would be interesting to take up from a relational approach. Might it prescribe going to war for some reason other than merely rebutting aggression against a territory or its citizens? Would relationality entail an obligation on a given country to support another one that has been attacked, if they have had close ties? What would it mean for obligations to support fellow soldiers, when their cause is not just or their means of fighting are unjust?

Let us turn away from questions about non-ideal justice, in which a wrong has already been done and the issues concern how to respond to it. Instead, consider now some ideal matters, i.e., principles that, if followed, would enable an agent to avoid wrongdoing in the first place.

When it comes to economic justice, for instance, how should property and opportunities be allocated so that no legitimate claims to compensation or punishment, let alone war, arise? How might the relational moral theory make sense of a requirement of equal opportunity to obtain education and employment? Would it prescribe a distribution of money and other kinds of wealth different from familiar consequentialist and Rawlsian principles?

I did briefly sketch an account of human rights in this book, and it would be natural to think that a state should enforce them. Does a commitment to human rights require a just state to be full-blown liberal and hence neutral about conceptions of the good life? Does the communal ethic also entail that, alongside human rights, there are some group rights of persons or animal rights that should also be enforced?

Finally, for now, there are questions about the just allocation of political power to be addressed. Until recently, most of the debate in English-speaking philosophy had been between those who think that the final authority to determine law should be had roughly either by a single party (or person), on the one hand, or by whichever party out of an array of competitors has won a majority of votes, on the other. However, it is becoming increasingly well known that African political philosophers have often advocated a 'non-party polity' (in the words of Wiredu 2000), by which the power to make law should be shared equally; by this approach, no law would be valid unless it were the object of a unanimous agreement amongst legislators. I briefly argued that the relational moral theory would support a consensual democracy (7.4), but could it do so in a way that responds to important objections from majoritarians or autocrats?

A comprehensive and coherent defence of answers to these questions and related ones is the natural next stage of work to undertake. My hope is that the reader agrees it would be revealing to develop such a relational theory of justice.[5]

[5] For some initial statements, see Metz (2014b, 2015b, 2016b, 2017c, 2019, 2020).

Epilogue

At the end of the first chapter (1.5), I noted that, since having moved to an African country, I have considered myself to have had a moral obligation to engage with its intellectual traditions when teaching and researching. I would have rightly felt guilt had I taught merely Western ethics to African students and contributed only Euro-American-Australasian perspectives to journals published in the sub-Saharan region. Having been principally trained as an analytic moral and political philosopher, I have been in a good position to articulate normative-theoretic interpretations of African morality, to evaluate these moral theories by appealing to intuitions, and to apply them to a range of practical controversies. Now, it would be welcome if the relational moral theory I have defended in this book could explain why I had a duty to make such a contribution to the field. And indeed it does. I have had an obligation of some weight to teach and research African philosophical ideas as I am particularly able to do so for a reason that is by now familiar to the reader. In the way that a newly trained doctor has an obligation of some weight to give something back to his country before emigrating (9.4.3) and a firm has a *pro tanto* duty to support the society in which it is based (12.3), so an academic has extra moral reason to transmit, interpret, and develop local cultures relative to non-local ones (11.2). Upon having come to relate communally with others, one acquires some obligation to sustain and enrich that relation with them. The book's central thesis prescribes its own composition.

A Relational Moral Theory: African Ethics in and beyond the Continent. Thaddeus Metz, Oxford University Press.
© Thaddeus Metz 2022. DOI: 10.1093/oso/9780198748960.003.0014

References

Abraham, Willie Emmanuel (1962) *The Mind of Africa*, Chicago, IL: The University of Chicago Press.

Adeyemi, Michael and Adeyinka, Augustus (2003) 'The Principles and Content of African Traditional Education', *Educational Philosophy and Theory*, 35: 425–40.

Adeyinka, Augustus and Ndwapi, Gaolekwe (2002) 'Education and Morality in Africa', *Pastoral Care in Education*, 20: 17–23.

Adler, Jonathan (2003) 'Knowledge, Truth, and Learning', in *A Companion to the Philosophy of Education*, Curren, Randall (ed.), Malden, MA: Blackwell, pp. 285–304.

Aja, Egbeke (1997) 'Crime and Punishment: An Indigenous African Experience', *Journal of Value Inquiry*, 31: 353–68.

Ake, Claude (1987) 'The African Context of Human Rights', *Africa Today*, 34: 5–12.

Anderson, Elizabeth (2007) 'Fair Opportunity in Education: A Democratic Equality Perspective', *Ethics*, 117: 595–622.

Andoh, C.T. (2011) 'Bioethics and the Challenges to its Growth in Africa', *Open Journal of Philosophy*, 1: 67–75.

Anedo, Onukwube (2012) 'A Cultural Analysis of Harmony and Conflict', *Unizik Journal of Arts and Humanities*, 13: 16–52.

Ani, Emmanuel Ifeanyi (2014) 'On Traditional African Consensual Rationality', *The Journal of Political Philosophy*, 22: 342–65.

Anyanwu, K.C. (1984) 'The Meaning of Ultimate Reality in Igbo Cultural Experience', *Ultimate Reality and Meaning*, 7: 84–101.

Anyanwu, K.C. (1987) 'The Idea of Art in African Thought', *Contemporary Philosophy: A New Survey*, 5, Dordrecht: Martinus Nijhoff Publishers, pp. 235–60.

Appiah, Kwame Anthony (1998) 'Ethical Systems, African', in *Routledge Encyclopedia of Philosophy*, Craig, Edward (ed.), London: Routledge.

Appiah, Kwame Anthony (2006) *Cosmopolitanism: Ethics in a World of Strangers*, New York: W. W. Norton and Company.

Asante, Molefi Kete (2003) *Afrocentricity*, rev. edn, Chicago, IL: African American Images.

Asouzu, Innocent (2004) *The Method and Principles of Complementary Reflection in and beyond African Philosophy*, Calabar: University of Calabar Press.

Ayittey, George B.N. (2006) *Indigenous African Institutions*, 2nd edn, Ardsley, NY: Transnational Publishers, Inc.

Badhwar, Neera Kapur (1991) 'Why It Is Wrong to Be Always Guided by the Best: Consequentialism and Friendship', *Ethics*, 101: 483–504.

Baier, Kurt (1965) *The Moral Point of View: A Rational Basis of Ethics*, New York: Random House.

Balogun, Oladele Abiodun (2008) 'The Idea of an "Educated Person" in Contemporary African Thought', *Journal of Pan-African Studies*, 2: 117–28.

Behrens, Kevin (2013) 'Towards an African Relational Environmentalism', in *Ontologized Ethics: A Critical Reader in African Meta-Ethics*, Imafidon, Elvis and Bewaji, John (eds), Lanham, MD: Lexington Books, pp. 55–72.

Bell, Daniel A. and Metz, Thaddeus (2011) 'Confucianism and *Ubuntu*: Reflections on a Dialogue between Chinese and African Traditions', *Journal of Chinese Philosophy*, 38 (supp. 1): 78–95.

Bell, Daniel A. and Mo, Yingchuan (2014) 'Harmony in the World 2013: The Ideal and the Reality', *Social Indicators Research*, 118: 797–818.

Bell, Richard (2002) *Understanding African Philosophy*, New York: Routledge.

Bewaji, John Ayotunde Isola (2004) 'Ethics and Morality in Yoruba Culture', in *A Companion to African Philosophy*, Wiredu, Kwasi (ed.), Oxford: Blackwell, pp. 396–403.

Bhengu, Mfuniselwa John (1996) *Ubuntu: The Essence of Democracy*, Cape Town: Novalis Press.

Bhengu, Mfuniselwa John (2006) *Ubuntu: The Global Philosophy for Humankind*, Cape Town: Lotsha Publications.

Biko, Steve (2004) *I Write What I Like*, Johannesburg: Picador Africa.

Bikopo, Deogratias and van Bogaert, Louis-Jacques (2010) 'Reflection on Euthanasia: Western and African Perspectives on the Death of a Chief', *Developing World Bioethics*, 10: 42–8.

Blum, Lawrence (1980) *Friendship, Altruism, and Morality*, London: Routledge & Kegan Paul.

Boon, Mike (2007) *The African Way: The Power of Interactive Leadership*, 3rd edn, Cape Town: Zebra Press.

Bujo, Bénézet (1997) *The Ethical Dimension of Community*, Nganda, Cecilia Namulondo (tr.), Nairobi: Paulines Publications.

Bujo, Bénézet (2001) *Foundations of an African Ethic: Beyond the Universal Claims of Western Morality*, McNeil, Brian (tr.), New York: Crossroad Publishers.

Bujo, Bénézet (2005) 'Differentiations in African Ethics', in *The Blackwell Companion to Religious Ethics*, Schweiker, William (ed.), Malden, MA: Blackwell, pp. 423–37.

Bujo, Bénézet (2015) 'Vatican II and the Challenge of Marriage and Family in Africa', in *Mission for Diversity*, Uzukwu, Elochukwu (ed.), Zurich: LIT Verlag, pp. 205–27.

Busia, Kofi Abrefa (1962) *The Challenge of Africa*, New York: Frederick A. Praeger, Inc.

Busia, Kofi Abrefa (1967) *Africa in Search of Democracy*, London: Routledge & Kegan Paul.

Carlston, Kenneth Smith (1968) *Social Theory and African Tribal Organization*, Urbana, IL: University of Illinois Press.

Chemhuru, Munamato (2016) 'Using the African Teleological View of Existence to Interpret Environmental Ethics', *Philosophia Africana*, 18: 41–51.

Chimakonam, Jonathan Okeke (2019) *Ezumezu: A System of Logic for African Philosophy and Studies*, Cham: Springer.

Constitutional Court of South Africa (1995) *The State versus T Makwanyane and M Mchunu*, CCT 3/94 [1995] ZACC 3, www.saflii.org/za/cases/ZACC/1995/3.html.

Cottingham, John (1983) 'Ethics and Impartiality', *Philosophical Studies*, 43: 83–99.

Dandala, Mvume (2009) 'Cows Never Die: Embracing African Cosmology in the Process of Economic Growth', in *African Ethics: An Anthology of Comparative and Applied Ethics*, Murove, Munyaradzi Felix (ed.), Pietermaritzburg: KwaZulu-Natal Press, pp. 259–77.

Davis, Michael (1992) *To Make the Punishment Fit the Crime: Essays in the Theory of Criminal Justice*, Boulder, CO: Westview Press.

De Waal, Frans (1996) *Good Natured*, Cambridge, MA: Harvard University Press.

Deng, Francis (2004) 'Human Rights in the African Context', in *A Companion to African Philosophy*, Wiredu, Kwasi (ed.), Oxford: Blackwell Publishing Ltd, pp. 499–508.

Dombrowski, Daniel (1997) *Babies and Beasts*, Chicago, IL: University of Illinois Press.
Dowling, Dolina and Seepe, Sipho (2003) 'Towards a Responsive Curriculum', in *A Tale of the Three Countries: Social Sciences Curriculum Transformations in Southern Africa*, Naudé, Piet and Cloete, Nico (eds), Lansdowne: Juta and Co. Pty Ltd, pp. 41–51.
Du Bois, W.E.B. (1897) 'The Conservation of Races', repr. in *The Souls of Black Folk*, Edwards, Brent Hayes (ed.), New York: Oxford University Press, 2007, pp. 179–88.
Du Bois, W.E.B. (1924) 'Little Portraits of Africa', *The Crisis*, 27: 273–4.
Dube, Musa (2009) 'I Am Because We Are: Giving Primacy to African Indigenous Values in HIV&AIDS Prevention', in *African Ethics: An Anthology of Comparative and Applied Ethics*, Murove, Munyaradzi Felix (ed.), Pietermaritzburg: University of KwaZulu-Natal Press, pp. 188–217.
Dzobo, Noah (1992) 'Values in a Changing Society: Man, Ancestors, and God', in *Person and Community; Ghanaian Philosophical Studies, I*, Wiredu, Kwasi and Gyekye, Kwame (eds), Washington, DC: Council for Research in Values and Philosophy, pp. 223–40.
Ejizu, Christopher (2011) 'African Traditional Religions and the Promotion of Community-Living in Africa', https://traditions-afripedia.fandom.com/wiki/AFRICAN_TRADITIONAL_RELIGIONS_AND_THE_PROMOTION_OF_COMMUNITY-LIVING_IN_AFRICA.
Enslin, Penny and Horsthemke, Kai (2004) 'Can *Ubuntu* Provide a Model for Citizenship Education in African Democracies?', *Comparative Education*, 40: 545–58.
Etieyibo, Edwin (2014) 'Post-Modern Thinking and African Philosophy', *Filosofia Theoretica*, 3: 67–82.
Etieyibo, Edwin (2017) 'Moral Education, *Ubuntu* and *Ubuntu*-Inspired Communities', *South African Journal of Philosophy*, 36: 311–25.
Eze, Michael Onyebuchi (2008) 'What Is African Communitarianism? Against Consensus as a Regulative Ideal', *South African Journal of Philosophy*, 27: 386–99.
Eze, Michael Onyebuchi and Metz, Thaddeus (2015) 'Emergent Issues in African Philosophy: A Dialogue with Kwasi Wiredu', *Philosophia Africana*, 17: 73–86.
Feinberg, Harvey and Solodow, Joseph (2002) 'Out of Africa', *Journal of African History*, 43: 255–61.
Flexner, Abraham (2017) *The Usefulness of Useless Knowledge*, Princeton, NJ: Princeton University Press.
Forde, Daryll (ed.) (1954) *African Worlds: Studies in the Cosmological Ideas and Social Values of African Peoples*, London: Oxford University Press.
Fortes, Meyer and Evans-Pritchard, Edward Evan (eds) (1940) *African Political Systems*, repr. London: Kegan Paul, 1994.
Frankena, William (1963) *Ethics*, Englewood Cliffs, NJ: Prentice-Hall.
Frey, R.G. (1983) *Rights, Killing, and Suffering*, Oxford: Basil Blackwell.
Friedman, Marilyn (1993) *What Are Friends for? Feminist Perspectives on Personal Relationships and Moral Theory*, Ithaca, NY: Cornell University Press.
Gade, Christian (2012) 'What Is *Ubuntu*? Different Interpretations among South Africans of African Descent', *South African Journal of Philosophy*, 31: 484–503.
Gädeke, Dorothea (2020) '*Is* and *Ought*? How the (Social) Ontological Circumscribes the Normative', *The Journal of Ethics*, 24: 509–25.
Gathogo, Julius (2008) 'African Philosophy as Expressed in the Concepts of Hospitality and *Ubuntu*', *Journal of Theology for Southern Africa*, 130: 39–53.
Gbadegesin, Segun (1991) *African Philosophy: Traditional Yoruba Philosophy and Contemporary African Realities*, New York: Peter Lang.

Gbadegesin, Segun (1998) 'Genetic Screening, Sickle Cell Anemia, and the African and African-American Perspectives', in *Genetic Knowledge: Values and Responsibility*, Kegley, J.A. (ed.), Lexington, KY: ICUS, pp. 183–95.

Gelfand, Michael (1973) *The Genuine Shona: Survival Values of an African Culture*, Gwelo, Rhodesia: Mambo Press.

Goleman, Daniel (2013) 'Rich People Just Care Less', *New York Times*, 5 October, http://opinionator.blogs.nytimes.com/2013/10/05/rich-people-just-care-less.

Grewal, Daisy (2012) 'How Wealth Reduces Compassion', *Scientific American*, 10 April, www.scientificamerican.com/article/how-wealth-reduces-compassion.

Gutmann, Amy (1995) 'Civic Education and Social Diversity', *Ethics*, 105: 557–79.

Gyekye, Kwame (1992) 'Traditional Political Ideas: Their Relevance to Development in Contemporary Africa', in *Person and Community: Ghanaian Philosophical Studies, I*, Wiredu, Kwasi and Gyekye, Kwame (eds), Washington, DC: Council for Research in Values and Philosophy, pp. 243–55.

Gyekye, Kwame (1995) *An Essay on African Philosophical Thought*, rev. edn, Philadelphia, PA: Temple University Press.

Gyekye, Kwame (1997) *Tradition and Modernity: Philosophical Reflections on the African Experience*, New York: Oxford University Press.

Gyekye, Kwame (2004) *Beyond Cultures: Ghanaian Philosophical Studies, III*, Washington, DC: The Council for Research in Values and Philosophy.

Gyekye, Kwame (2010) 'African Ethics', in *The Stanford Encyclopedia of Philosophy*, Zalta, Edward (ed.), http://plato.stanford.edu/archives/fall2010/entries/african-ethics.

Gyekye, Kwame (2013) *Philosophy, Culture and Vision: African Perspectives*, Accra: Sub-Saharan Publishers.

Habermas, Jürgen (1987) *The Theory of Communicative Action, 2: A Critique of Functionalist Reason*, McCarthy, Thomas (tr.), Boston, MA: Beacon Press.

Hamminga, Bert (2005) 'Epistemology from the African Point of View', in *Knowledge Cultures: Comparative Western and African Epistemology*, Hamminga, Bert (ed.), Amsterdam: Rodopi, pp. 57–84.

Harding, Sandra (1987) 'The Curious Coincidence of Feminine and African Moralities', repr. in *African Philosophy: An Anthology*, Eze, Emmanuel Chukwudi (ed.), Malden, MA: Blackwell, 1998, pp. 360–72.

Hart, H.L.A. (1961) *The Concept of Law*, Oxford: Oxford University Press.

Helm, Bennett (2013) 'Friendship', in *The Stanford Encyclopedia of Philosophy*, Zalta, Edward (ed.), http://plato.stanford.edu/archives/fall2013/entries/friendship.

Higgins, John (2000) 'Academic Freedom in the New South Africa', *Boundary 2*, 27: 97–119.

Hirst, Paul (1974) *Knowledge and the Curriculum*, London: Routledge.

Hoagland, Sarah (1991) 'Some Thoughts about Caring', in *Feminist Ethics*, Card, Claudia (ed.), Lawrence, KS: University of Kansas.

Horsthemke, Kai (2015) *Animals and African Ethics*, New York: Palgrave Macmillan.

Horsthemke, Kai (2018) *Animal Rights Education*, Cham: Palgrave Macmillan.

Horsthemke, Kai and Enslin, Penny (2005) 'Is There a Distinctly and Uniquely African Philosophy of Education?', in *African(a) Philosophy of Education: Reconstructions and Deconstructions*, Waghid, Yusef et al. (eds), Stellenbosch: Department of Education Policy Studies, Stellenbosch University, pp. 54–75.

Hountondji, Paulin (1996) *African Philosophy: Myth and Reality*, 2nd edn, Evans, Henri (tr.), Bloomington, IN: Indiana University Press.

Hurka, Thomas (1993) *Perfectionism*, Oxford: Oxford University Press.

Idowu, William (2006) 'African Jurisprudence and the Reconciliation Theory of Law', *Cambrian Law Review*, 37: 1–16.

Ikuenobe, Polycarp (2006) *Philosophical Perspectives on Communalism and Morality in African Traditions*, Lanham, MD: Lexington Books.

Ikuenobe, Polycarp (2016) 'The Communal Basis for Moral Dignity: An African Perspective', *Philosophical Papers*, 45: 437–69.

Imafidon, Elvis (2013) 'On the Ontological Foundation of a Social Ethics in African Tradition', in *Ontologized Ethics: New Essays in African Meta-Ethics*, Imafidon, Elvis and Bewaji, John Ayotunde Isola (eds), Lanham, MD: Lexington Books, pp. 37–54.

Imafidon, Elvis and Bewaji, John Ayotunde Isola (eds) (2013) *Ontologized Ethics: New Essays in African Meta-Ethics*, Lanham, MD: Lexington Books.

Iroegbu, Pantaleon (2005a) 'Beginning, Purpose and End of Life', in *Kpim of Morality Ethics*, Iroegbu, Pantaleon and Echekwube, Anthony (eds), Ibadan: Heinemann Educational Books, pp. 440–5.

Iroegbu, Pantaleon (2005b) 'Right to Life and the Means to Life: Human Dignity', in *Kpim of Morality Ethics*, Iroegbu, Pantaleon and Echekwube, Anthony (eds), Ibadan: Heinemann Educational Books, pp. 446–9.

Iroegbu, Pantaleon (2007) 'Individual–Community Dialectics in Communalism', in *Perspectives on African Communalism*, Odimegwu, Ike (ed.), Victoria: Trafford Publishing, pp. 142–58.

Isike, Christopher and Uzodike, Ufo Okeke (2011) 'Towards an Indigenous Model of Conflict Resolution: Reinventing Women's Roles as Traditional Peacebuilders in Neo-Colonial Africa', *African Journal on Conflict Resolution*, 11: 32–58.

Jahn, Janheinz (1961) *Muntu: An Outline of Neo-African Culture*, Greene, Marjorie (tr.), London: Faber and Faber.

Jonathan, Ruth (2006) *Academic Freedom, Institutional Autonomy and Public Accountability in Higher Education*, Pretoria: Council on Higher Education.

Jones, Ward and Metz, Thaddeus (2015) 'The Politics of Doing Philosophy in Africa', *South African Journal of Philosophy*, 34: 538–50.

Kant, Immanuel (1785) *Groundwork of the Metaphysics of Morals*, Gregor, Mary (tr.), in *Immanuel Kant: Practical Philosophy*, Gregor, Mary (ed.), Cambridge: Cambridge University Press, 1996, pp. 37–108.

Kant, Immanuel (1793) 'On the Common Saying: That May Be Correct in Theory, But It Is of No Use in Practice', Gregor, Mary (tr.), in *Immanuel Kant: Practical Philosophy*, Gregor, Mary (ed.), Cambridge: Cambridge University Press, 1996, pp. 273–309.

Kant, Immanuel (1797) *The Metaphysics of Morals*, Gregor, Mary (tr.), in *Immanuel Kant: Practical Philosophy*, Gregor, Mary (ed.), Cambridge: Cambridge University Press, 1996, pp. 353–603.

Kasenene, Peter (1994) 'Ethics in African Theology', in *Doing Ethics in Context: South African Perspectives*, Villa-Vicencio, Charles and de Gruchy, John (eds), Cape Town: David Philip, pp. 138–47.

Kasenene, Peter (1998) *Religious Ethics in Africa*, Kampala: Fountain Publishers.

Kasenene, Peter (2000) 'African Ethical Theory and the Four Principles', in *Cross-Cultural Perspectives in Medical Ethics*, Veatch, R.M. (ed.), Sudbury, MA: Jones and Bartlett, pp. 347–57.

Kasoma, Francis P. (1996) 'The Foundations of African Ethics (Afriethics) and the Professional Practice of Journalism: The Case for Society-Centred Media Morality', *Africa Media Review*, 10: 93–116.

Kaunda, Kenneth (1966) *A Humanist in Africa*, London: The Camelot Press Ltd.

Kayange, Grivas Muchineripi (2018) *Meaning and Truth in African Philosophy*, Cham: Springer.

Kekes, John (1981) 'Morality and Impartiality', *American Philosophical Quarterly*, 18: 295–303.

Kelly, Morgan (2000) 'Inequality and Crime', *The Review of Economics and Statistics*, 82: 530–9.

Kennett, Jeanette (2002) 'Autism, Empathy and Moral Agency', *Philosophical Quarterly*, 52: 340–57.

Kenyatta, Jomo (1965) *Facing Mount Kenya*, New York: Vintage.

Khoza, Reuel (2006) *Let Africa Lead: African Transformational Leadership for 21st Century Business*, Johannesburg: Vezubuntu.

Kigongo, James (2002) 'The Relevance of African Ethics to Contemporary African Society', in *Ethics, Human Rights and Development in Africa: Ugandan Philosophical Studies*, Dalfovo, A.T. (ed.), Washington, DC: Council for Research in Values and Philosophy, pp. 51–65.

Kiss, Elizabeth and Euben, J. Peter (eds) (2010) *Debating Moral Education: Rethinking the Role of the Modern University*, Durham, NC: Duke University Press.

Kleingeld, Pauline and Brown, Eric (2013) 'Cosmopolitanism', in *The Stanford Encyclopedia of Philosophy*, Zalta, Edward (ed.), https://plato.stanford.edu/entries/cosmopolitanism.

Klosko, George (1992) *The Principle of Fairness and Political Obligation*, Lanham, MD: Rowman & Littlefield.

Koenane, Mojalefa (2019) 'Economic Development in Africa through the Stokvel System', *Filosofia Theoretica*, 8: 109–24.

Koestler, Arthur (1967) *The Ghost in the Machine*, New York: Macmillan.

Kohlberg, Lawrence (1984) *The Psychology of Moral Development*, San Francisco, CA: Harper & Row.

Kohlberg, Lawrence (1986) 'A Current Statement on Some Theoretical Issues', in *Lawrence Kohlberg: Consensus and Controversy*, Modgil, Sohan and Modgil, Celia (eds), London: The Falmer Press, pp. 485–546.

Kraemer-Mbula, Erika et al. (eds) (2020) *Transforming Research Excellence: New Ideas from the Global South*, Cape Town: African Minds.

Krige, J.D. and Krige, E.J. (1954) 'The Lovedu of the Transvaal', in *African Worlds: Studies in the Cosmological Ideas and Social Values of African Peoples*, Forde, Daryll (ed.), Oxford: Oxford University Press, pp. 55–82.

Krog, Antjie (2008) '"This Thing Called Reconciliation": Forgiveness as Part of an Interconnectedness-towards-Wholeness', *South African Journal of Philosophy*, 27: 353–66.

Küng, Hans and Kuschel, Karl-Joseph (1993) *Global Ethic: The Declaration of the Parliament of the World's Religions*, Bowden, John (tr.), New York: Continuum.

LaFollette, Hugh (1995) *Personal Relationships: Love, Identity, and Morality*, Oxford: Blackwell.

Lamola, John (2019) 'Will We Ever Have a Genuine African Philosophy?', *Social Epistemology Review and Reply Collective*, 8: 39–45.

Legesse, Asmarom (2001) *Oromo Democracy: An Indigenous African Political System*, Lawrenceville, NJ: The Red Sea Press.

LenkaBula, Puleng (2008) 'Beyond Anthropocentricity—*Botho/Ubuntu* and the Quest for Economic and Ecological Justice in Africa', *Religion and Theology*, 15: 375–94.

Leopold, Aldo (1968) *A Sand County Almanac*, 2nd edn, New York: Oxford University Press.
Letseka, Moeketsi (2000) 'African Philosophy and Educational Discourse', in *African Voices in Education*, Higgs, Philip et al. (eds), Cape Town: Juta, pp. 179–93.
Lombardi, Joseph L. (1991) 'Filial Gratitude and God's Right to Command', *The Journal of Religious Ethics*, 19: 93–118.
Lutz, David (2009) 'African *Ubuntu* Philosophy and Global Management', *Journal of Business Ethics*, 84: 313–28.
Macedo, Stephan (1990) *Liberal Virtues: Citizenship, Virtue, and Community in Liberal Constitutionalism*, Oxford: Oxford University Press.
Macpherson, Cheryl and Macklin, Ruth (2010) 'Symposium Editorial: African Perspectives', *Developing World Bioethics*, 10: 30–3.
Magesa, Laurenti (1997) *African Religion: The Moral Traditions of Abundant Life*, Maryknoll, NY: Orbis Books.
Mandela, Nelson (2006) '*Ubuntu* Told by Nelson Mandela', www.youtube.com/watch?v= HED4h00xPPA.
Mandela, Nelson (2012) *Notes to the Future: Words of Wisdom*, Hatang, S.K. and Venter, Sahm (eds), New York: Atria.
Mandela, Nelson (2013) *Nelson Mandela by Himself: The Authorised Book of Quotations*, Hatang, S.K. and Venter, Sahm (eds), Johannesburg: Pan Macmillan.
Mangena, Fainos (2009) 'The Search for an African Feminist Ethic', *Journal of International Women's Studies*, 11: 18–30.
Manzini, Nompumelelo Zinhle (2018) 'Menkiti's Normative Communitarian Conception of Personhood as Gendered, Ableist and Anti-Queer', *South African Journal of Philosophy*, 37: 18–33.
Masolo, Dismas (2010) *Self and Community in a Changing World*, Bloomington, IN: University of Indiana Press.
Matolino, Bernard (2018) *Consensus as Democracy in Africa*, Grahamstown, South Africa: NISC [Pty] Ltd.
Matolino, Bernard and Kwindingwi, Wenceslaus (2013) 'The End of *Ubuntu*', *South African Journal of Philosophy*, 32: 197–205.
Mawere, Munyaradzi (2011) 'Possibilities for Cultivating African Indigenous Knowledge Systems (IKSs): Lessons from Selected Cases of Witchcraft in Zimbabwe', *Journal of Gender and Peace Development*, 1: 91–100.
Mbigi, Lovemore (2007) 'The Hunter's Spirit in Leadership: An African Wounded Soul Theory Perspective', in *Diversity: The Coming of Age of a Continent*, April, Kurt and Shockley, Marylou (eds), London: Palgrave Macmillan, pp. 157–63.
Mbigi, Lovemore and Maree, Jenny (2005) *Ubuntu: The Spirit of African Transformation Management*, Randburg: Knowres Publishing.
Mbiti, John (1975) *Introduction to African Religion*, New York: Praeger.
Mbiti, John (1990) *African Religions and Philosophy*, 2nd edn, Oxford: Heinemann.
Mboti, Nyasha (2015) 'May the Real Ubuntu Please Stand Up?', *Journal of Media Ethics*, 30: 125–47.
McCarty, L.P. (2011) 'Cosmopolitan Education', *Colleagues*, 6: 6–7.
Mearsheimer, John (1998) 'The Aims of Education', *Philosophy and Literature*, 22: 137–55.
Menkiti, Ifeanyi (1984) 'Person and Community in African Traditional Thought', in *African Philosophy: An Introduction*, 3rd edn, Wright, Richard (ed.), Lanham, MD: University Press of America, pp. 171–81.

Menkiti, Ifeanyi (2004) 'On the Normative Conception of a Person', in *A Companion to African Philosophy*, Wiredu, Kwasi (ed.), Oxford: Blackwell, pp. 324–31.
Menkiti, Ifeanyi (2017) 'Community, Communism, Communitarianism: An African Intervention', in *The Palgrave Handbook of African Philosophy*, Afolayan, Adeshina and Falola, Toyin (eds), New York: Palgrave Macmillan, pp. 461–73.
Metz, Thaddeus (2002) 'Realism and the Censure Theory of Punishment', *Archives for Philosophy of Law and Social Philosophy*, 85 (supp.): 117–29.
Metz, Thaddeus (2007) 'Toward an African Moral Theory', *Journal of Political Philosophy*, 15: 321–41. Revised edition published in *Themes, Issues and Problems in African Philosophy*, Ukpokolo, Isaac (ed.), London: Palgrave Macmillan, 2017, pp. 97–119.
Metz, Thaddeus (2009) 'Higher Education, Knowledge for its Own Sake, and an African Moral Theory', *Studies in Philosophy and Education*, 28: 517–36.
Metz, Thaddeus (2012) '"Giving the World a More Human Face": Human Suffering in African Thought and Philosophy', in *Perspectives on Human Suffering*, Malpas, Jeff and Lickiss, Norelle (eds), Dordrecht: Springer, pp. 49–62.
Metz, Thaddeus (2013a) *Meaning in Life: An Analytic Study*, Oxford: Oxford University Press.
Metz, Thaddeus (2013b) 'The Ethics of Swearing: The Implications of Moral Theories for Oath-Breaking in Economic Contexts', *Review of Social Economy*, 71: 228–48.
Metz, Thaddeus (2014a) 'African Values and Human Rights as Two Sides of the Same Coin', *African Human Rights Law Journal*, 14: 306–21.
Metz, Thaddeus (2014b) 'African Values, Human Rights and Group Rights: A Philosophical Foundation for the Banjul Charter', in *African Legal Theory and Contemporary Problems*, Onazi, Oche (ed.), Dordrecht: Springer, pp. 131–51.
Metz, Thaddeus (2015a) 'African Ethics and Journalism Ethics: News and Opinion in Light of *Ubuntu*', *Journal of Media Ethics*, 30: 74–90.
Metz, Thaddeus (2015b) 'An African Egalitarianism: Bringing Community to Bear on Equality', in *The Equal Society: Essays on Equality in Theory and Practice*, Hull, George (ed.), Lanham, MD: Rowman & Littlefield, pp. 185–208.
Metz, Thaddeus (2016a) 'Confucian Harmony from an African Perspective', *African and Asian Studies*, 15: 1–22.
Metz, Thaddeus (2016b) 'An African Theory of Social Justice: Relationship as the Ground of Rights, Resources and Recognition', in *Distributive Justice Debates in Political and Social Thought*, Boisen, Camilla and Murray, Matt (eds), Abingdon: Routledge, pp. 171–90.
Metz, Thaddeus (2017a) 'Values in China as Compared to Africa: Two Conceptions of Harmony', *Philosophy East and West*, 67: 441–65.
Metz, Thaddeus (2017b) 'The Ethics and Politics of the Brain Drain: A Communal Alternative to Liberal Perspectives', *South African Journal of Philosophy*, 36: 101–14.
Metz, Thaddeus (2017c) 'Replacing Development: An Afro-Communal Approach to Global Justice', *Philosophical Papers*, 46: 111–37.
Metz, Thaddeus (2018) 'What Is the Essence of an Essence? Comparing Afro-Relational and Western-Individualist Ontologies', *Synthesis Philosophica*, 65: 209–24.
Metz, Thaddeus (2019) 'Reconciliation as the Aim of a Criminal Trial: *Ubuntu*'s Implications for Sentencing', *Constitutional Court Review*, 9: 113–34.
Metz, Thaddeus (2020) 'An African Theory of Just Causes for War', in *Comparative Just War Theory*, Cordeiro-Rodrigues, Luis and Singh, Danny (eds), Lanham, MD: Rowman & Littlefield, pp. 131–55.

Metz, Thaddeus (2022a) 'What Africa Can Bring to the World', in *General History of Africa, Volume 9: Global Africa*, Chenntouf, Tayeb (ed.), Geneva: UNESCO, ch. 22.
Metz, Thaddeus (2022b) 'Virtue in African Ethics as Living Harmoniously', in *The Virtue of Harmony*, Li, Chenyang and Düring, Dascha (eds), New York: Oxford University Press, pp. 207–29.
Metz, Thaddeus and Gaie, Joseph (2010) 'The African Ethic of *Ubuntu/Botho*: Implications for Research on Morality', *Journal of Moral Education*, 39: 273–90.
Metz, Thaddeus and Miller, Sarah Clark (2016) 'Relational Ethics', in *The International Encyclopedia of Ethics*, LaFollette, Hugh (ed.), Malden, MA: Blackwell Publishing Ltd, pp. 1–10.
Mkhize, Nhlanhla (2008) '*Ubuntu* and Harmony: An African Approach to Morality and Ethics', in *Persons in Community: African Ethics in a Global Culture*, Nicolson, Ronald (ed.), Pietermaritzburg: University of KwaZulu-Natal Press, pp. 35–44.
Mnyaka, Mluleki and Motlhabi, Mokgethi (2005) 'The African Concept of *Ubuntu/Botho* and its Socio-Moral Significance', *Black Theology*, 3: 215–37.
Mofuoa, Khali (2014) 'Applying *Ubuntu-Botho* African Ethics to Stakeholder Corporate Social Responsibility', *Management Research*, 12: 222–39.
Mokgoro, Yvonne (1998) '*Ubuntu* and the Law in South Africa', *Potchefstroom Electronic Law Journal*, 1: 15–26.
Molefe, Motsamai (2015) 'A Rejection of Humanism in African Moral Tradition', *Theoria*, 62: 59–77.
Molefe, Motsamai (2019) *An African Philosophy of Personhood, Morality, and Politics*, Cham: Palgrave Macmillan.
Molefe, Motsamai (2020) *An African Ethics of Personhood and Bioethics*, Cham: Palgrave Macmillan.
Molema, S.M. (1920) *The Bantu: Past and Present*, Edinburgh: Edinburgh University Press.
Msila, Vuyisile (2014) 'African Leadership Models in Education', *Anthropologist*, 18: 1105–14.
Msila, Vuyisile (2015) *Ubuntu: Shaping the Current Workplace with (African) Wisdom*, Randburg: Knowres Publishing.
Mulago, Vincent (1991) 'Traditional African Religion and Christianity', in *African Traditional Religions in Contemporary Society*, Olupona, Jacob (ed.), New York: Paragon House, pp. 119–34.
Mungwini, Pascah (2019) *Indigenous Shona Philosophy: Reconstructive Insights*, Grahamstown, South Africa: NISC [Pty] Ltd.
Murove, Munyaradzi Felix (2004) 'An African Commitment to Ecological Conservation: The Shona Concepts of *Ukama* and *Ubuntu*', *The Mankind Quarterly*, 45: 195–215.
Murove, Munyaradzi Felix (2007) 'The Shona Ethic of *Ukama* with Reference to the Immortality of Values', *The Mankind Quarterly*, 48: 179–89.
Murove, Munyaradzi Felix (2009a) 'The Incarnation of Max Weber's Protestant Ethic and the Spirit of Capitalism in Post-Colonial African Economic Discourse: The Quest for an African Economic Ethic', in *African Ethics: An Anthology of Comparative and Applied Ethics*, Murove, Munyaradzi Felix (ed.), Pietermaritzburg: University of KwaZulu-Natal Press, pp. 221–37.
Murove, Munyaradzi Felix (2009b) 'African Bioethics: An Exploratory Discourse', in *African Ethics: An Anthology of Comparative and Applied Ethics*, Murove, Munyaradzi Felix (ed.), Pietermaritzburg: University of KwaZulu-Natal Press, pp. 157–77.
Murove, Munyaradzi Felix (2016) *African Moral Consciousness*, London: Austin Macauley Publishers Ltd.

Murungi, John (2004) 'The Question of an African Jurisprudence', in *A Companion to African Philosophy*, Wiredu, Kwasi (ed.), Malden, MA: Blackwell, pp. 519–26.
Mutwa, Credo (1964) *Indaba, My Children*, repr. Edinburgh: Payback Press, 1998.
Narayan, Uma (1995) 'Colonialism and Its Others: Considerations on Rights and Care Discourses', *Hypatia*, 10: 133–40.
Ncube, Lisa (2010) '*Ubuntu*: A Transformative Leadership Philosophy', *Journal of Leadership Studies*, 4: 77–82.
Ndlovu, Priscilla Mtungwa (2016) *Discovering the Spirit of Ubuntu Leadership*, London: Palgrave Macmillan.
Ngwainmbi, Emmanuel (2009) 'Abela', in *Encyclopedia of African Religion*, Asante, Molefi Kete and Mazama, Ama (eds), Los Angeles, CA: Sage Publications, pp. 2–3.
Nisbett, Richard (2003) *The Geography of Thought: How Asians and Westerners Think Differently... and Why*, New York: Free Press.
Nkondo, Gessler Muxe (2007) '*Ubuntu* as a Public Policy in South Africa: A Conceptual Framework', *International Journal of African Renaissance Studies*, 2: 88–100.
Nkrumah, Kwame (1970) *Consciencism*, 2nd edn, New York: Monthly Review Press.
Nkulu-N'Sengha, Mutombo (2009) '*Bumuntu*', in Asante, Molefi Kete and Mazama, Ama (eds), *Encyclopedia of African Religion*, Los Angeles, CA: Sage, pp. 142–7.
Nozick, Robert (1989) *The Examined Life*, New York: Simon and Schuster.
Nussbaum, Barbara (2003) '*Ubuntu* and Business: Reflections and Questions', *World Business Academy Perspectives*, 17: 1–16.
Nussbaum, Martha (2002) 'Education for Citizenship in an Era of Global Connection', *Studies in Philosophy and Education*, 21: 289–303.
Nussbaum, Martha (2006) 'The Moral Status of Animals', *Chronicle of Higher Education*, 52 (22): B6–8.
Nussbaum, Martha (2012) *Not for Profit: Why Democracy Needs the Humanities*, Princeton, NJ: Princeton University Press.
Nwala, T. Uzodinma (1985) *Igbo Philosophy*, Lagos: Lantern Books.
Nyerere, Julius (1968) *Ujamaa: Essays on Socialism*, New York: Oxford University Press.
Nze, Chukwuemeka (2007) 'Aspects of African Communalism', in *Perspectives on African Communalism*, Odimegwu, Ike (ed.), Victoria: Trafford Publishing, pp. 588–604.
Odimegwu, Ike (2008) *Integrative Personhood: A Communalist Metaphysical Anthropology*, Berlin: LIT Verlag.
Ogbujah, Columbus (2007) 'The Individual in African Communalism', in *Perspectives on African Communalism*, Odimegwu, Ike (ed.), Victoria: Trafford Publishing, pp. 127–41.
Oguejiofor, Josephat Obi (2007) 'How African Is Communalism?', in *Perspectives on African Communalism*, Odimegwu, Ike (ed.), Victoria: Trafford Publishing, pp. 5–23.
Ogugua, Ikechukwu (2007) 'The Metaphysical Basis of African Communalism', in *Perspectives on African Communalism*, Odimegwu, Ike (ed.), Victoria: Trafford Publishing, pp. 24–33.
Okem, Andrew Emmanuel and Stanton, Anne (2016) 'Contextualising the Cooperative Movement in Africa', in *Theoretical and Empirical Studies on Cooperatives*, Okem, Andrew Emmanuel (ed.), Cham: Springer, pp. 15–26.
Okyere-Manu, Beatrice (2016) 'Overpopulation and the Lifeboat Metaphor: A Critique from an African Worldview', *International Studies in the Philosophy of Science*, 30: 279–89.
Oladipo, Olusegun (2004) 'Religion in African Culture: Some Conceptual Issues', in *A Companion to African Political Philosophy*, Wiredu, Kwasi (ed.), Oxford: Blackwell Publishing Ltd, pp. 356–63.

Omoregbe, Joseph (2005) 'Ethics in Traditional African Societies', in *Kpim of Morality Ethics*, Iroegbu, Pantaleon and Echekwube, Anthony (eds), Ibadan: Heinemann Educational Books, pp. 36–42.

Onah, Godfrey (2012) 'The Meaning of Peace in African Traditional Religion and Culture', http://beeshadireed.blogspot.com/2012/08/the-meaning-of-peace-in-african.html.

O'Neill, Onora (1989) *Constructions of Reason*, Cambridge: Cambridge University Press.

Onwuanibe, Richard (1984) 'The Human Person and Immortality in Ibo Metaphysics', in *African Philosophy: An Introduction*, 3rd edn, Wright, Richard (ed.), Lanham, MD: University Press of America, pp. 183–93.

Onyibor, Marcel (2007) 'The Freedom of the Individual in African Communalism', in *Perspectives on African Communalism*, Odimegwu, Ike (ed.), Victoria: Trafford Publishing, pp. 159–73.

Oruka, Henry Odera (1997) *Practical Philosophy: In Search of an Ethical Minimum*, Nairobi: East African Educational Publishers.

Oruka, Henry Odera and Juma, Calestous (1994) 'Ecophilosophy and Parental Earth Ethics', in *Philosophy, Humanity and Ecology*, Oruka, Henry Odera (ed.), Nairobi: ACTS, pp. 115–29.

Owolabi, Kolowole (2001) 'The Quest for Method in African Philosophy: A Defense of the Hermeneutic-Narrative Approach', *Philosophical Forum*, 32: 147–63.

Oyowe, Oritsegbubemi (2013) 'Personhood and Social Power in African Thought', *Alternation*, 20: 203–28.

Oyowe, Oritsegbubemi (2018) 'Is, Ought, and All: In Defense of a Method', in *Method, Substance, and the Future of African Philosophy*, Etieyibo, Edwin (ed.), Cham: Palgrave Macmillan, pp. 161–84.

Oyowe, Oritsegbubemi and Yurkivska, Olga (2014) 'Can a Communitarian Concept of African Personhood Be Both Relational and Gender-Neutral?', *South African Journal of Philosophy*, 33: 85–99.

Parfit, Derek (1984) *Reasons and Persons*, Oxford: Oxford University Press.

Paris, Peter (1995) *The Spirituality of African Peoples: The Search for a Common Moral Discourse*, Minneapolis, MN: Fortress Press.

Parker, Ben (2003) 'Back on the Chain Gang: Some Difficulties in Developing a (South) African Philosophy of Education', *Journal of Education*, 30: 23–40.

Paul II, Pope John (1995) *The Gospel of Life (Evangelium Vitae): On the Value and Inviolability of Human Life*, Washington, DC: USCCB Publishing.

Peters, R.S. (1966) *Ethics and Education*, London: Allen & Unwin.

Praeg, Leonhard (2014) *A Report on Ubuntu*, Pietermaritzburg: University of KwaZulu-Natal Press.

Rakotsoane, Francis and van Niekerk, Anton (2017) 'Human Life Invaluableness: An Emerging African Bioethical Principle', *South African Journal of Philosophy*, 36: 252–62.

Ramose, Mogobe (2001) 'An African Perspective on Justice and Race', *Polylog*, 3, http://them.polylog.org/3/frm-en.htm.

Ramose, Mogobe (2003) 'The Ethics of *Ubuntu*', in *The African Philosophy Reader*, 2nd edn, Coetzee, P.H. and Roux, A.P.J. (eds), London: Routledge, pp. 379–87.

Ramose, Mogobe (2005) *African Philosophy through Ubuntu*, rev. edn, Harare: Mond Books.

Ramose, Mogobe (2007) 'But Hans Kelsen Was Not Born in Africa', *South African Journal of Philosophy*, 26: 347–55.

Rawls, John (1988) 'The Priority of Right and Ideas of the Good', *Philosophy and Public Affairs*, 17: 251–76.

Rawls, John (1999) *A Theory of Justice*, rev. edn, Cambridge, MA: Harvard University Press.
Regan, Tom (2004) *The Case for Animal Rights*, 2nd edn, Berkeley, CA: University of California Press.
Richardson, Henry (2012) *Moral Entanglements: The Ancillary-Care Obligations of Medical Researchers*, Oxford: Oxford University Press.
Richardson, Henry and Belsky, Leah (2004) 'The Ancillary Care Responsibilities of Medical Researchers: An Ethical Framework for Thinking about the Clinical Care That Researchers Owe their Subjects', *Hastings Center Report*, 34: 25–33.
Samkange, Stanlake and Samkange, Tommie Marie (1980) *Hunhuism or Ubuntuism: A Zimbabwean Indigenous Political Philosophy*, Harare: Graham Publishing Company.
Samuel, Olusegun and Fayemi, Ademola (2020) 'A Critique of Thaddeus Metz's Modal Relational Account of Moral Status', *Theoria*, 67: 28–44.
Seepe, Sipho (ed.) (1998) *Black Perspective(s) on Tertiary Institutional Transformation*, Florida Hills: Vivlia Publishers and the University of Venda.
Senghor, Léopold Sédar (1964) *On African Socialism*, Cook, Mercer (tr.), New York: Praeger.
Senior, Jennifer (2010) 'All Joy and No Fun: The Paradox of Modern Parenthood', *New York Times*, 2 July, https://nymag.com/news/features/67024.
Setiloane, Gabriel (1976) *The Image of God among the Sotho-Tswana*, Rotterdam: Balkema.
Setlhodi, Itumeleng (2019) '*Ubuntu* Leadership: An African Panacea for Improving School Performance', *Africa Education Review*, 16: 126–42.
Shutte, Augustine (2001) *Ubuntu: An Ethic for the New South Africa*, Cape Town: Cluster Publications.
Siame, Chisanga (2000) '"Two Concepts of Liberty" through African Eyes', *Journal of Political Philosophy*, 8: 53–67.
Siegel, Harvey (1998) *Educating Reason: Rationality, Critical Thinking, and Education*, New York: Routledge.
Silberbauer, George (1991) 'Ethics in Small-Scale Societies', in *A Companion to Ethics*, Singer, Peter (ed.), Oxford: Basil Blackwell, pp. 14–28.
Sindima, Henry (1989) 'Community of Life', *The Ecumenical Review*, 41: 537–51.
Singer, Peter (1993) *Practical Ethics*, 2nd edn, Cambridge: Cambridge University Press.
Slack, Catherine et al. (2005) 'Provision of HIV Treatment in HIV Preventive Vaccine Trials: A Developing Country Perspective', *Social Science and Medicine*, 60: 1197–208.
Slote, Michael (2007) *The Ethics of Care and Empathy*, New York: Routledge.
Sogolo, Godwin (1993) *Foundations of African Philosophy: A Definitive Analysis of Conceptual Issues in African Thought*, Ibadan: Ibadan University Press.
Stobie, Melissa and Slack, Catherine (2010) 'Treatment Needs in HIV Prevention Trials: Using Beneficence to Clarify Sponsor-Investigator Responsibilities', *Developing World Bioethics*, 10: 150–7.
Stone, Christopher (1972) 'Should Trees Have Standing?', *South California Law Review*, 45: 450–501.
Stone, Christopher (1985) 'Should Trees Have Standing? Revisited', *South California Law Review*, 59: 1–154.
Sulmasy, Daniel (1999) 'What Is an Oath and Why Should a Physician Swear One?', *Theoretical Medicine and Bioethics*, 20: 329–46.
Tangwa, Godfrey (1996) 'Bioethics: An African Perspective', *Bioethics*, 10: 183–200.
Tangwa, Godfrey (2005) 'The HIV/AIDS Pandemic, African Traditional Values and the Search for a Vaccine in Africa', in *Ethics and AIDS in Africa*, van Niekerk, Anton and Kopelman, Loretta (eds), Claremont: David Philip Publishers, pp. 179–89.

Tangwa, Godfrey (2010) *Elements of African Bioethics in a Western Frame*, Bameda: Langaa Research and Publishing CIG.

Taringa, Nisbert (2006) 'How Environmental Is African Traditional Religion?', *Exchange*, 35: 191–214.

Taringa, Nisbert (2007) 'Possibilities and Limitations for Intercultural Dialogue from the Perspective of *Ubuntu* Philosophy', *Swedish Missiological Themes*, 95: 185–96.

Taylor, Paul (1986) *Respect for Nature*, Princeton, NJ: Princeton University Press.

Tempels, Placide (1959) *Bantu Philosophy*, 2nd edn, King, Colin (tr.), Paris: Présence Africaine.

Tosam, Mbih Jerome (2014) 'The Relevance of Kom Ethics to African Development', *International Journal of Philosophy*, 2: 36–47.

Tshivhase, Mpho (2018) 'Love as the Foundation of *Ubuntu*', *Synthesis Philosophica*, 65: 197–208.

Tutu, Desmond (1999) *No Future without Forgiveness*, New York: Random House.

Uduma, Uduma Oji and Nweke, Victor (2018) '*Ndubuisi*: An Igbo-African Understanding of the Value of Human Life and its Implications for the Death Penalty Question', in *The Death Penalty from an African Perspective*, Mangena, Fainos and Chimakonam, Jonathan Okeke (eds), Wilmington, DE: Vernon Press, pp. 29–60.

Ukagba, George (2005) 'Afroxiology: Ethical Study of African Values', in *Kpim of Morality Ethics*, Iroegbu, Pantaleon and Echekwube, Anthony (eds), Ibadan: Heinemann Educational Books, pp. 179–89.

Unah, Jim (2014) 'Finding Common Grounds for a Dialogue between African and Chinese Ethics', in *Ontologized Ethics: New Essays in African Meta-Ethics*, Imafidon, Elvis and Bewaji, John (eds), Lanham, MD: Lexington Books, pp. 107–20.

United States Catholic Church (2003) *Catechism of the Catholic Church*, 2nd edn, New York: Doubleday.

van Niekerk, Jason (2007) 'In Defence of an Autocentric Account of *Ubuntu*', *South African Journal of Philosophy*, 26: 64–8.

Velleman, David (1999) 'Love as a Moral Emotion', *Ethics*, 109: 338–74.

Verhoef, Heidi and Michel, Claudine (1997) 'Studying Morality within the African Context', *Journal of Moral Education*, 26: 389–407.

Villa-Vicencio, Charles (2009) *Walk with Us and Listen: Political Reconciliation in Africa*, Washington, DC: Georgetown University Press.

Waks, Leonard (2009) 'Reason and Culture in Cosmopolitan Education', *Educational Theory*, 59: 589–604.

Warren, Mary Anne (1973) 'On the Moral Status of Abortion', *The Monist*, 57: 43–61.

Warren, Mary Anne (2003) 'Moral Status', in *A Companion to Applied Ethics*, Frey, R.G. and Wellman, Christopher (eds), Malden, MA: Blackwell, pp. 439–50.

Wenger, Etienne (1998) *Communities of Practice*, Cambridge: Cambridge University Press.

White, John (2010) *The Aims of Education Restated*, London: Routledge.

Wielenberg, Erik (2004) 'Egoism and *Eudaimonia*-Maximization in the Nicomachean Ethics', *Oxford Studies in Ancient Philosophy*, 26: 277–95.

Wilkinson, Richard and Pickett, Kate (2009) *The Spirit Level: Why More Equal Societies Almost Always Do Better*, Harmondsworth: Penguin.

Wiredu, Kwasi (1980) *Philosophy and an African Culture*, Cambridge: Cambridge University Press.

Wiredu, Kwasi (1992) 'The Moral Foundations of an African Culture', in *Person and Community: Ghanaian Philosophical Studies, I*, Wiredu, Kwasi and Gyekye, Kwame (eds), Washington, DC: Council for Research in Values and Philosophy, pp. 193–206.

Wiredu, Kwasi (1996) *Cultural Universals and Particulars: An African Perspective*, Bloomington, IN: Indiana University Press.

Wiredu, Kwasi (2000) 'Democracy and Consensus in African Traditional Politics: A Plea for a Non-Party Polity', *Polylog*, 2, http://them.polylog.org/2/fwk-en.htm.

Wiredu, Kwasi (2004) 'Prolegomena to an African Philosophy of Education', *South African Journal of Higher Education*, 18: 17–26.

Wiredu, Kwasi (2008) 'Social Philosophy in Postcolonial Africa: Some Preliminaries Concerning Communalism and Communitarianism', *South African Journal of Philosophy*, 27: 332–9.

Wiredu, Kwasi (2009) 'An Oral Philosophy of Personhood: Comments on Philosophy and Orality', *Research in African Literatures*, 40: 8–18.

Woermann, Minka and Engelbrecht, Schalk (2019) 'The *Ubuntu* Challenge to Business: From Stakeholders to Relationholders', *Journal of Business Ethics*, 157: 27–44.

Wolf, Susan (1982) 'Moral Saints', *Journal of Philosophy*, 79: 419–39.

Yurkivska, Olga (2001) 'A Question Mark against *Ubuntu*: Comparisons with Russian Communitarians', in *Protest and Engagement: Philosophy after Apartheid at an Historically Black South African University*, Giddy, Patrick (ed.), Washington, DC: Council for Research in Values and Philosophy, pp. 83–102.

Index